IMAGES
of America

COWTOWN RODEO

I0806209

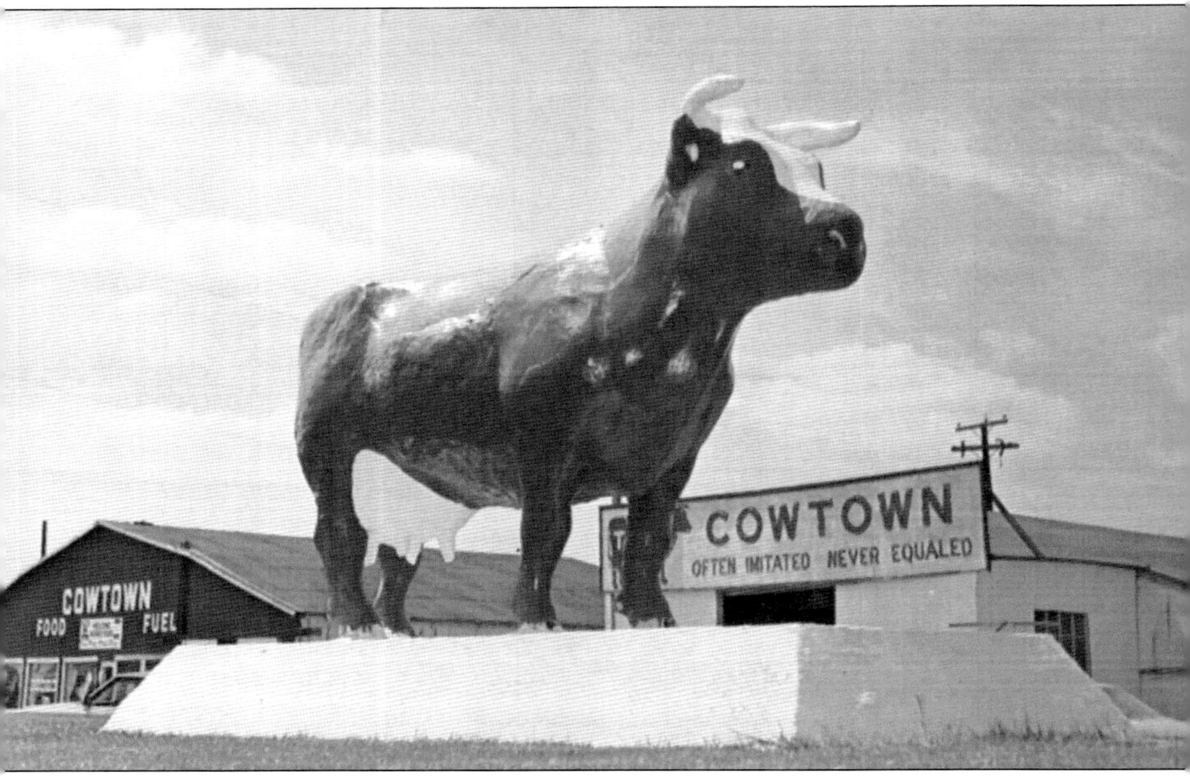

Look for the Cow. Route 40 in Woodstown and Pilesgrove is a main roadway that is heavily traveled not just by locals, but also by commuters and vacationers. Traffic increases significantly in the summertime, when people are traveling to the Jersey Shore and Delaware beaches. For years, the Cowtown cow has been a highly visible landmark. (Courtesy of the Harris family.)

On the Cover: Howard Harris III, owner of Cowtown until 1978, competes in a saddle bronc event at Cowtown. In saddle bronc riding, a horse tries to buck the rider off. This picture was snapped mid-buck; the horse's hind legs are poised to kick upward. (Courtesy of the Harris family.)

IMAGES
of America

COWTOWN RODEO

Angela Speakman

ARCADIA
PUBLISHING

ISBN 978-1-4671-2148-4

Published by Arcadia Publishing
Charleston, South Carolina

Printed in the United States of America

Library of Congress Control Number: 2013949420

For all general information, please contact Arcadia Publishing:
Telephone 843-853-2070
Fax 843-853-0044
E-mail sales@arcadiapublishing.com
For customer service and orders:
Toll-Free 1-888-313-2665

Visit us on the Internet at www.arcadiapublishing.com

To all the cowboys and cowgirls, and to one cowboy in particular: Stoney Harris

Contents

Acknowledgments

I am so grateful to the Harris family—Grant, Betsy, Katy, and Courtney—for helping me learn about their family history. This book would have been impossible without their help and guidance. All images used in this book come from the Harris family unless otherwise noted. Also, I would not have been able to piece it all together without Cowtown experts Alice Mae Shivers, Emily Walker, Jimmy Lee Walker, Lee Curry, Joe and Judy Merola, and Lora Lowry.

In addition to the family and friends of Cowtown, I would like to thank Annette Devitt at the 4-H Rutgers Cooperative Extension, April Luciano and the Salem County Public Archives, the staff of the *South Jersey Times*, and Don and Megen Brovero at Wolves' Den Farm.

This book would not have come to fruition without having spent 16 years working with my summer family of Rebekah Johnson, Suzanne Zigo, Travis Zigo, Ernie Bickford, Alec Zigo, Ryan Zigo, Carol Robinson, Megan Dillon, Nolan Concannon, Amanda Bozzelli, Marge Owen, and the rest of the Cowtown Cowboy Outfitters–Rodeo Division alumni.

And last, but not least, I cannot say thank you enough to two special people for all their help: Jim Mascola III and Julie Demarest. With both of them in my corner, I will always succeed.

INTRODUCTION

For as long as I can remember, my summer memories include Cowtown. A place like Cowtown is special because it is more than just a flea market with a huge cowboy standing in front of it. It is more than just a tourist destination that includes a show. To me, it is the smell of summertime. It is talking with out-of-towners whose eyes light up when they describe how fast a barrel racer and her horse moved in the arena. It is watching kids roll down a grassy hill and giggle at the bottom. It is a piece of history that happens to be in my backyard.

When people think of New Jersey, rodeo is not one of the first things that comes to mind. Most people equate the Garden State with city living, where the houses are built up, not across, or with sprawling suburbia. Many do not know that we have sprawling farmland and quite a bit of wide-open space left in Salem County and the counties that surround it. Outsiders probably do not realize that, while we are within a few hours of several major metropolitan areas, there are still pockets of country life and aspects of simpler living that Salem Countians try to preserve and promote. Perhaps it is one of our best-kept secrets.

Howard Amos Harris, the man that started it all, moved to Woodstown in 1908. After limited success with automobile auctions in Woodstown, he shifted his focus to livestock, which was in high demand and short supply. Traveling salesmen would sell the livestock, but the community needed something more stable. By 1926, a successful weekly livestock auction was run by Howard and his son Amos Howard "Stoney" Harris in the center of Woodstown. The Harris men were true entrepreneurs. They saw a need, they saw a way to fill it, and then they went after it. The auction led to the market, which was well received by the community. By the time 1930 rolled around, Woodstown had a thriving weekly auction and marketplace, but it did not stop there.

The Salem County Fair had fallen apart after World War I. The Harris men, Stoney in particular, saw another opportunity. Stoney worked with the Salem County Fair and revived the annual event, which included a rodeo. Hundreds of community members attended the fair and rodeo. Woodstown had been a town that needed more livestock, more market choices, and entertainment. In less than five years time, Cowtown had provided all of it.

By the end of the 1930s, Cowtown had grown significantly. In 1940, the whole operation moved to its current location on Route 40 in Pilesgrove. It worked out; there were complaints about the livestock smell in town, and Cowtown needed to expand anyway (some say that the Cowtown cow statue's rear faces town on purpose because of those complaints, but others claim it faces that way to welcome the traffic from the Delaware Memorial Bridge). World War II resulted in a hiatus for the rodeo and fair, but the auction and market continued.

The livestock auctions got bigger. People, including many butchers, were coming from farther and farther away to purchase cattle and horses. Stoney started importing livestock, drawing from his own ranch in Wyoming and other ranches in the West. The livestock was delivered to Cowtown by ranch hands and cowboys. After the war was over, Cowtown had a plethora of livestock and cowboys to ride in the rodeo. It was time for Cowtown to add some entertainment.

Rodeos had really taken hold of the West, and the popularity of cowboys and the sport were spreading across the country, especially to the East Coast. Cowtown had already been filled once with scores of people excited to watch bronc and bull riding at the fair. Stoney and his son Howard Amos Harris III brought the rodeo back to Cowtown. And it has been there ever since.

The Cowtown Rodeo, a Professional Rodeo Cowboys Association (PRCA)–sanctioned rodeo, is held weekly and is the oldest one in the country. It is nestled into a rural community in New Jersey, which happens to be the most densely populated state in the country. There are many people out there that probably would not believe it until they saw it for themselves, but it is true nonetheless.

The success of Harris Sales Co. was not simply luck. It was a direct result of vision, hard work, and grit. In its nearly 60 years of operation, Cowtown has continued to grow and shift as the needs of community did the same. In that time, a new arena was built, Saturday shopping was added, a new cow was christened, the auction ended, and many other things have changed since Howard Amos Harris and his son Stoney called that first auction in 1926. But, with a fascinating past, present, and future, Cowtown remains.

One

Family and Friends of Cowtown

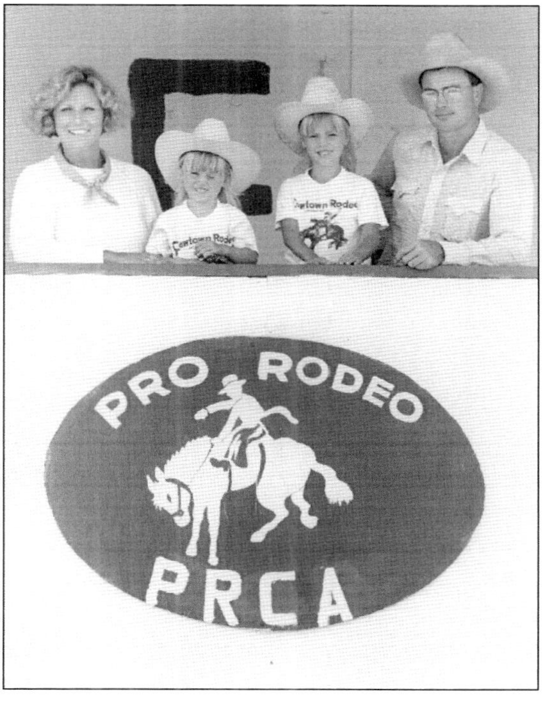

Cowtown Family Portrait. "Often imitated, never equaled," reads the sign visible from Route 40 outside of Woodstown, New Jersey, simply stating what anyone that has ever visited Cowtown already knows. In the 1920s, the Harris family launched what is now known as Cowtown. Grant and Betsy Harris, pictured here, bought Cowtown from Grant's parents, Howard Amos Harris III and Irene Harris, in 1978. Howard and Irene had purchased Cowtown from Howard's parents, Stoney and Marie Harris. Stoney and his father, Howard Amos Harris, started it all when they launched a livestock auction in the 1920s. The history behind Cowtown is as much a history of a family as it is of a business. Since 1978, Grant, Betsy, and daughters Courtney (right) and Katy (left) have lived on the home ranch, outside of Woodstown. Cowtown has always and will continue to be a family operation and a unique South Jersey attraction.

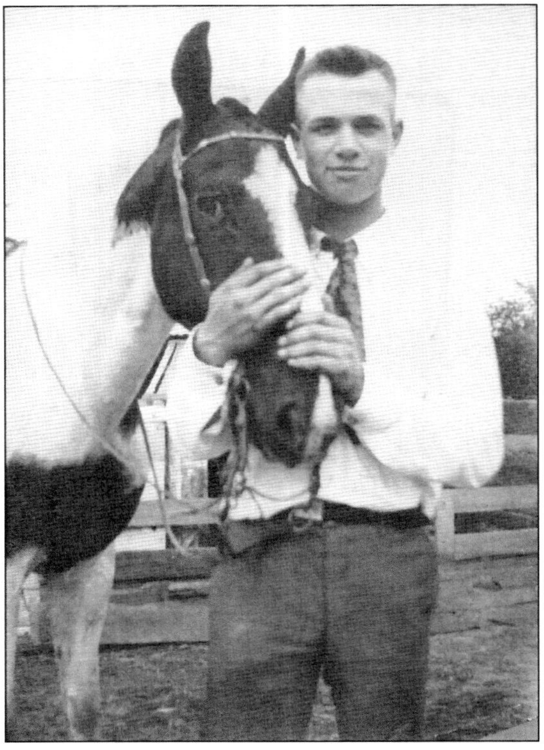

The Force behind Cowtown. A young Stoney Harris stands with his horse Billy. Stoney's nickname came from his high school football days. Most people said hitting him was like hitting a stone wall. Without Stoney's vision, Cowtown would not exist as it does today.

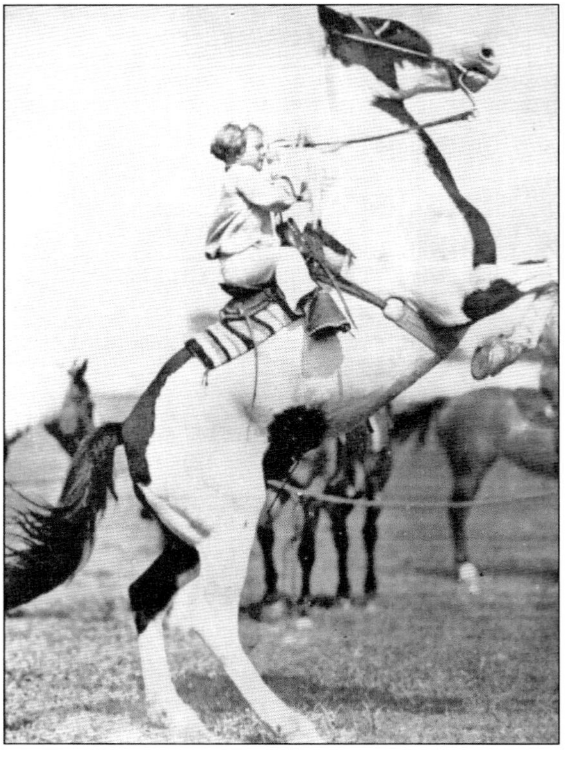

A Girl and her Horse. This picture of young Henrietta Harris Boland, Stoney Harris's daughter and Howard Harris III's sister, on a horse was featured in the 1938 Salem County Fair Rodeo program. The annual rodeo program was over 40 pages long and provided rodeo attendees with important information about rodeo rules and purse amounts.

FAMILY ON HORSEBACK. Three generations of Harris men are seated on a horse. From left to right, infant Howard Amos Harris III, Howard Amos Harris Sr., and Stoney Harris pose for the camera. The rodeo continues to be a family-run business, owned and operated by the Harris family.

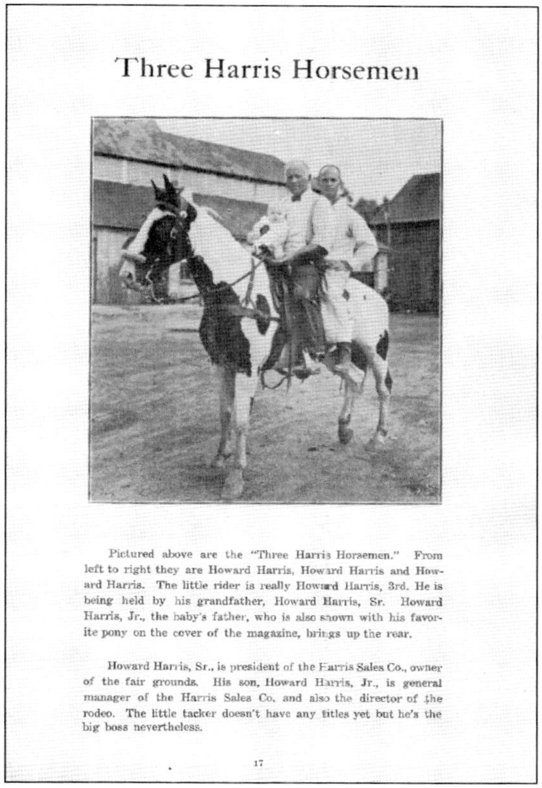

Three Harris Horsemen

Pictured above are the "Three Harris Horsemen." From left to right they are Howard Harris, Howard Harris and Howard Harris. The little rider is really Howard Harris, 3rd. He is being held by his grandfather, Howard Harris, Sr. Howard Harris, Jr., the baby's father, who is also shown with his favorite pony on the cover of the magazine, brings up the rear.

Howard Harris, Sr., is president of the Harris Sales Co., owner of the fair grounds. His son, Howard Harris, Jr., is general manager of the Harris Sales Co. and also the director of the rodeo. The little tacker doesn't have any titles yet but he's the big boss nevertheless.

17

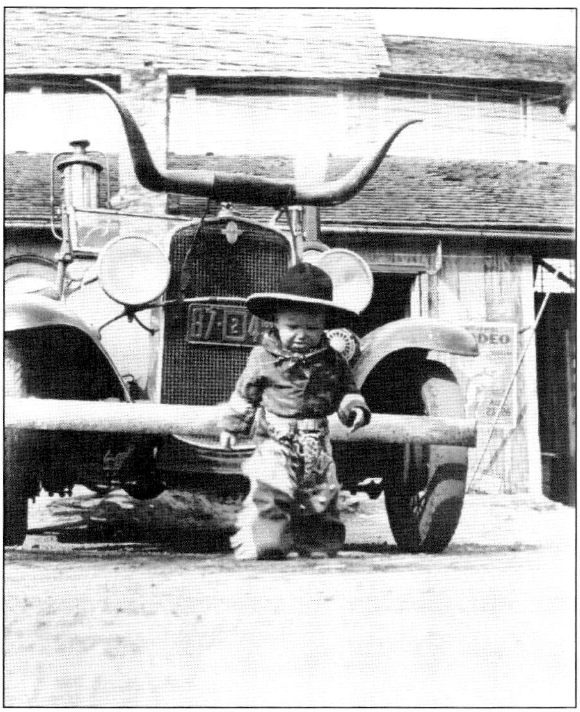

LITTLE COWBOY. Around the age of three, Howard Amos Harris III (Stoney's son) is dressed as a cowboy. To the right of the car, an advertisement promoting the rodeo hangs at Cowtown. The rodeo was revived in the late 1920s in conjunction with the annual Salem County Fair. This photograph was taken in the mid-1930s.

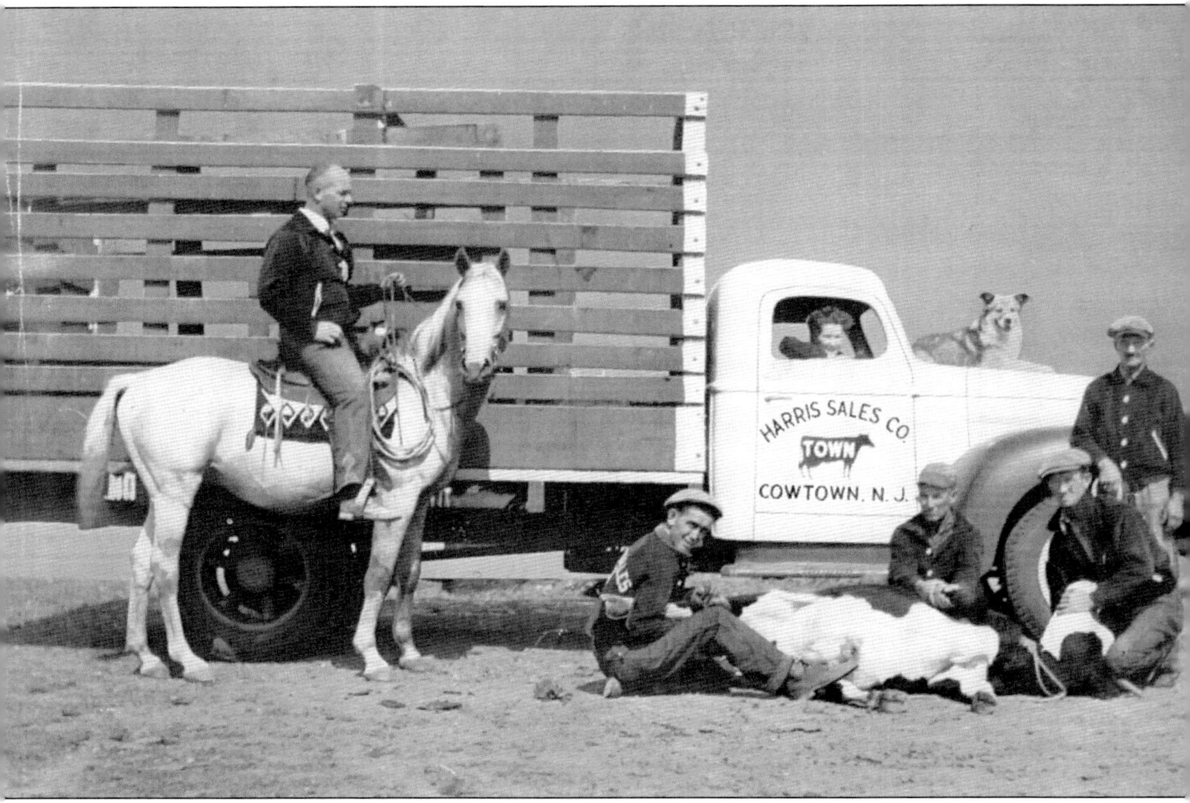

Harris Sales Co. Cowtown owner Stoney Harris (left) sits on his horse Cappy-Tan in a posed portrait from 1944. If Stoney was on a horse, it was usually Cappy-Tan, who was one of his favorite horses. From left to right, Charles Ridgway, Bill Bell, and Cap Ridgway kneel next to a tied cow, while Woody Van Meter stands behind them. The cow was likely already sold or about to be sold. Lavinia Duffy leans out of the truck window. The Cowtown logo, which is still the logo today, is painted on the side of the truck. All seen here, including Lark the dog, were Cowtown staff. Even though Lark was a four-legged member of the staff, he was just as important as his two-legged counterparts. It is believed that Lark alerted Stoney to the Cowtown Sale Barn fire in 1946. (Courtesy of Edna Crispin and the Harris family.)

Cowtown in Italy. In 1944, the world was at war. The Kelly family is a local farm family in Salem County. Three of the Kelly boys were old enough to go to war, but Edward and Martin Kelly had to stay behind and work the farm. William "Bill" Kelly went off to war and used the jeep pictured here to deliver ammunition. He took a little bit of Cowtown with him. Bill returned safely to the family farm after the war.

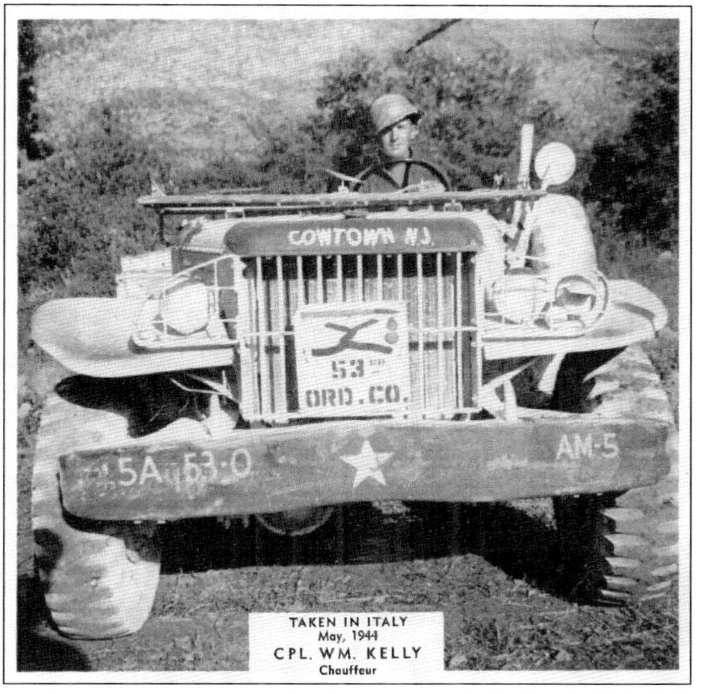

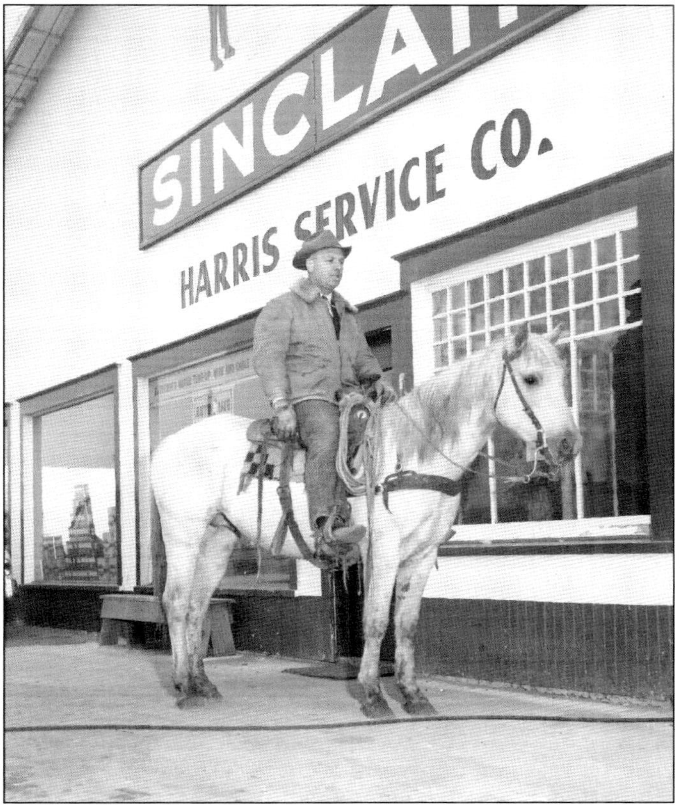

Cars in South Jersey. Stoney Harris sits on his horse in front of the family's service station. Automobile auctioneering was how Stoney's father, Howard Harris, came to founding Cowtown. Automobile auctions were not booming; however, there was a real need in rural South Jersey for livestock. The service station was opened in the 1940s after the livestock auction moved to Route 40.

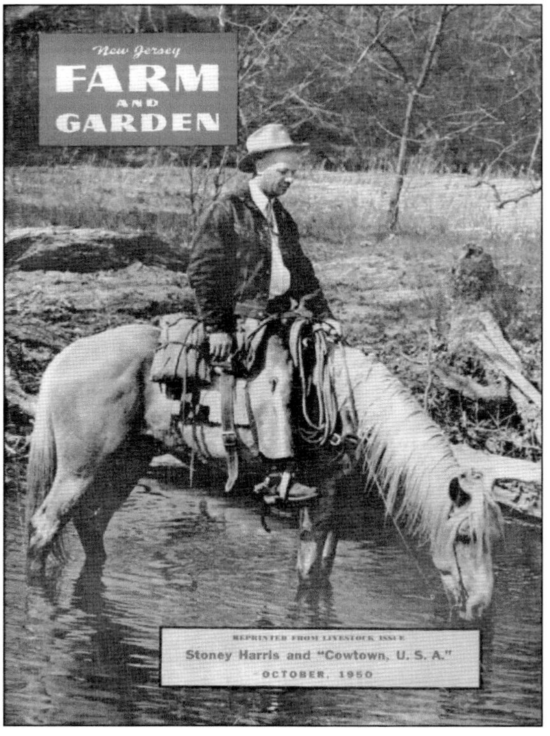

PRESS FOR STONEY. Stoney Harris was featured on the cover of a 1950 issue of *New Jersey Farm and Garden* magazine. Even though he was born and raised in South Jersey, his purchase of a ranch in Wyoming in 1938 actually helped him grow the Cowtown operation. In order to expand the business, he had to bring livestock in from the West. (Courtesy of Emily Walker.)

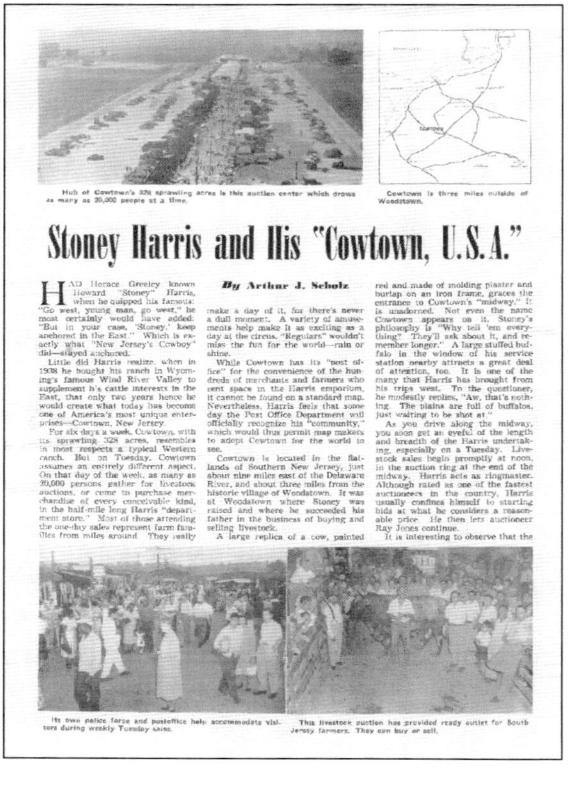

Hub of Cowtown's 328 sprawling acres is this auction center which draws as many as 20,000 people at a time.

Cowtown is three miles outside of Woodstown.

Stoney Harris and His "Cowtown, U.S.A."

By Arthur J. Scholz

HAD Horace Greeley known Howard "Stoney" Harris, when he quipped his famous: "Go west, young man, go west," he most certainly would have added: "But in your case, 'Stoney,' keep anchored in the East." Which is exactly what "New Jersey's Cowboy" did—stayed anchored.

Little did Harris realize, when in 1938 he bought his ranch in Wyoming's famous Wind River Valley to supplement his cattle interests in the East, that only two years hence he would create what today has become one of America's most unique enterprises—Cowtown, New Jersey.

For six days a week, Cowtown, with its sprawling 328 acres, resembles in most respects a typical Western ranch. But on Tuesday, Cowtown assumes an entirely different aspect. On that day of the week, as many as 20,000 persons gather for livestock auctions, or come to purchase merchandise of every conceivable kind, in the half-mile long Harris "department store." Most of those attending the one-day sales represent farm families from miles around. They really make a day of it, for there's never a dull moment. A variety of amusements help make it as exciting as a day at the circus. "Regulars" wouldn't miss the fun for the world—rain or shine.

While Cowtown has its "post office" for the convenience of the hundreds of merchants and farmers who rent space in the Harris emporium, it cannot be found on a standard map. Nevertheless, Harris feels that some day the Post Office Department will officially recognize his "community," which would thus permit map makers to adopt Cowtown for the world to see.

Cowtown is located in the flatlands of Southern New Jersey, just about nine miles east of the Delaware River, and about three miles from the historic village of Woodstown. It was at Woodstown where Stoney was raised and where he succeeded his father in the business of buying and selling livestock.

A large replica of a cow, painted red and made of molding plaster and burlap on an iron frame, graces the entrance to Cowtown's "midway." It is unadorned. Not even the name Cowtown appears on it. Stoney's philosophy is "Why tell 'em everything? They'll ask about it, and remember longer." A large stuffed buffalo in the window of his service station nearby attracts a great deal of attention, too. It is one of the many that Harris has brought from his trips west. To the questioner, he modestly replies, "Aw, that's nothing. The plains are full of buffalos, just waiting to be shot at."

As you drive along the midway, you soon get an eyeful of the length and breadth of the Harris undertaking, especially on a Tuesday. Livestock sales begin promptly at noon, in the auction ring at the end of the midway. Harris acts as ringmaster. Although rated as one of the fastest auctioneers in the country, Harris usually confines himself to starting bids at what he considers a reasonable price. He then lets auctioneer Ray Jones continue.

It is interesting to observe that the

Its own police force and postoffice help accommodate visitors during weekly Tuesday sales.

This livestock auction has provided ready outlet for South Jersey farmers. They can buy or sell.

QUITE THE CHARACTER. Stoney Harris has been described as a person with a "larger than life" personality. In the magazine article, author Arthur J. Scholz refers to Stoney as a "showman" and a "ringmaster." Scholz reports that Stoney felt best in "dungarees" and a "10 gallon hat." (Courtesy of Emily Walker.)

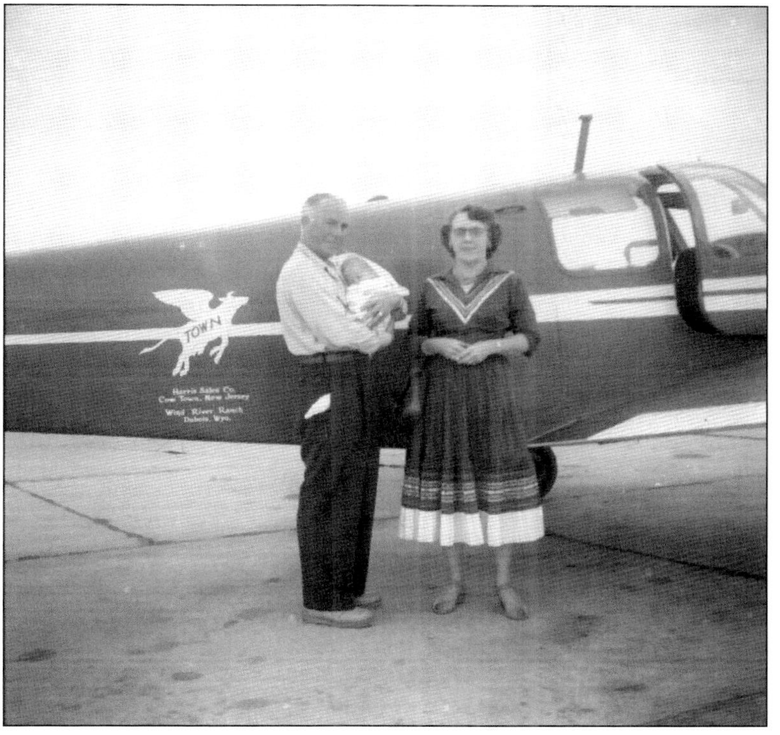

COWTOWN IN THE AIR. The Cowtown plane stopped in Fort Wayne, Indiana, in 1954. Underneath the flying cow, Cowtown, New Jersey, and the Wind River Ranch in DuBois, Wyoming, are listed. The Harris family had strong ties to both locations. Stoney Harris loved flying planes. In addition to his trips west, he was frequently spotted in the air flying around Salem County.

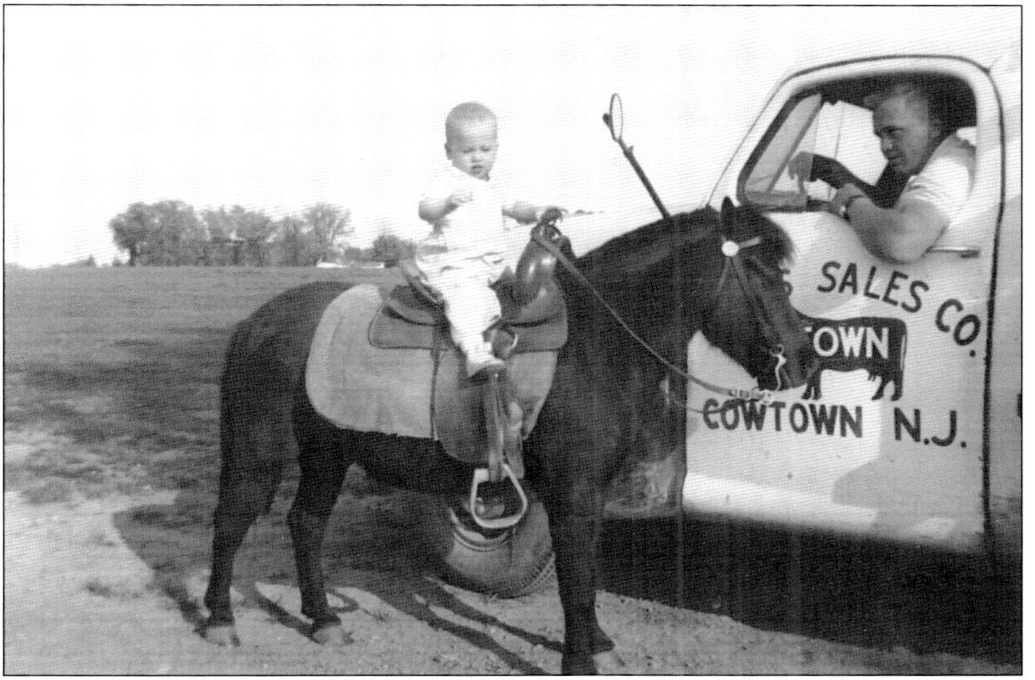

A YOUNG RIDER. In 1955, a young Grant Harris sits on Blackie the pony outside of the home ranch at Cowtown. Grant's father, Howard Harris III, looks on from the Cowtown truck. Even if their feet could not reach the stirrups, Harris family children were able to try out the saddle.

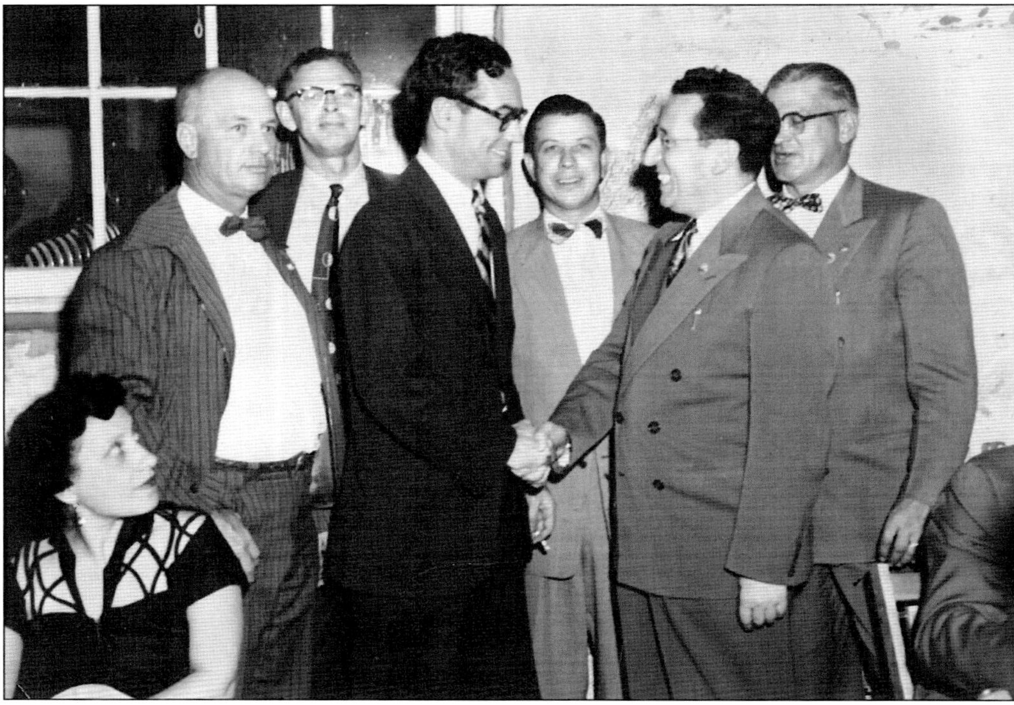

A Presence in Politics. Stoney Harris, an entrepreneur that was interested in politics, was involved in many projects and organizations. Malcom Forbes (center with glasses, shaking hands) is pictured here campaigning for governor in 1957. Stoney (left, in striped suit) joined him at the appearance. Forbes did not win the election; afterwards, he focused on *Forbes* magazine rather than continue to pursue politics.

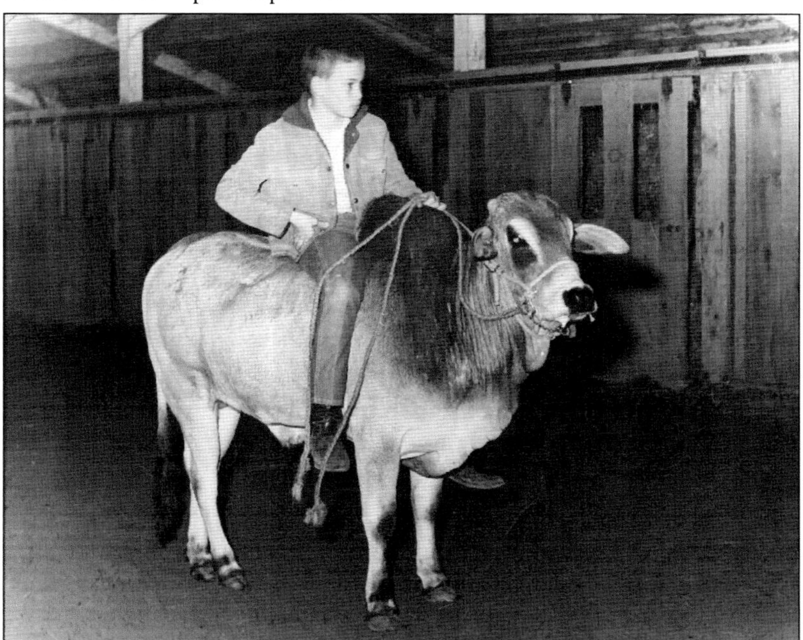

It is not a Horse. Normally, bull riding is synonymous with danger, but a bull can be trained just like other livestock. Here, Grant Harris, current owner of Cowtown, sits on a trained bull around the age of nine. Life at Cowtown involved and continues to involve livestock of all types.

A FAMILY OF RIDERS. Whether it was the auction, the market, or the rodeo, Cowtown was often a family affair. The Harris family was certainly no exception. Grant (left) was a competitor at Cowtown, much like his father, Howard (right). Both were rodeo competitors from young ages, but they both gave up the professional circuit to manage the Cowtown operation.

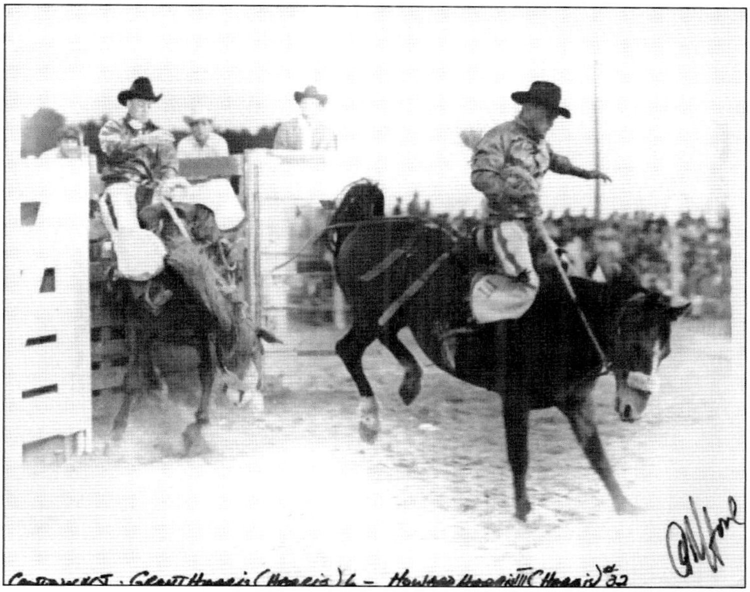

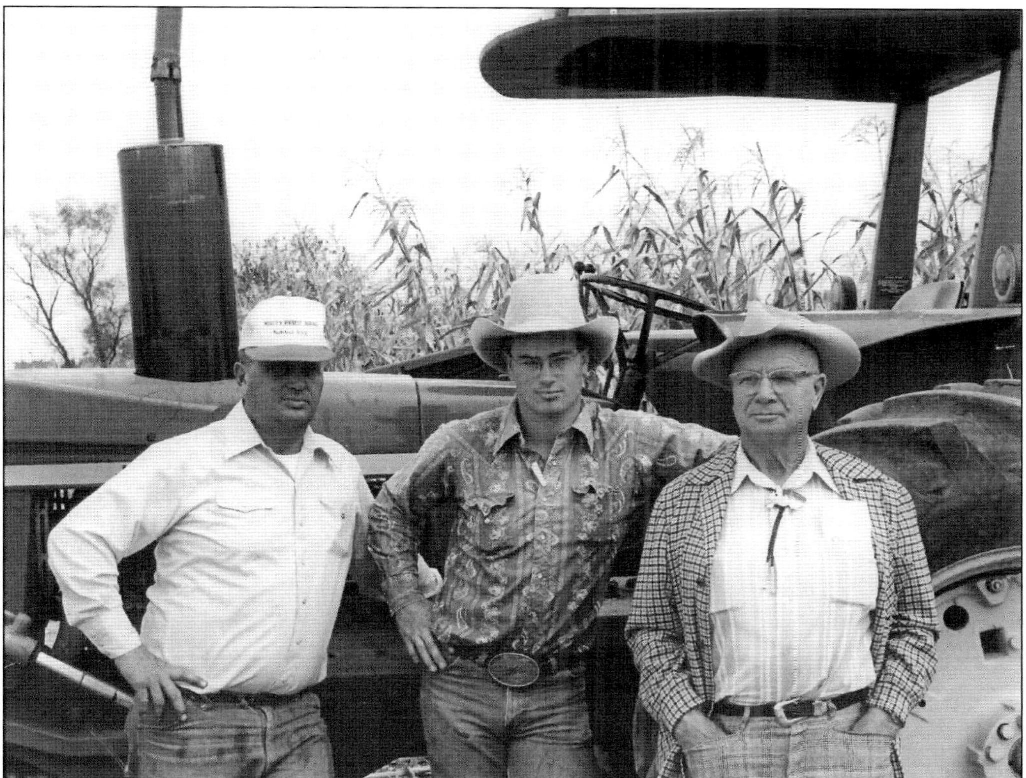

FARMING AT COWTOWN. Three generations of Harris men stand beside a John Deere tractor in a Cowtown cornfield. John Deere tractors were a favorite of Stoney Harris. The Cowtown operations and pastures are on hundreds of acres owned by the Harris family. From left to right are Howard, Grant, and Stoney Harris.

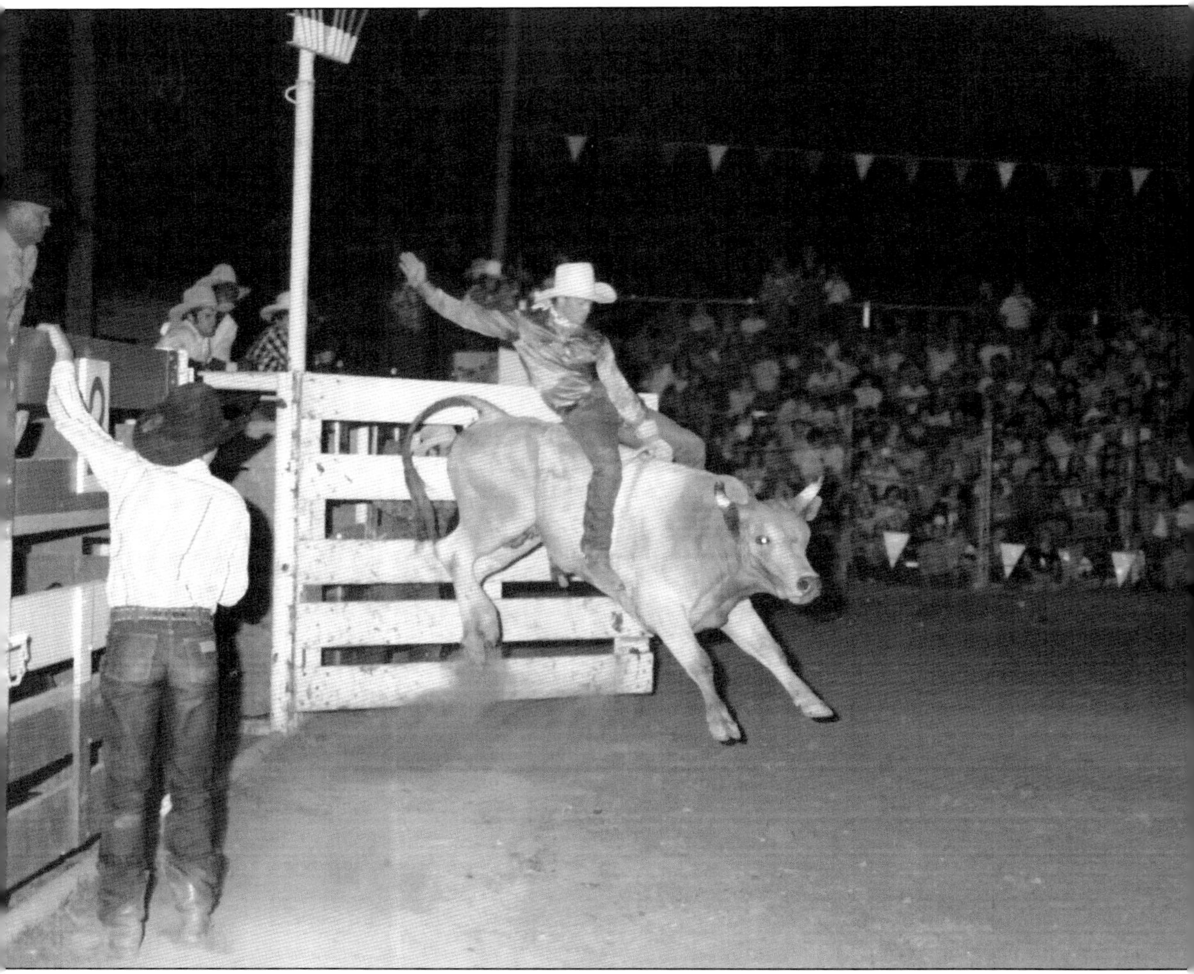

Becoming a Professional. Grant Harris, pictured here riding a bull, was just eight years old when he won the Junior Bull Riding Championship. He received his Professional Rodeo Cowboys Association (PRCA) card at the age of 17. Today, PRCA card applicants must be at least 18 to qualify for membership. Also, applicants must designate a rodeo circuit when applying.

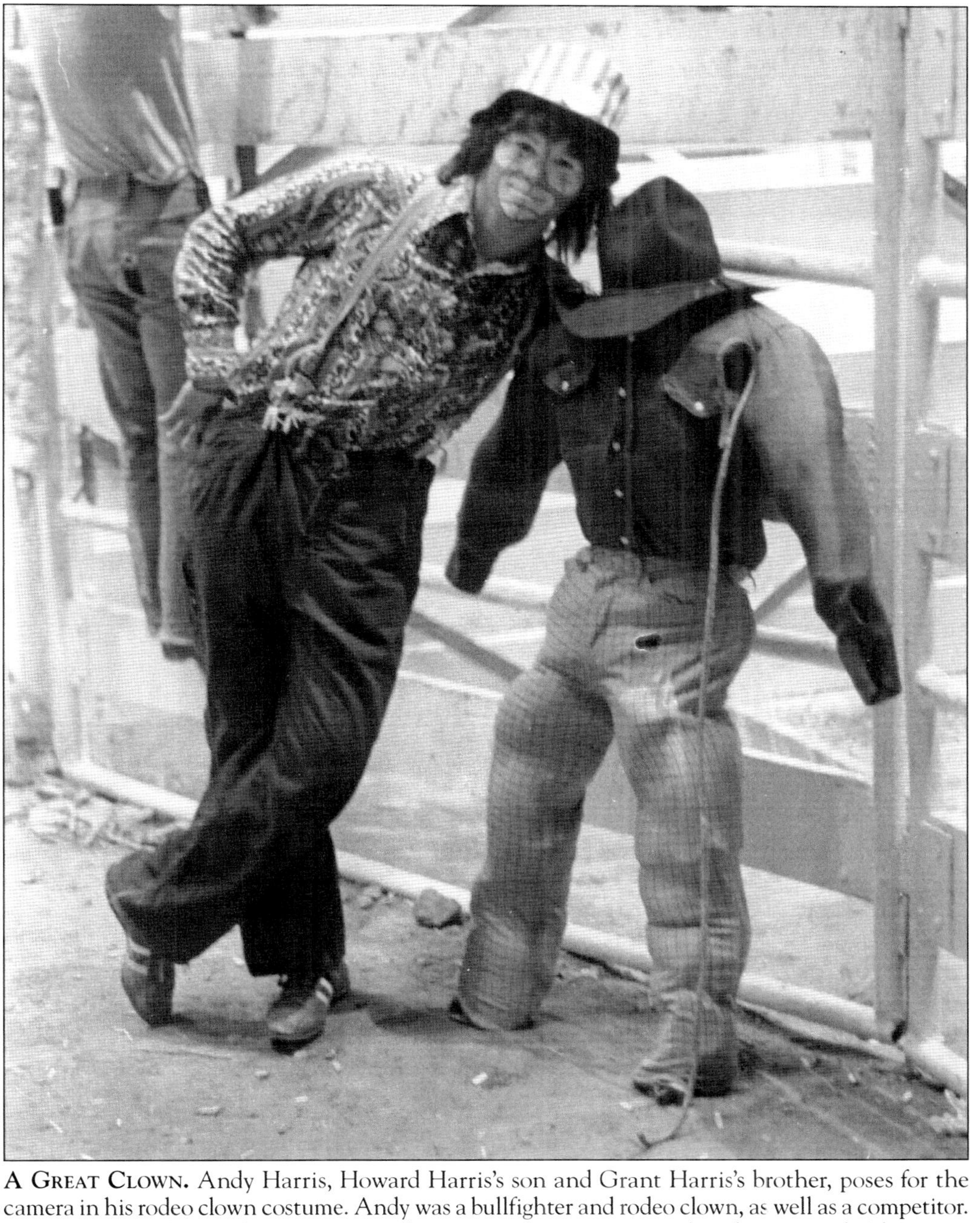

A Great Clown. Andy Harris, Howard Harris's son and Grant Harris's brother, poses for the camera in his rodeo clown costume. Andy was a bullfighter and rodeo clown, as well as a competitor. Today, most professional competitors only compete in one event, rather than several. Also, most bullfighters today do not compete in events.

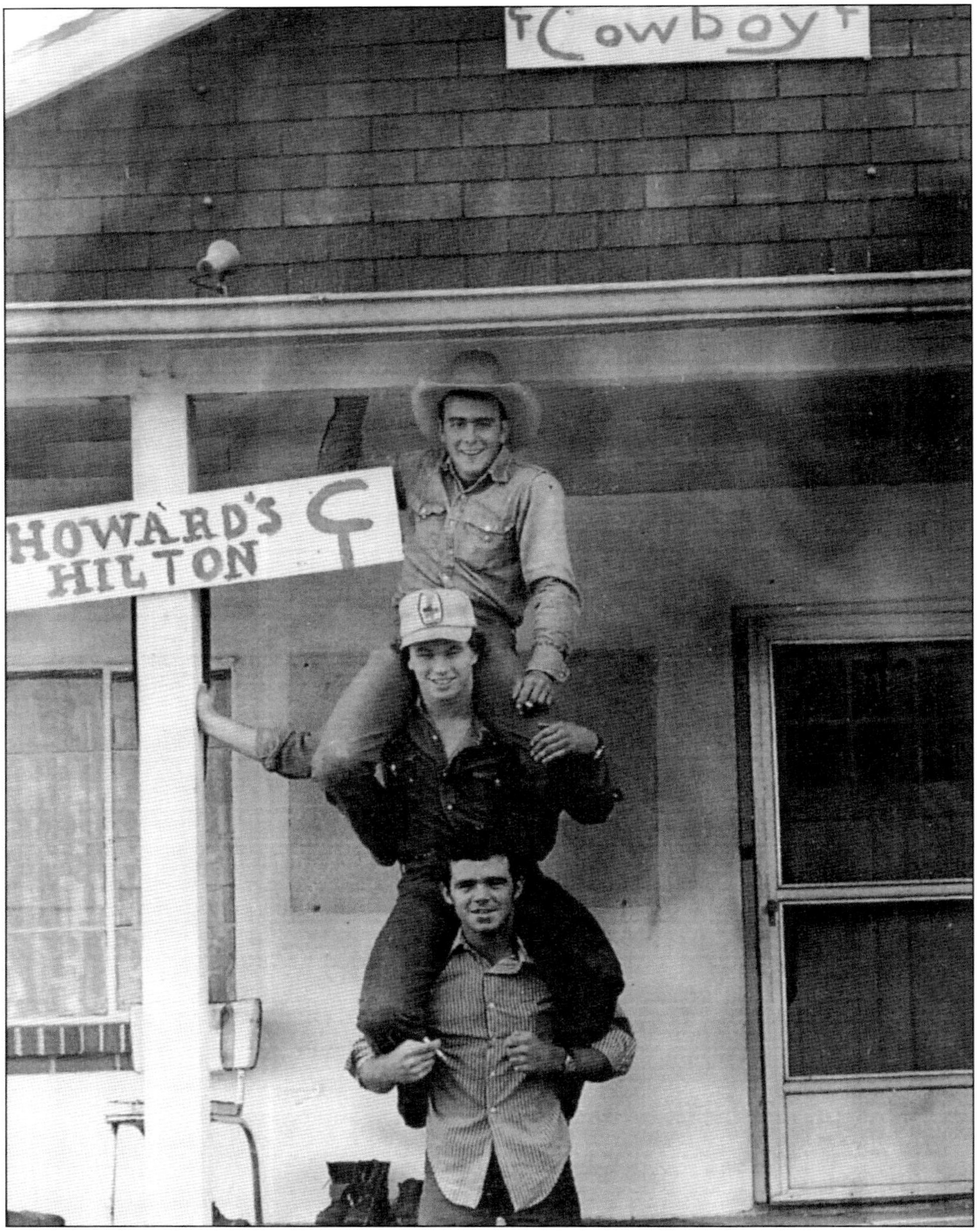

Cowboy Lodging. Howard's Hilton, as it was affectionately referred to, provided lodging for cowboys when they came to town to compete in the rodeo. On the handmade sign, presumably written in red, there was a rodeo symbol. The rodeo brand symbol is a "C" leading into a "T." Cowboys would stay at Howard's Hilton all summer long year after year. While there, some would work on the ranch and practice for professional competition. Before being used as Howard's Hilton, it was the New Jersey State Troopers barracks. Currently, it is the Ranch Hope Thrift Shop, which is still located on the Cowtown property. The thrift shop uses proceeds to fund services for at-risk youth in the community. Seen here, from top to bottom, are Pat McCary, Andy Harris, and Dennis Shierman, who were horsing around for the camera. (Courtesy of Pat McCary.)

THE FIRST CATTLE DRIVE. Gen. "Mad" Anthony Wayne was singled out by George Washington and sent on a mission to get supplies for the Revolutionary Army at Valley Forge. General Wayne crossed the Delaware River into Salem County in 1778 and rounded up what he could, including 150 head of cattle. The weather worsened, and the British were getting closer to the general and his men.

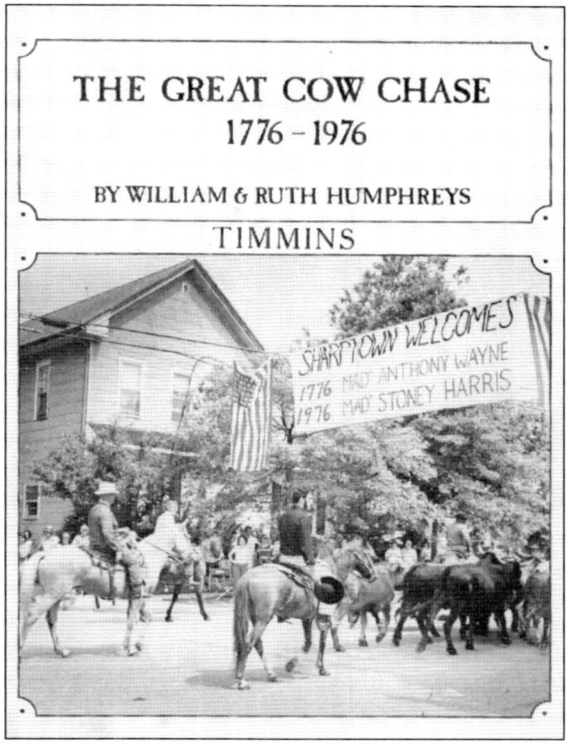

THE CATTLE DRIVE ROUTE. In order to get supplies to the men in Valley Forge, Wayne had to plot out a cattle drive that became known as "the Great Cow Chase." Stoney Harris and his team of men reenacted the cattle drive with 50 head of cattle to pay homage to General Wayne during the bicentennial celebration.

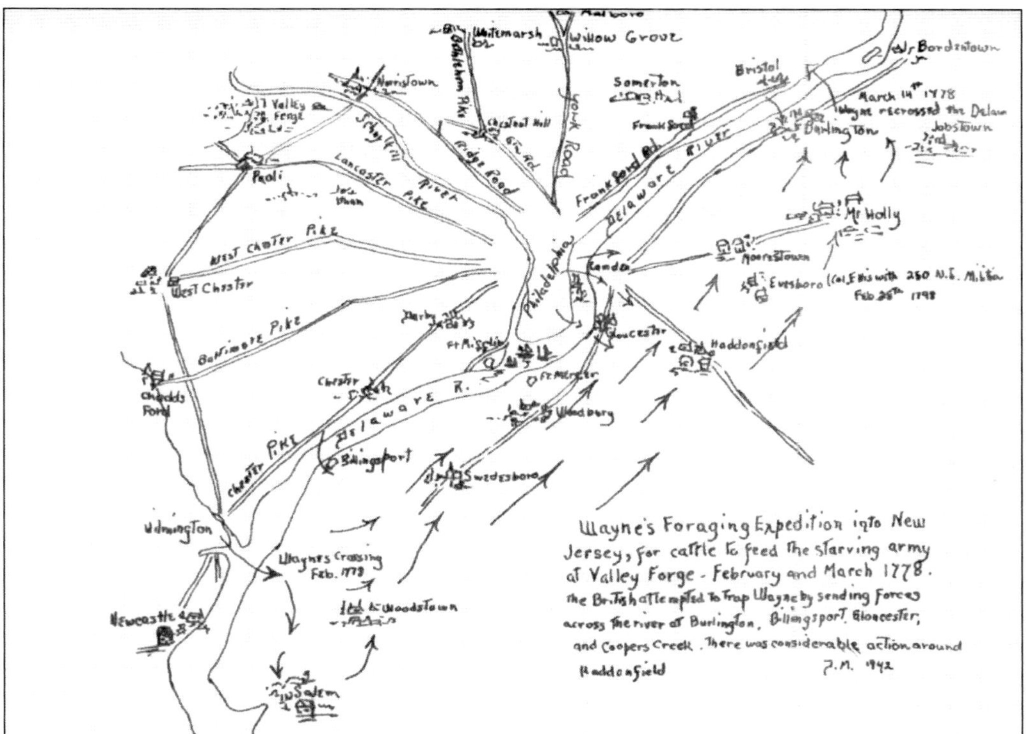

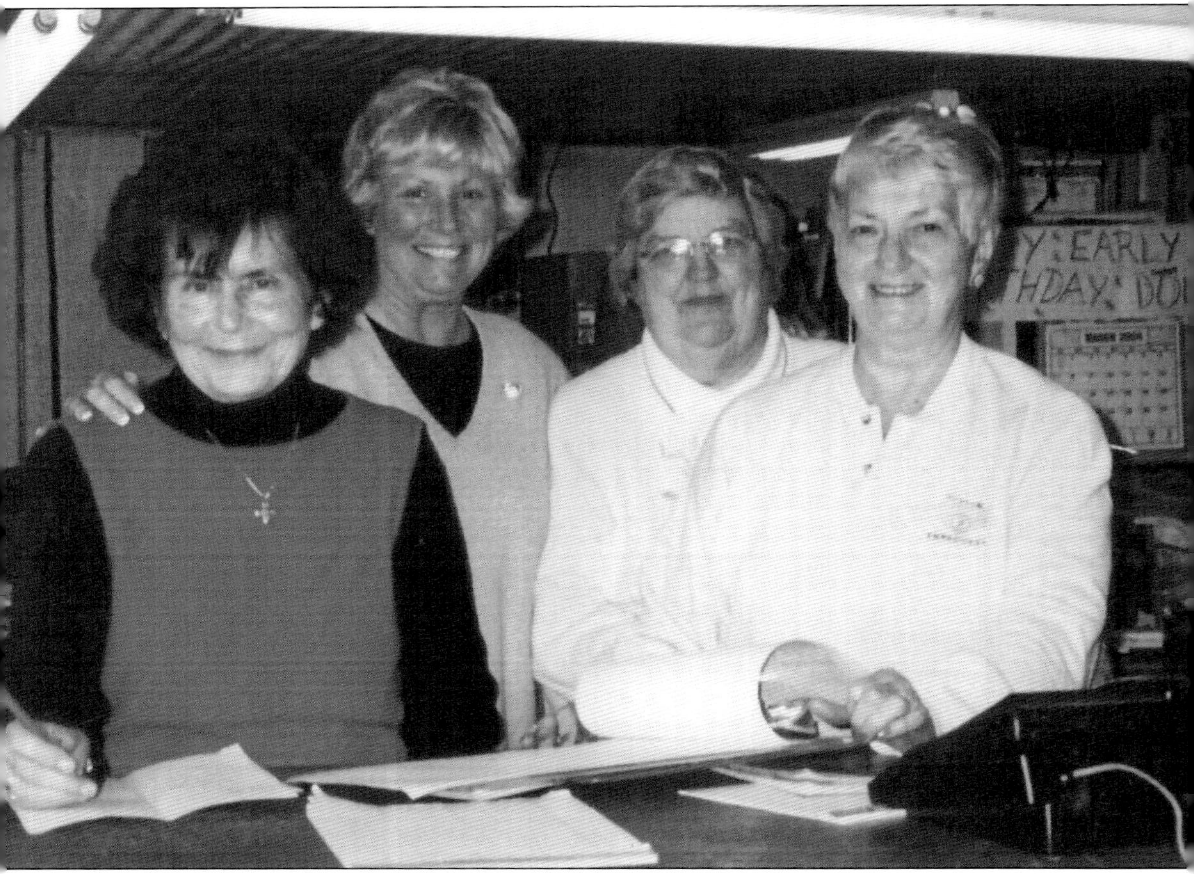

TAKING CARE OF BUSINESS. The Cowtown office staff handles the administrative side of the Cowtown business. From left to right, Emily Walker, Betsy Harris, Alice Shivers, and Francis Hiles pose for a picture in the sale barn office. Even though there are no longer auctions at Cowtown, the office remains busy because of the four-month rodeo season and the year-round market. (Courtesy of Emily Walker.)

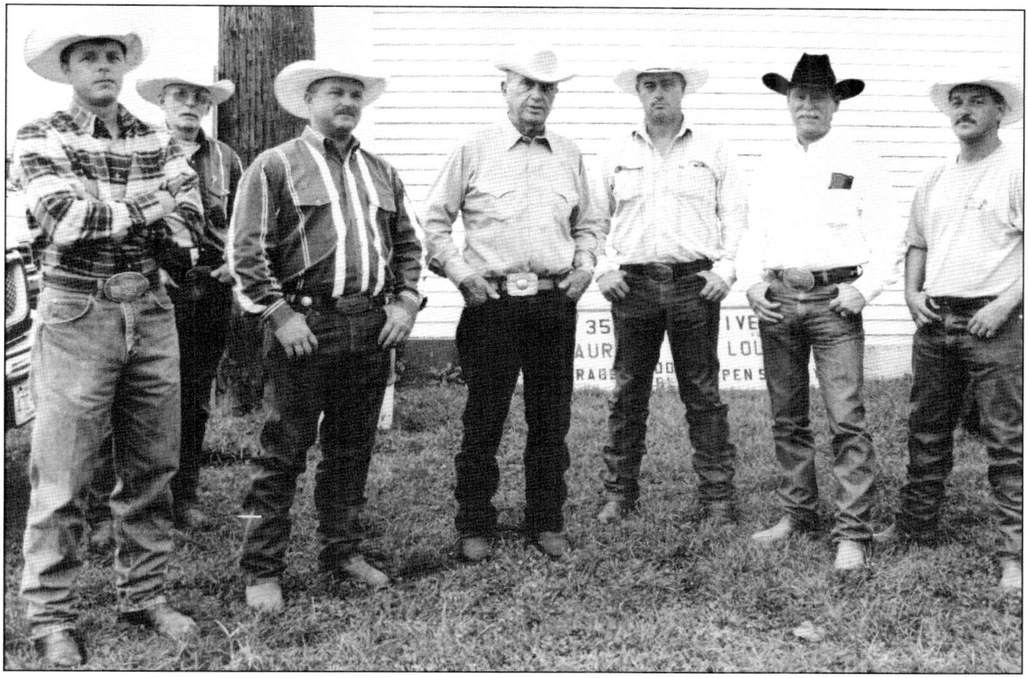

The Hat of Choice. The cowboy hat is the item of apparel most associated with rodeo. There are many different styles to choose from, like the Cattleman and the Gambler. From left to right, Mark DeSiato, Bill Gerhardt, David Schaeffer, Howard Harris, Grant Harris, Dusty Cleveland, and Kary Nelson pose for the camera with the right hat for the rodeo. (Photography by Carl Virgilio; courtesy of the Harris family.)

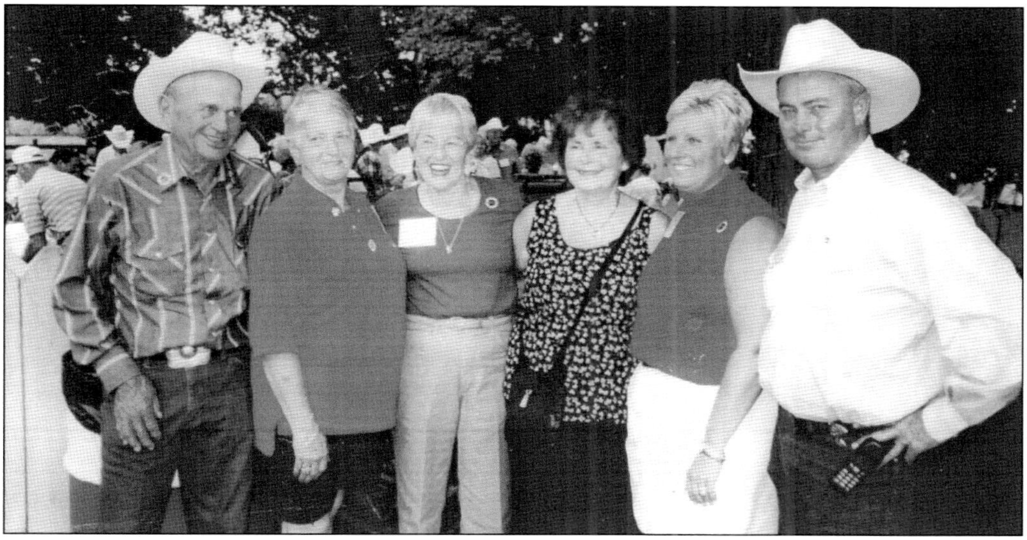

Relaxing at the Rodeo. Just like any working group, Cowtown competitors and staff form lifelong friendships. The uniqueness of the working environment and the perils involved with rodeo sometimes intensify those bonds. The Harris family, Cowtown staff, and rodeo participants enjoy events like the Cowtown reunion to catch up with old friends and reminisce. (Courtesy of Emily Walker.)

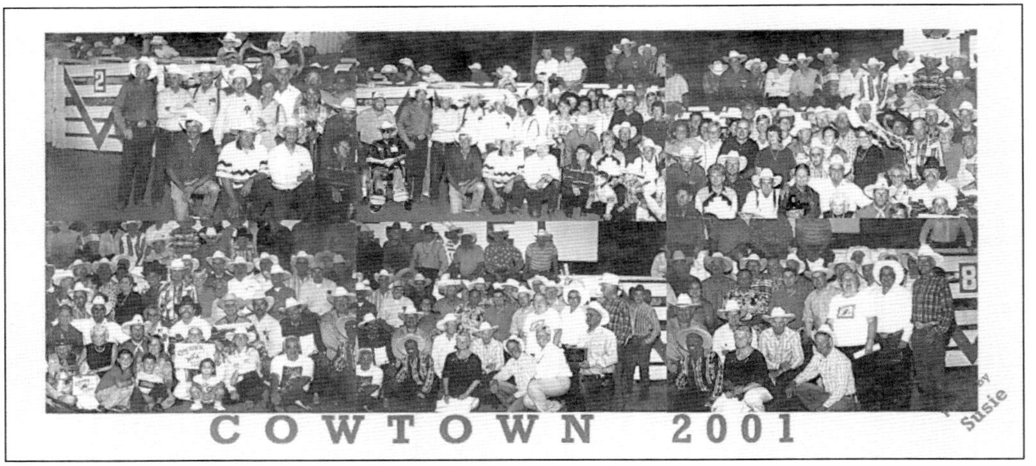

First Reunion at Cowtown. Cowtown had hosted nearly 50 years of summertime rodeo events for thousands of competitors. The Harrises decided to invite everyone back to Cowtown for an evening of friends and fun. Because the first reunion was a success, a second reunion was held in 2005, marking the 50th year of the Cowtown Rodeo.

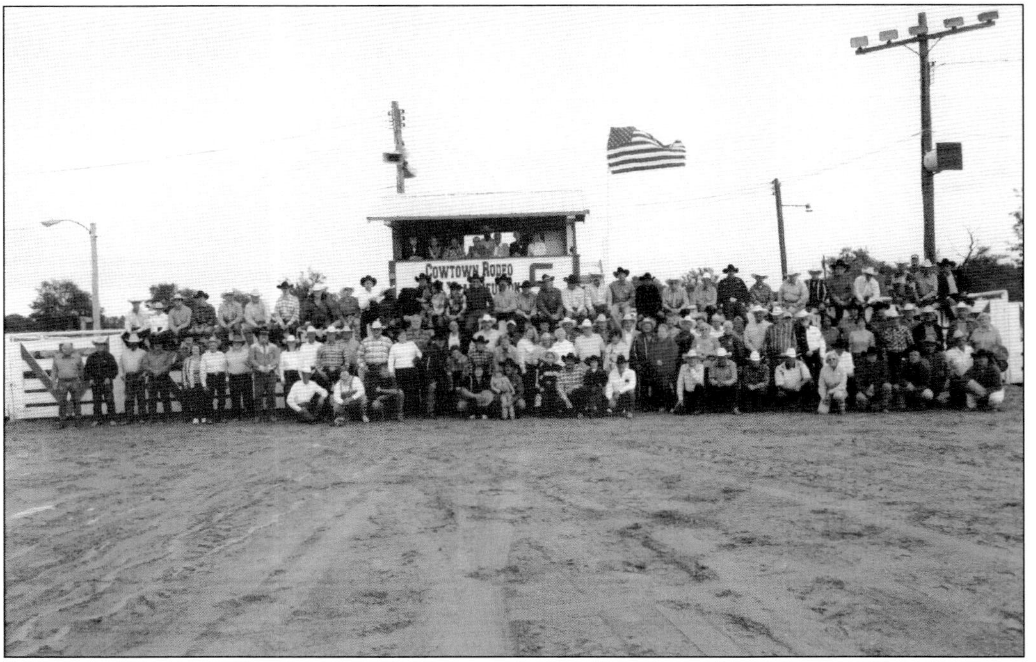

Second Reunion at Cowtown. The reunion was held on September 23–24, 2005. Cowtown hosted dinner, dancing, and fireworks to honor the rodeo competitors that had come through Cowtown over the years. Some riders would make the trek to Cowtown every year to compete. The reunion even included an invitation for all rodeo alumni to attend the last rodeo of the season. Former rodeo competitors and staff came to South Jersey from all over the country to attend the event.

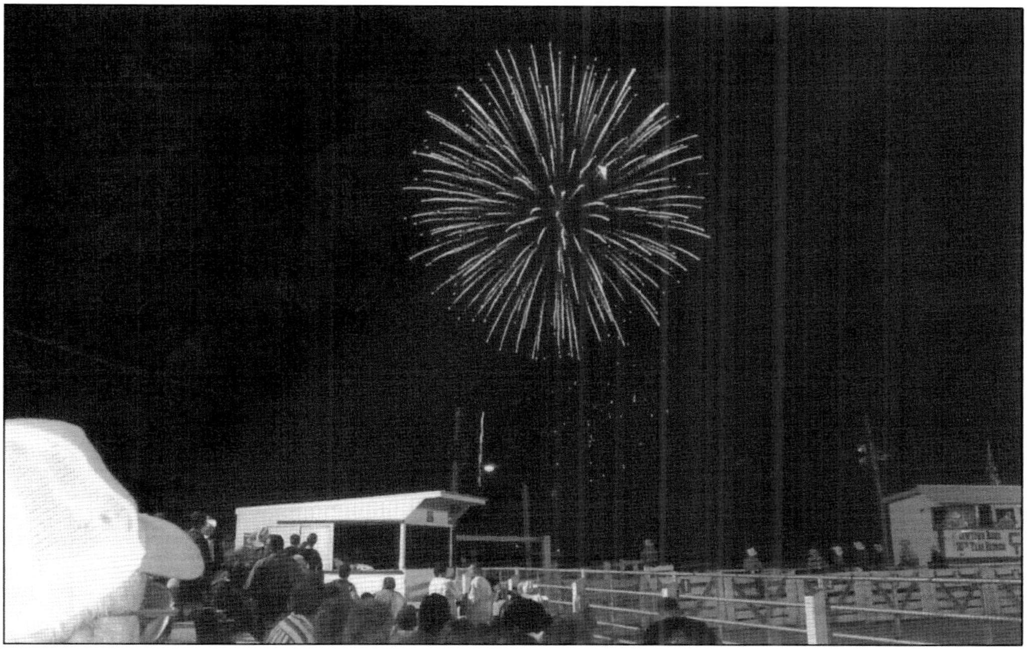

Bright Lights. A fireworks show was organized at Cowtown for the 2005 reunion. The fireworks changed the typical spectator experience. Usually at the rodeo, attendees cannot take their eyes off of the arena because of the exciting events occurring in it. The fireworks show over the announcer's booth and bucking chutes was a memorable experience.

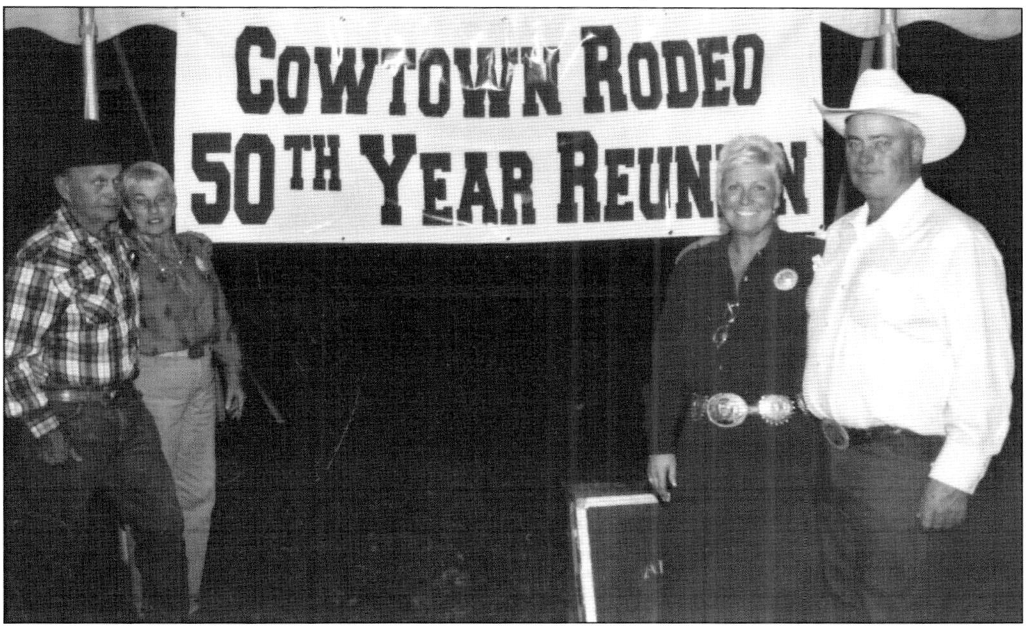

Old Friends Gather. The reunion was hosted to get the Cowtown family together, and over 500 people attended. There were stories of fond memories of riding and competing exchanged between old friends throughout the reunion. Howard and Irene Harris (left) and Betsy and Grant Harris (right) pose next to the reunion banner.

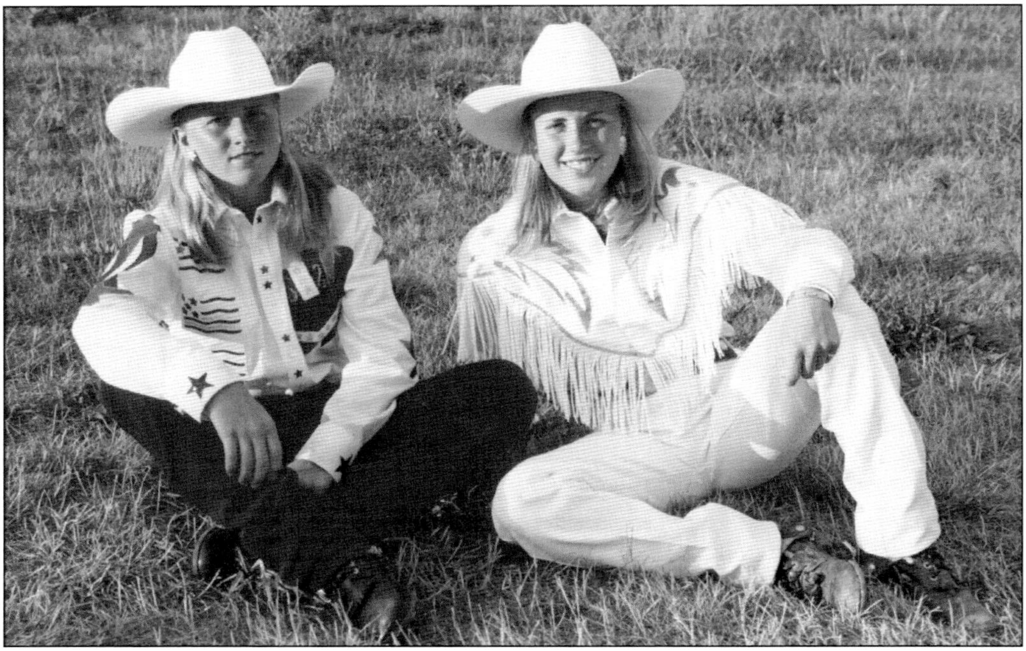

CONTINUING THE TRADITION. Courtney Harris Morehead and Katy Harris Griscom, daughters of Grant and Betsy, grew up on the Cowtown home ranch, outside of Woodstown. They often worked in the Cowtown office, at the auction, and at the rodeo. Both Courtney and Katy also frequently carried flags in the rodeo grand entry. Courtney is married to Jake Morehead of the Three Hills Rodeo Company in Bernard, Iowa. Katy is married to R.J. Griscom and continues the family business at Cowtown.

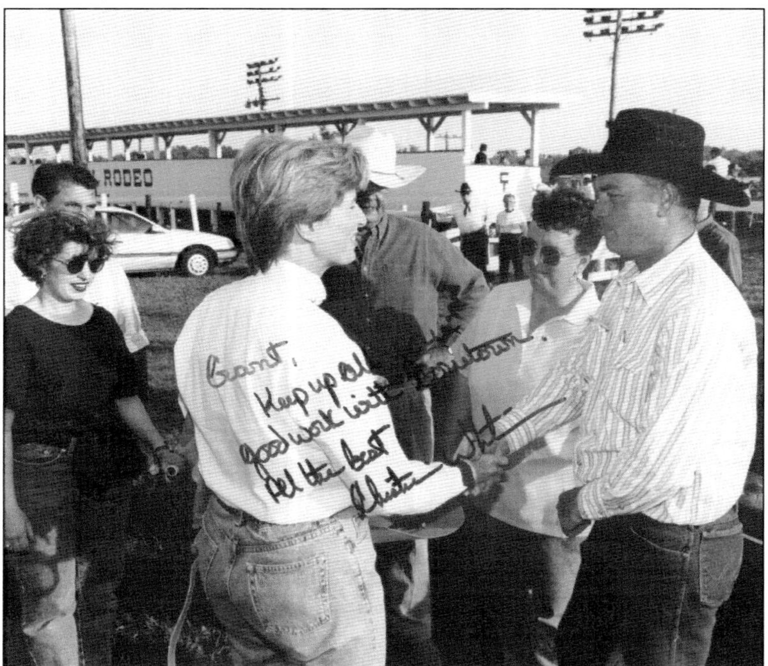

A HIGH-PROFILE ATTENDEE. Christine Todd Whitman was the 50th governor of New Jersey, serving from 1994 to 2001. Governor Whitman was known to love horses and attended the Cowtown Rodeo. She is seen here shaking hands with Cowtown owner Grant Harris. Many celebrities and high-profile people have attended the Cowtown Rodeo.

Two

The Livestock Auction

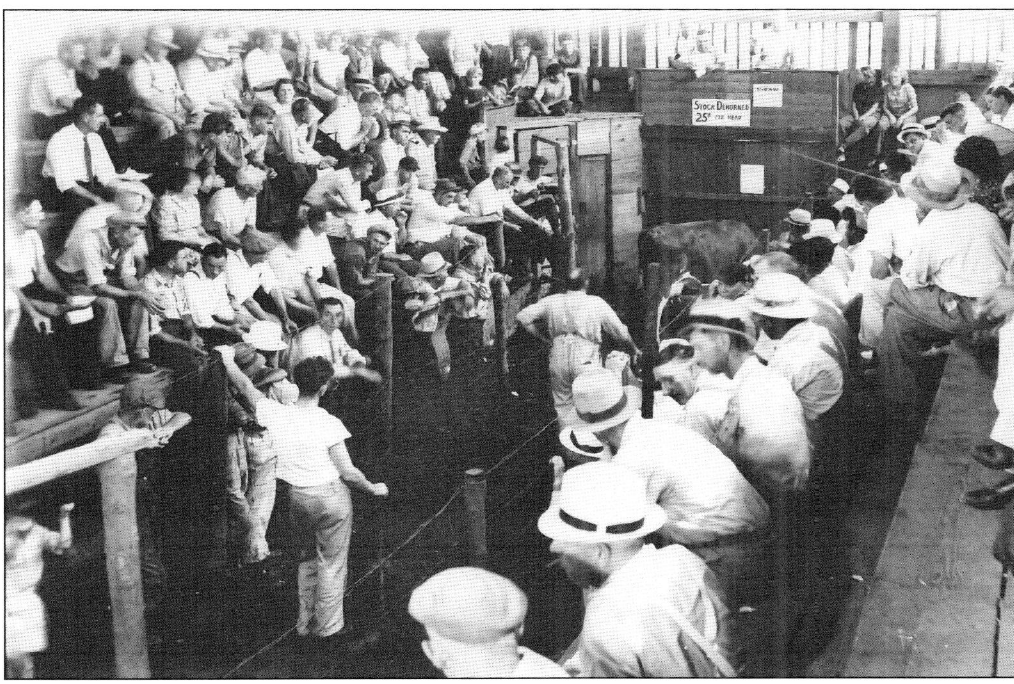

Stock Dehorned, 25¢. The auction ring seen here was the original ring in Woodstown. This summertime auction in the 1930s was well attended. Howard Amos Harris, the founder of Cowtown and Stoney Harris's father, sent Stoney to auctioneering school so he would be able to preside over the auctions. The auction did not move to the current location in Pilesgrove until 1940.

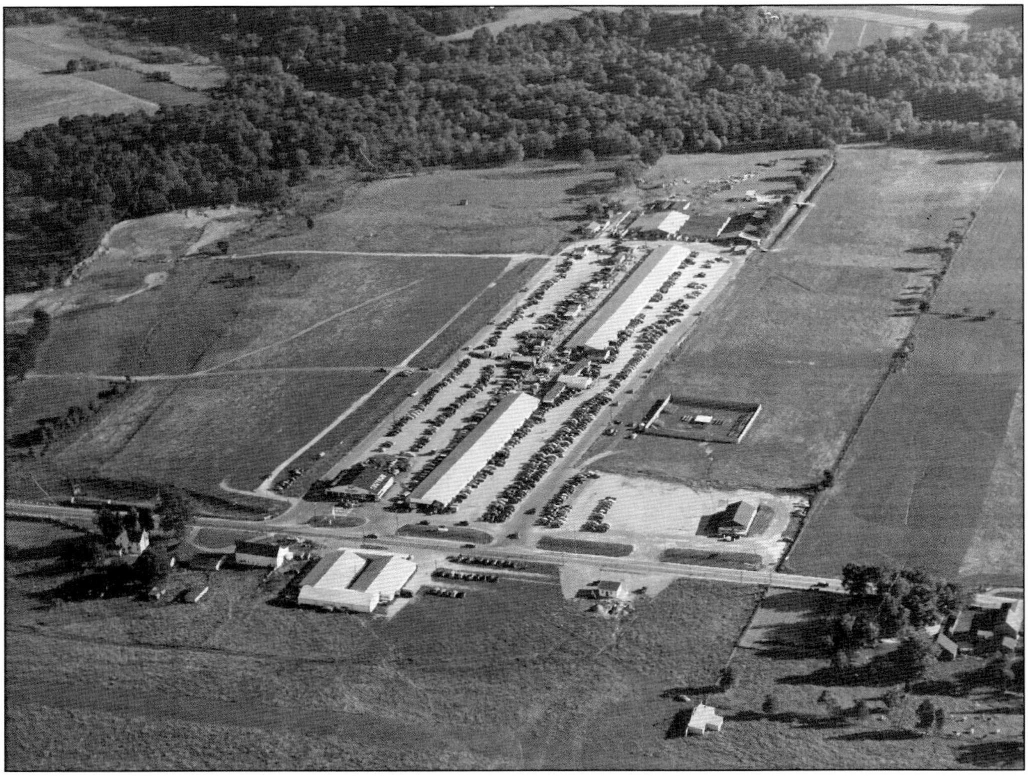

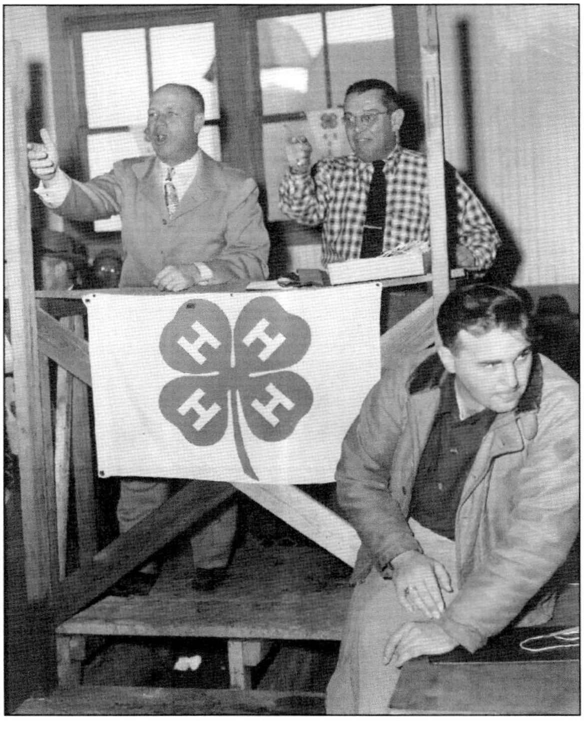

Move to Pilesgrove. Cowtown was originally located in the heart of Woodstown. After some complaints from several townspeople about the traffic and the livestock smell, the Cowtown operation moved to its current location on Route 40. Technically, the property is located in Pilesgrove Township, but many continue to associate Cowtown with Woodstown.

At the State Fair. Stoney Harris (far left) acts as an auctioneer for 4-H in Flemington, New Jersey, at the state fair in the 1940s. An organization administered by the National Institute of Food and Agriculture, 4-H was and continues to be an educational youth organization. The "H" in 4-H stands for head, hands, heart, and health. (Courtesy of the Harris family and the *Newark News*.)

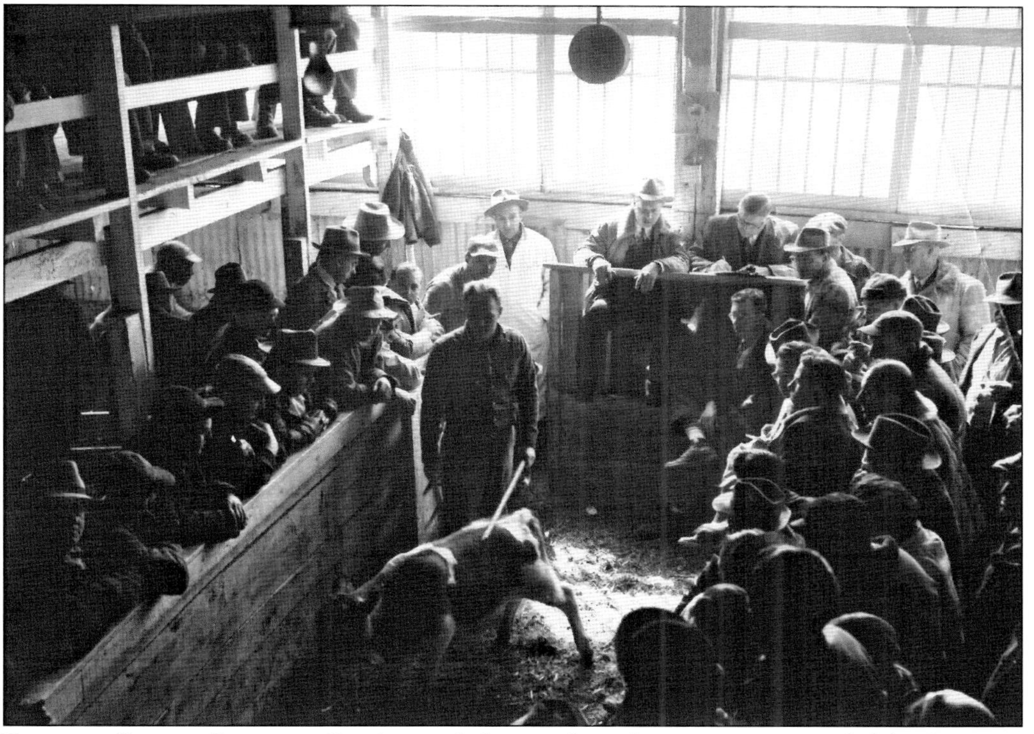

Everyone Goes to Cowtown. People, mostly farmers, from the tristate area attended the Cowtown auctions on Tuesdays. As the auction grew, so did its reach. Eventually, the auction became a well-known event and attracted people from up and down the East Coast. Stoney Harris sits at the head of the ring (left) next to auction clerk Albert Carman (right).

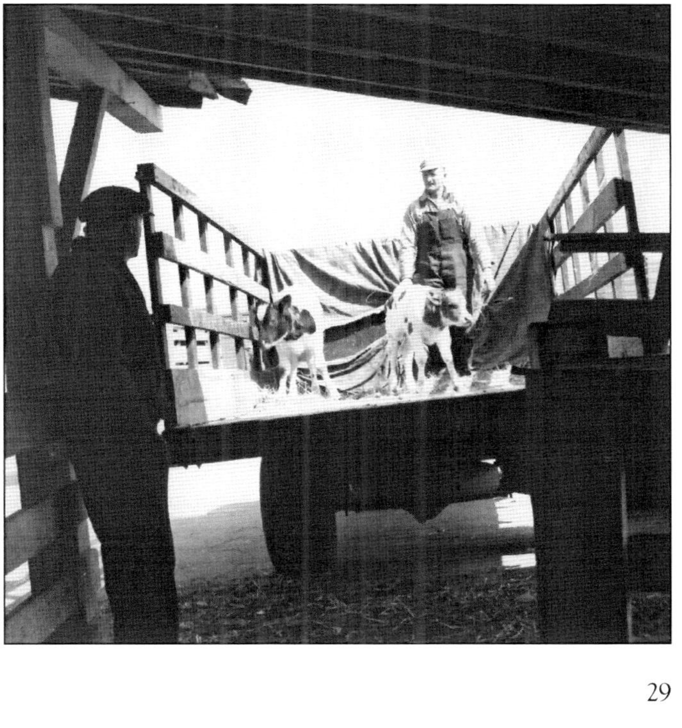

Cowtown Affects Market Prices. Tuesdays were the busiest days at Cowtown because they were auction days. Thousands would attend the Tuesday livestock auctions at Cowtown. The auction order always stayed the same: cows and steers, hogs, and then horses and mules. The prices at Cowtown actually helped to set the market prices in and around South Jersey.

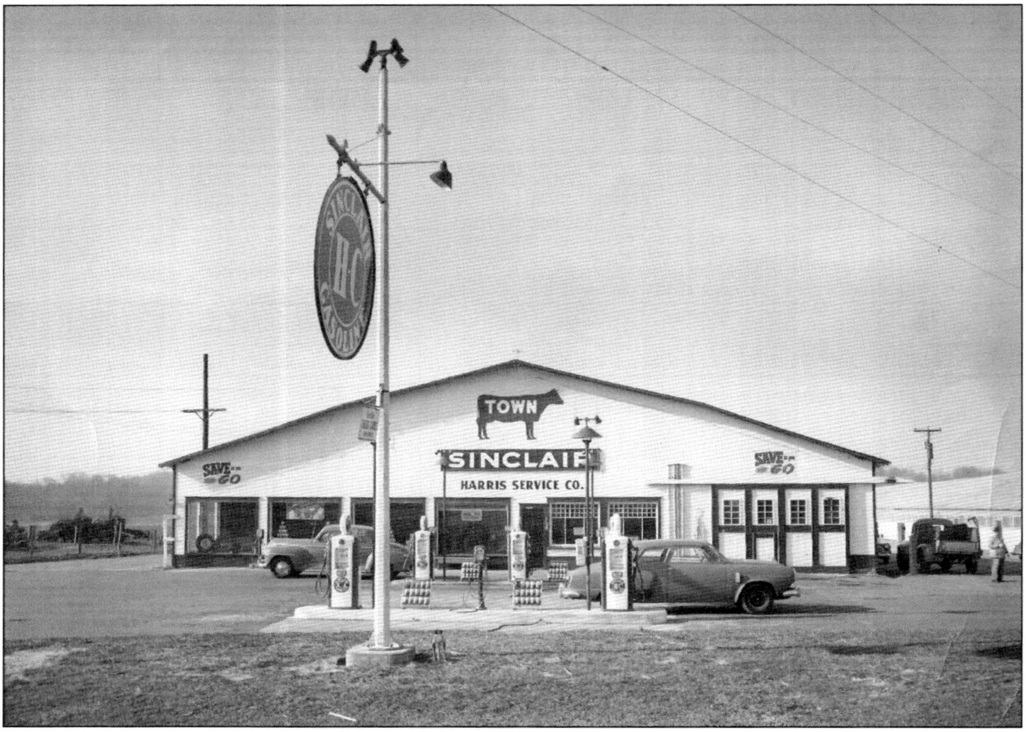

Introducing Automobiles. Before Howard Amos Harris founded the livestock auction, he was in the automobile auction business. In Salem County, livestock proved to be in higher demand than automobiles. However, the Harris family kept auto service and gasoline sales as a part of Cowtown for many years.

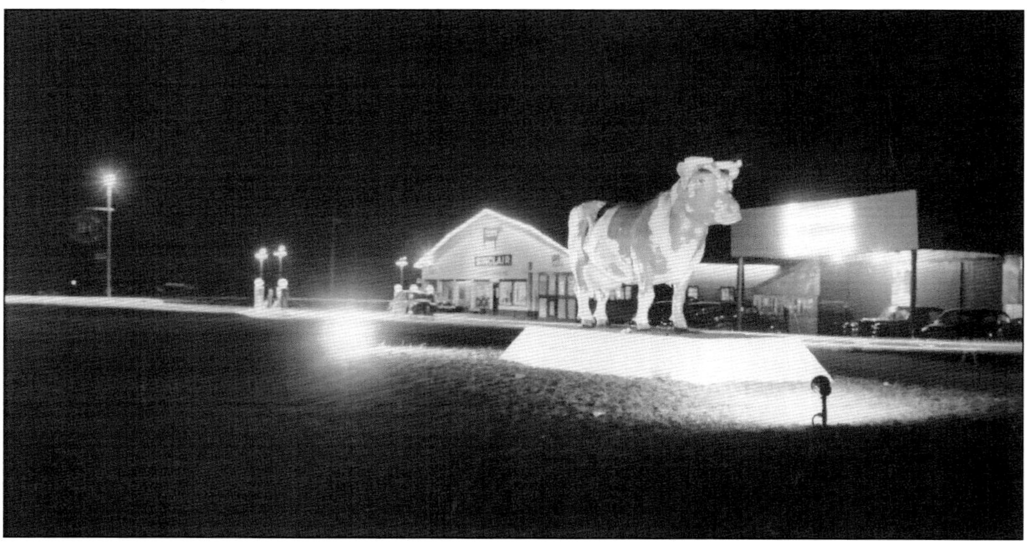

Seeing Red. The Harris Service Co. station was located on Route 40 outside of Woodstown. The iconic red cow, the original cow, sits in front of the station in the picture. The original cow was an Angus-Holstein and was painted red because it was Stoney's favorite color. The cow was replaced with a newer model in the 1980s.

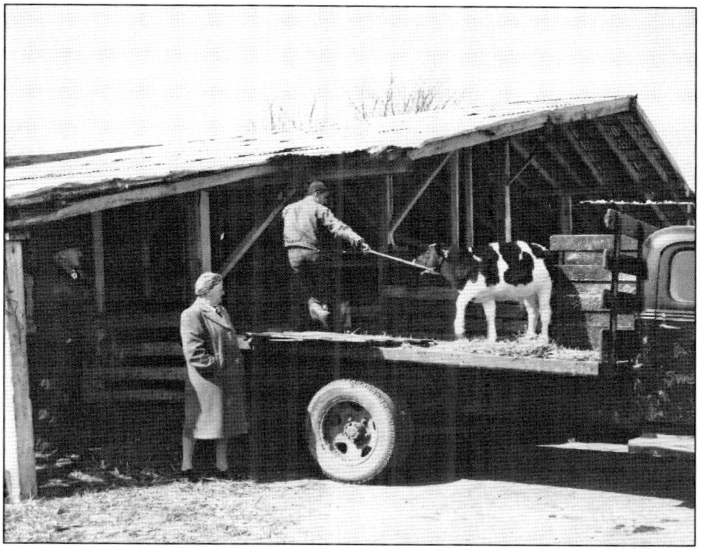

Brought to Auction. Agnes McCann looks on as a calf that she raised is unloaded from the truck. The calf was being brought to auction. The McCann farm was in Swedesboro, New Jersey, which is located in a neighboring South Jersey county. Calves were sold by the pound, as opposed to being sold by the head. (Courtesy of Katherine McCann.)

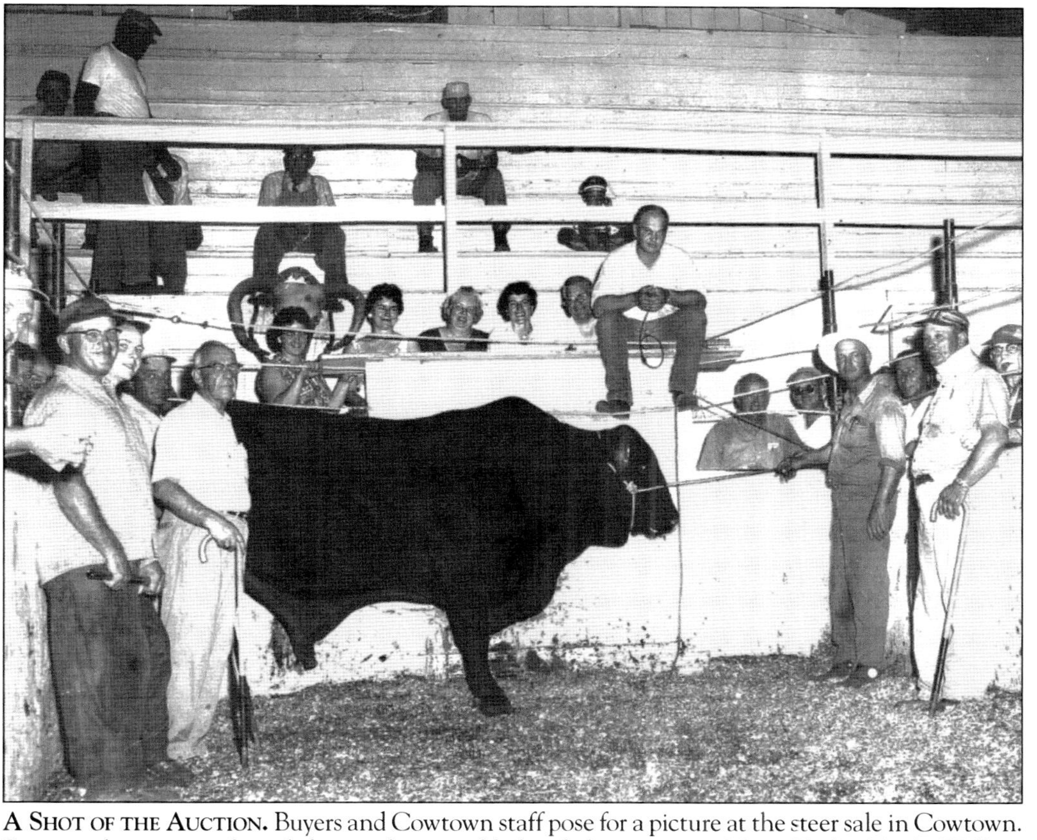

A Shot of the Auction. Buyers and Cowtown staff pose for a picture at the steer sale in Cowtown. Seen in the picture, from left to right seated behind the steer, are Mary Blight, Emily Walker, Alice Layton, Irene Harris, Albert Carman, and Howard Harris. Standing to the right of the steer, from left to right, are Stoney Harris and Bill Dare, and standing to the left of the steer, also from left to right, are Ralph Kilmore, Richard Dolbow, Harry Finlaw, and Albert Finlaw.

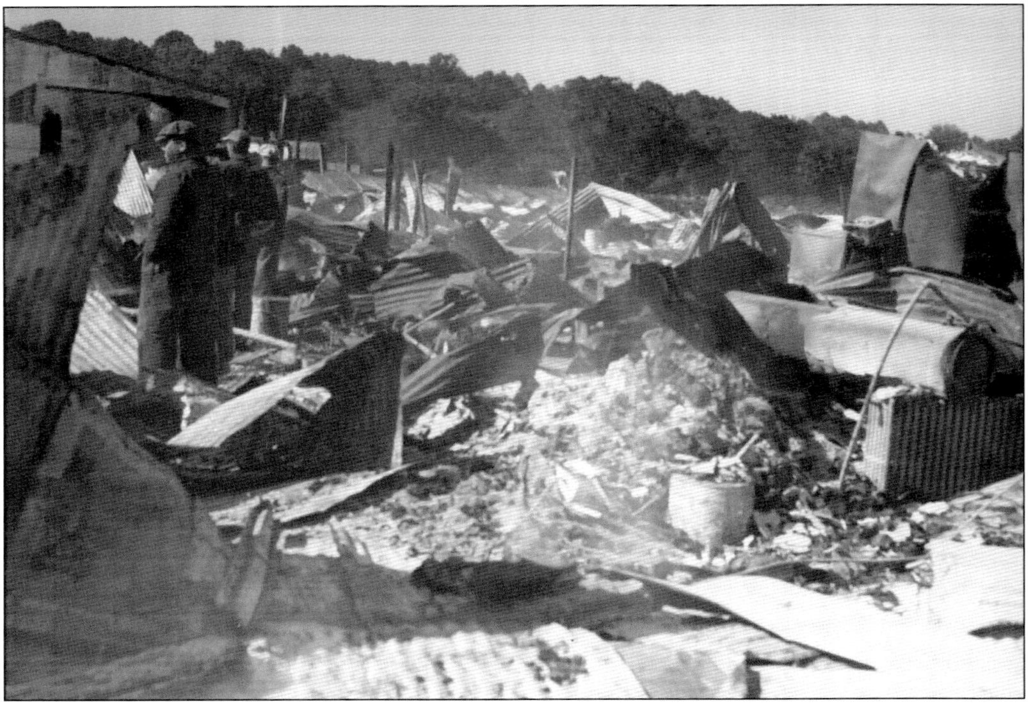

Fire at Cowtown. A fire destroyed the sale barn in October 1946. Some of the Cowtown cows were lost in the fire. Even though materials were in short supply because of World War II, the community banded together and quickly located supplies to rebuild. The reconstruction of the sale barn included only a small amount of salvageable materials. Most supplies, like lumber and nails, had to be purchased new, which was a daunting task because of the war. Supplies were purchased from multiple businesses in local counties because quantities were limited at each store. The new sale barn was built in less than a week. It was, in fact, ready for the auction by the Tuesday after the fire. The community was integral in the effort to have the sale barn ready for use.

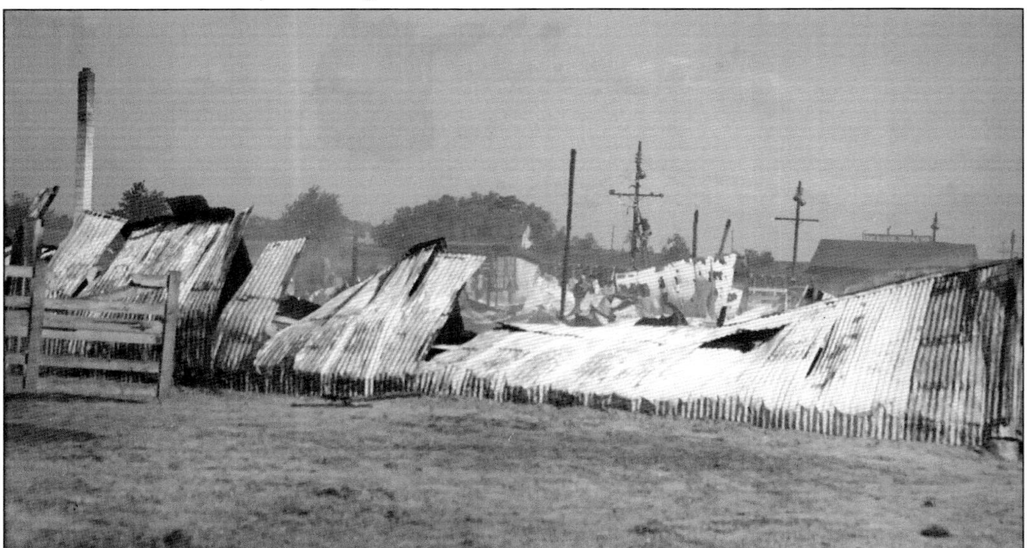

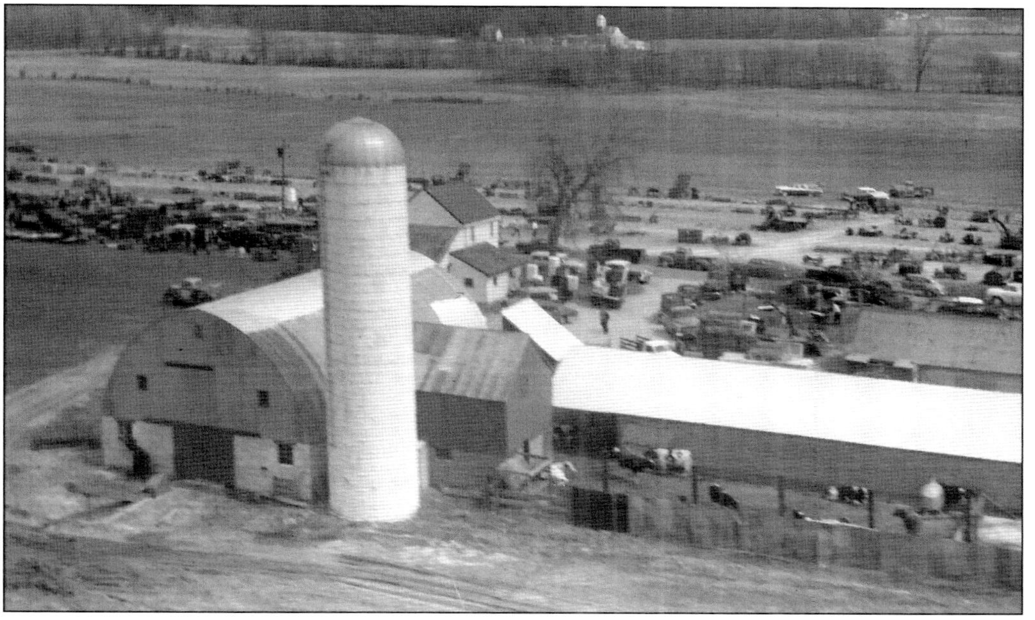

Farm Equipment Auction. Stoney Harris was not just an auctioneer at Cowtown; he was also well known in New Jersey as an auctioneer. He ran the auction at Walter Tarpine's equipment sale each year. It is likely that Stoney took these aerial pictures, as he very much enjoyed photography and often hopped in the Cowtown plane.

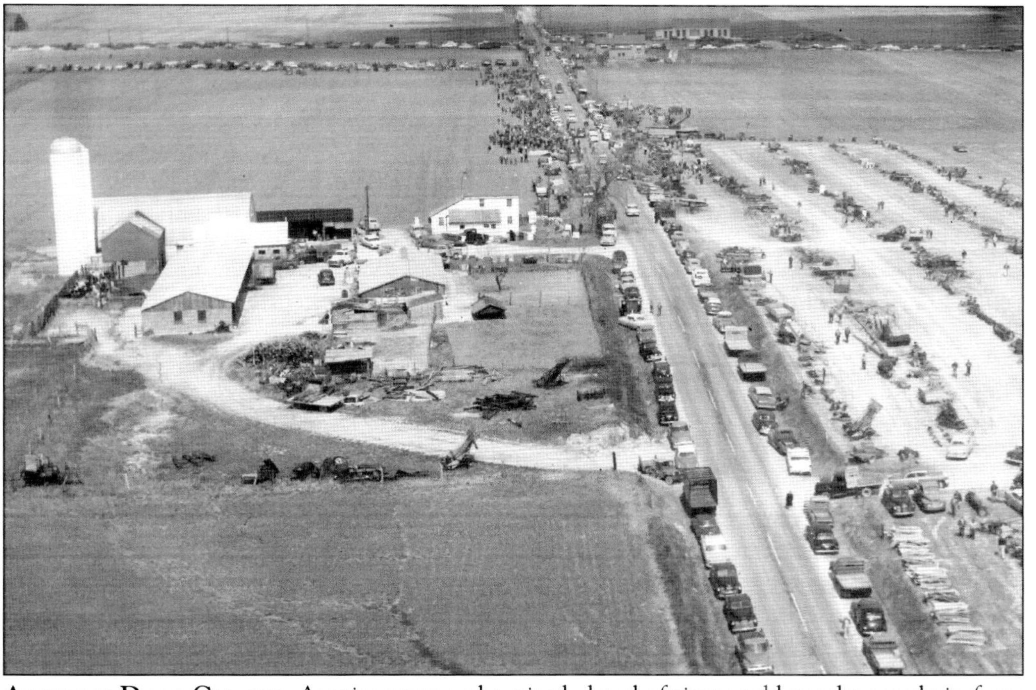

Auctions Drew Crowds. Auctions were advertised ahead of time and brought people in from surrounding communities. Hundreds of people attended this annual sale, seen here in the 1950s, which took place in Upper Pittsgrove Township, less than 10 miles from Cowtown.

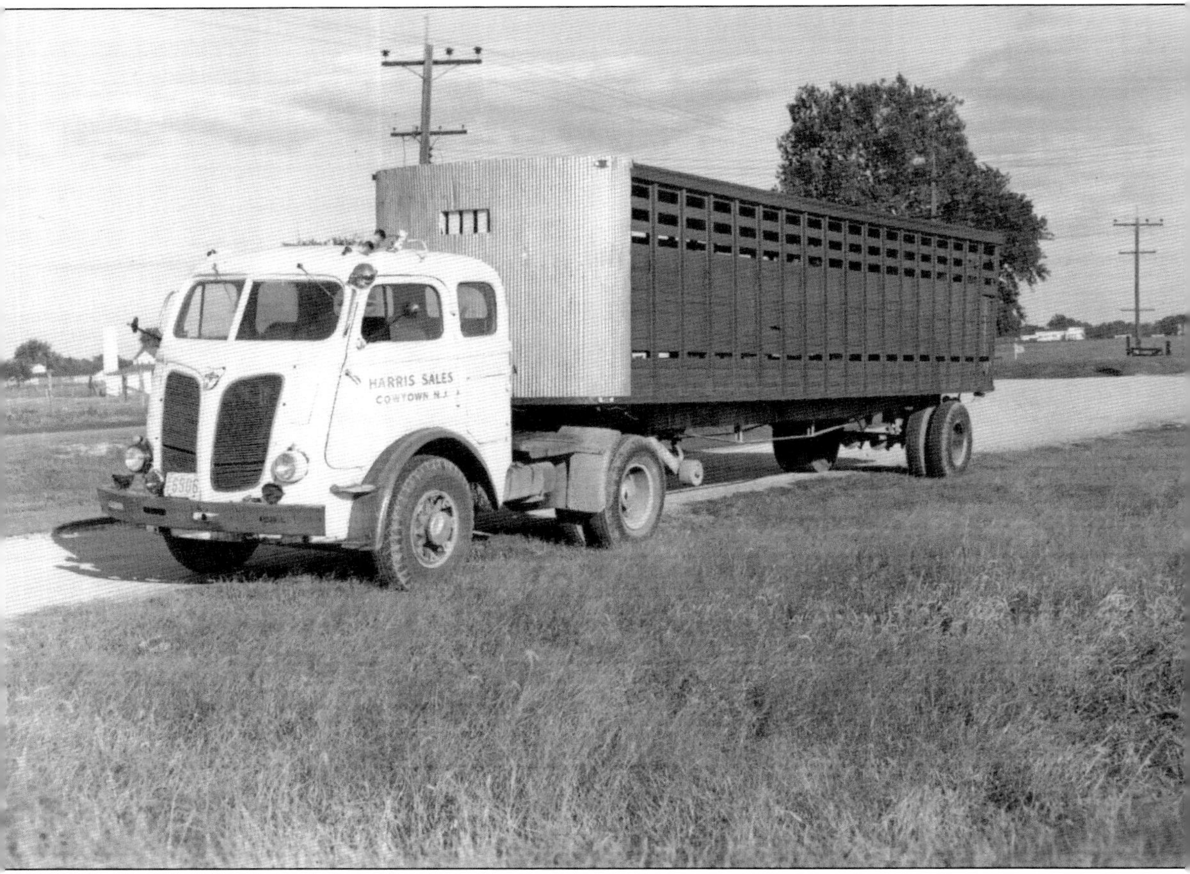

Changing Hands, Changing Names. This Cowtown truck would have been used to haul cattle to the slaughterhouse after auction. Larger purchases of livestock, namely cattle, would warrant transportation to the slaughterhouse for butchers who were purchasing in higher quantities. "Harris Sales" is painted on the side on the side of the truck. Today, Cowtown is a catchall phrase for the location, the flea market, and the rodeo. When Stoney Harris bought Cowtown from his father, Howard Amos Harris Sr., the auction and auctioneering services were called Harris Sales Co., and it was known as an operation located at Cowtown. Later, the auction and market was sold by Stoney to his son Howard Amos Harris III, and the operation continued as Harris Sales Co. Then, Stoney bought the business back from his son, and the name of the operation eventually morphed into Cowtown.

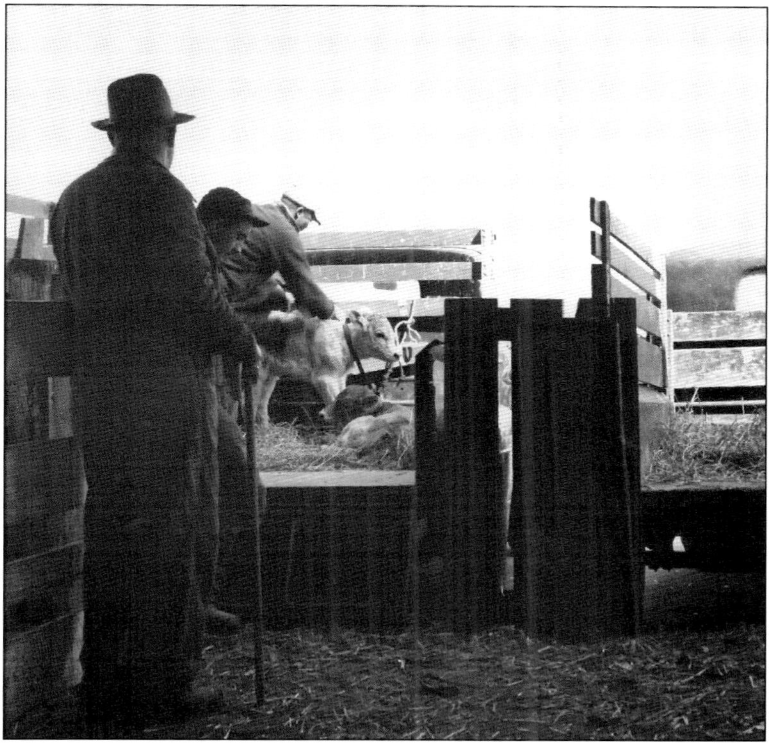

CALF PROCEDURE. Jack Ferguson stands next to two calves. After calves were brought to auction, their ears were tagged. Next, they were placed on the scale and weighed to be sold by the pound. Most of the buyers were butchers who would take the calves at the conclusion of the auction.

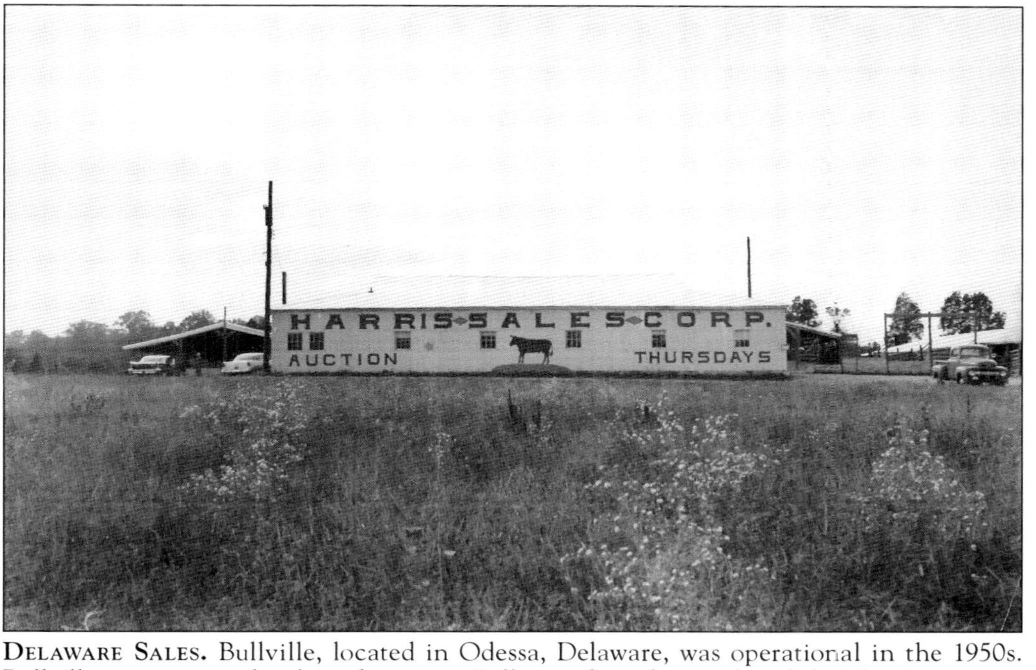

DELAWARE SALES. Bullville, located in Odessa, Delaware, was operational in the 1950s. Bullville auctions ran for about four years. Sellers and vendors preferred the Tuesday auction at the New Jersey location, so the customer base did not grow enough to support the Thursday Delaware auctions.

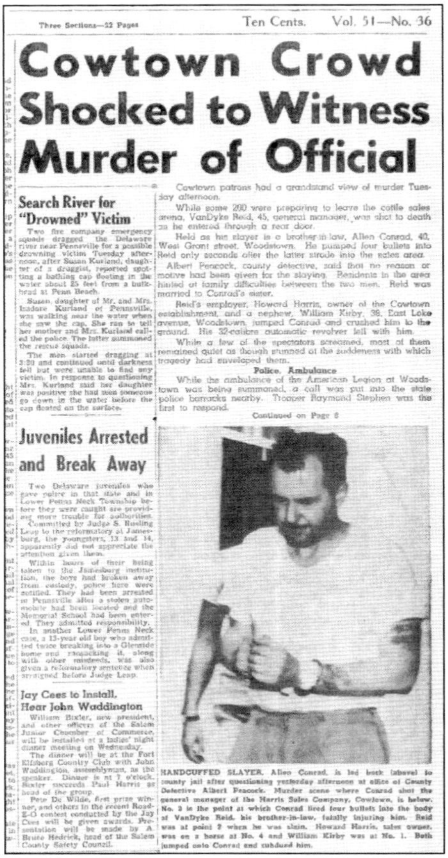

Three Sections—32 Pages Ten Cents. Vol. 51—No. 36

Cowtown Crowd Shocked to Witness Murder of Official

Cowtown patrons had a grandstand view of murder Tuesday afternoon.

While some 200 were preparing to leave the cattle sales arena, VanDyke Reid, 45, general manager, was shot to death as he entered through a rear door.

Held as his slayer is a brother-in-law, Allen Conrad, 40, West Grant street, Woodstown. He pumped four bullets into Reid only seconds after the latter strode into the sales area.

Albert Peacock, county detective, said that no reason or motive had been given for the slaying. Residents in the area hinted at family difficulties between the two men. Reid was married to Conrad's sister.

Reid's employer, Howard Harris, owner of the Cowtown establishment, and a nephew, William Kirby, 38, East Lake avenue, Woodstown, jumped Conrad and crushed him to the ground. His 32-calibre automatic revolver fell with him.

While a few of the spectators screamed, most of them remained quiet as though stunned at the suddenness with which tragedy had enveloped them.

Police, Ambulance

While the ambulance of the American Legion at Woodstown was being summoned, a call was put into the state police barracks nearby. Trooper Raymond Stephen was the first to respond.

Continued on Page 8

HANDCUFFED SLAYER. Allen Conrad, is led back (above) to county jail after questioning yesterday afternoon at office of County Detective Albert Peacock. Murder scene where Conrad shot the general manager of the Harris Sales Company, Cowtown, is below. No. 3 is the point at which Conrad fired four bullets into the body of VanDyke Reid, his brother-in-law, fatally injuring him. Reid was at point 2 when he was slain. Howard Harris, sales owner, was on a horse at No. 4 and William Kirby was at No. 1. Both jumped onto Conrad and subdued him.

Search River for "Drowned" Victim

Two fire company emergency squads dragged the Delaware river near Pennsville for a possible drowning victim Tuesday afternoon, after Susan Kurland, daughter of a druggist, reported spotting a bathing cap floating in the water about 25 feet from a bulkhead at Penn Beach.

Susan, daughter of Mr. and Mrs. Isadore Kurland of Pennsville, was walking near the water when she saw the cap. She ran to tell her mother and Mrs. Kurland called the police. The latter summoned the rescue squads.

The men started dragging at 3:30 and continued until darkness fell but were unable to find any victim. In response to questioning Mrs. Kurland said her daughter was positive she had seen someone go down in the water before the cap floated on the surface.

Juveniles Arrested and Break Away

Two Delaware juveniles who gave police in that state and in Lower Penns Neck Township before they were caught are providing more trouble for authorities.

Committed by Judge S. Rusling Leap to the reformatory at Jamesburg, the youngsters, 13 and 14, apparently did not appreciate the attention given them.

Within hours of their being taken to the Jamesburg institution, the boys had broken away from custody, police here were notified. They had been arrested at Pennsville after a stolen automobile had been located and the Memorial School had been entered. They admitted responsibility.

In another Lower Penns Neck case, a 13-year old boy who admitted twice breaking into a Glenside home and ransacking it, along with other misdeeds, was also given a reformatory sentence when arraigned before Judge Leap.

Jay Cees to Install, Hear John Waddington

William Bixler, new president, and other officers of the Salem Junior Chamber of Commerce, will be installed at a ladies' night dinner meeting on Wednesday.

The dinner will be at the Fort Elfsborg Country Club with John Waddington, assemblyman, as the speaker. Dinner is at 7 o'clock. Bixler succeeds Paul Harris as head of the group.

Pete De Wilde, first prize winner, and others in the recent Road-E-O contest conducted by the Jay Cees will be given awards. Presentation will be made by A. Bruce Hedrick, head of the Salem County Safety Council.

MURDER AT COWTOWN. The Cowtown livestock auction made the front page of the local paper in June 1955. VanDyke Reid was shot and killed during the auction by his brother-in-law Allen Conrad. Stoney Harris and Bill Kirby, also of the Harris Sales Co., subdued Conrad after he shot Reid four times. (Courtesy of Salem County Public Archives.)

HAY FOR SALE. The auctions at Cowtown were not restricted to livestock. The hay sale ran from early November until supplies diminished in the spring. Here, trucks filled with hay are lined up at the start of the auction. Items to be auctioned were determined based on availability from the sellers and interest from the buyers.

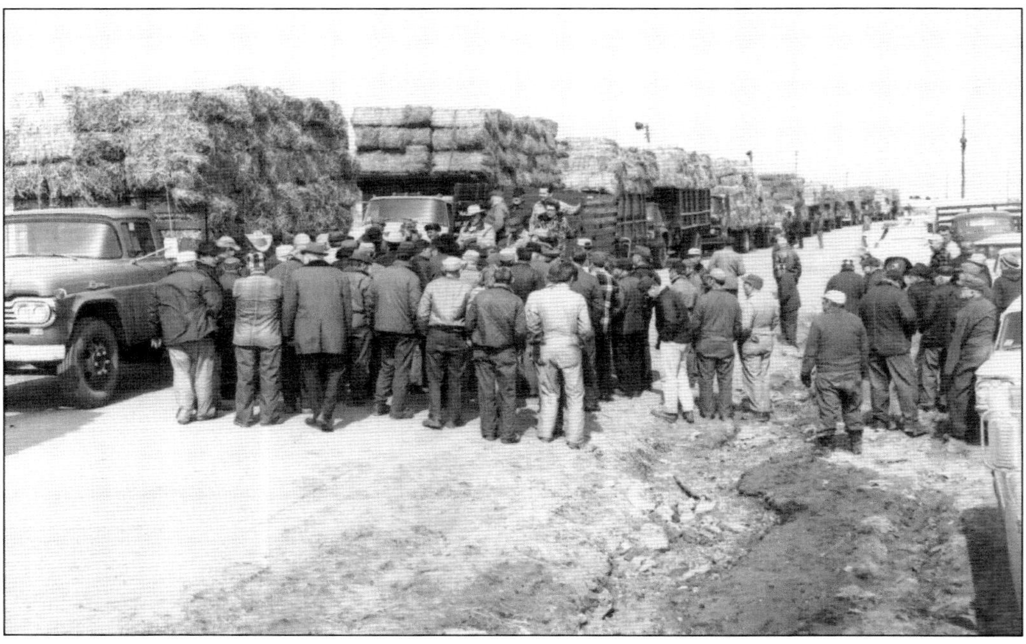

PIGS FOR SALE. The livestock auction was held all year long. The wintertime crowd here awaits the next pig. Boards ran above the pigpens to allow potential buyers to see the pigs before deciding to purchase. Stoney Harris (bent over) was the auctioneer. Auctioneers attend school (most of the Harris family auctioneers attended schools in the Midwest) to be able to conduct live auctions.

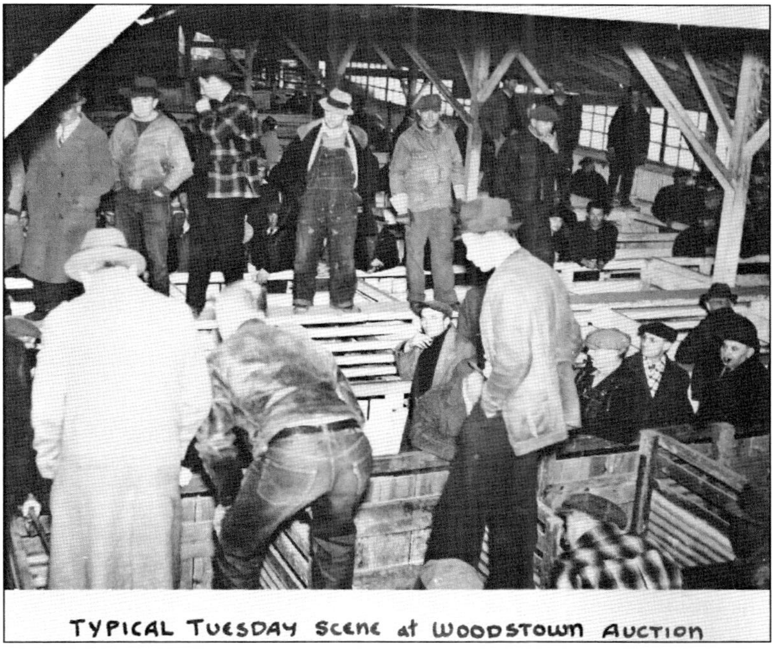

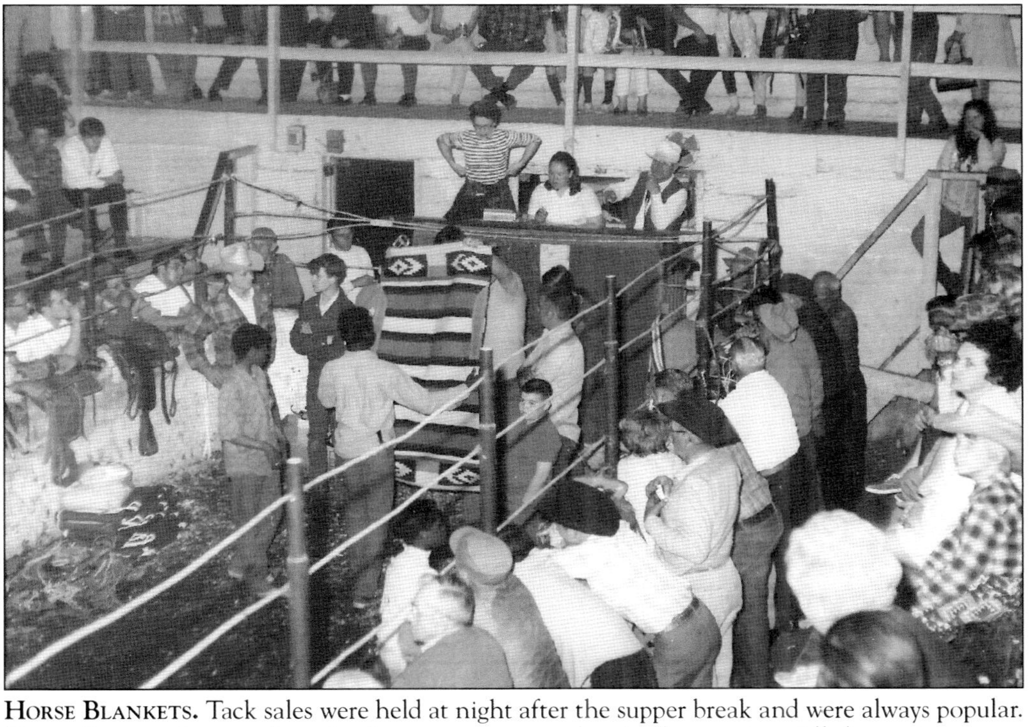

HORSE BLANKETS. Tack sales were held at night after the supper break and were always popular. Depending on what was for sale, they sometimes ran late in the evening. All the auctions were done on consignment. Seated at the table in the auction ring, from left to right, are Marie Harris, Charlotte Lippincott, and Stoney Harris.

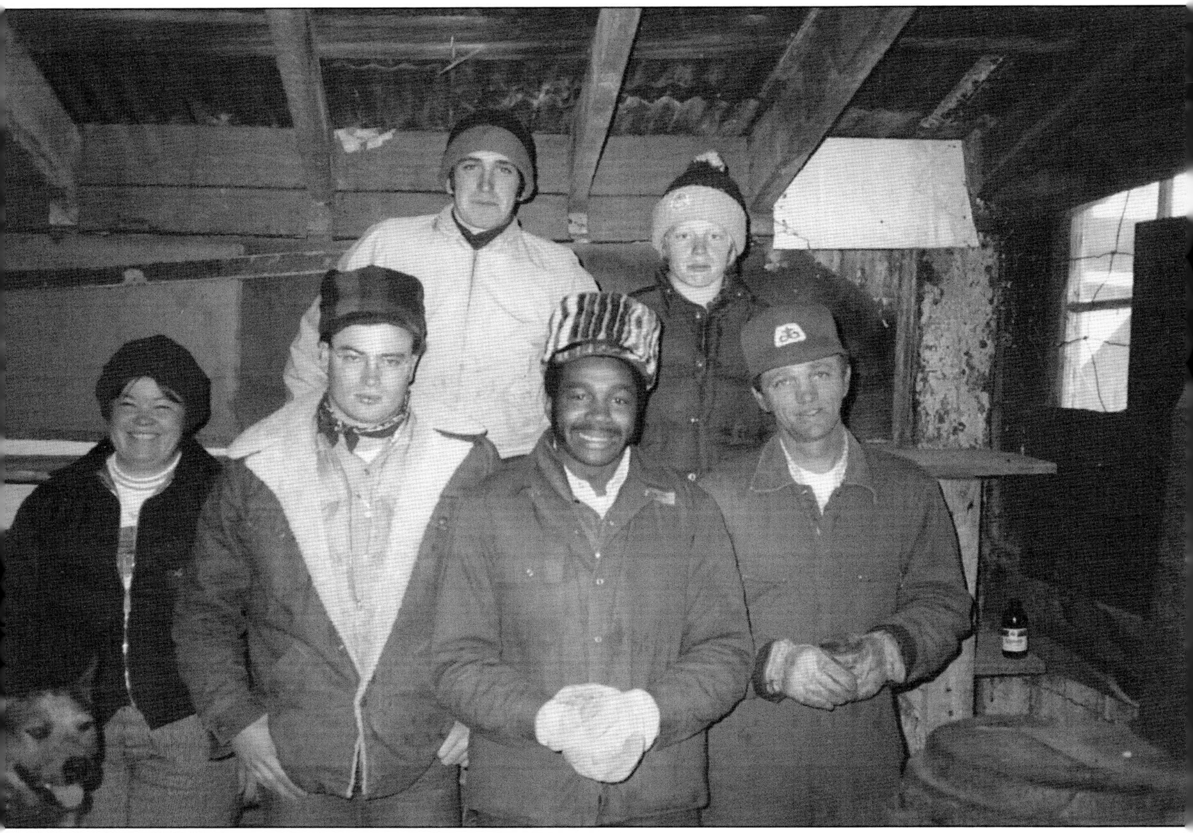

Eggs for Sale. An egg house was located in the sale barn, and eggs were sold on Tuesdays. Pictured here from left to right are (first row) Charlotte Lippincott, Grant Harris, Jimmy Lee Walker, and Corn Fowler; (second row) Bob Buffington and Scott Fowler.

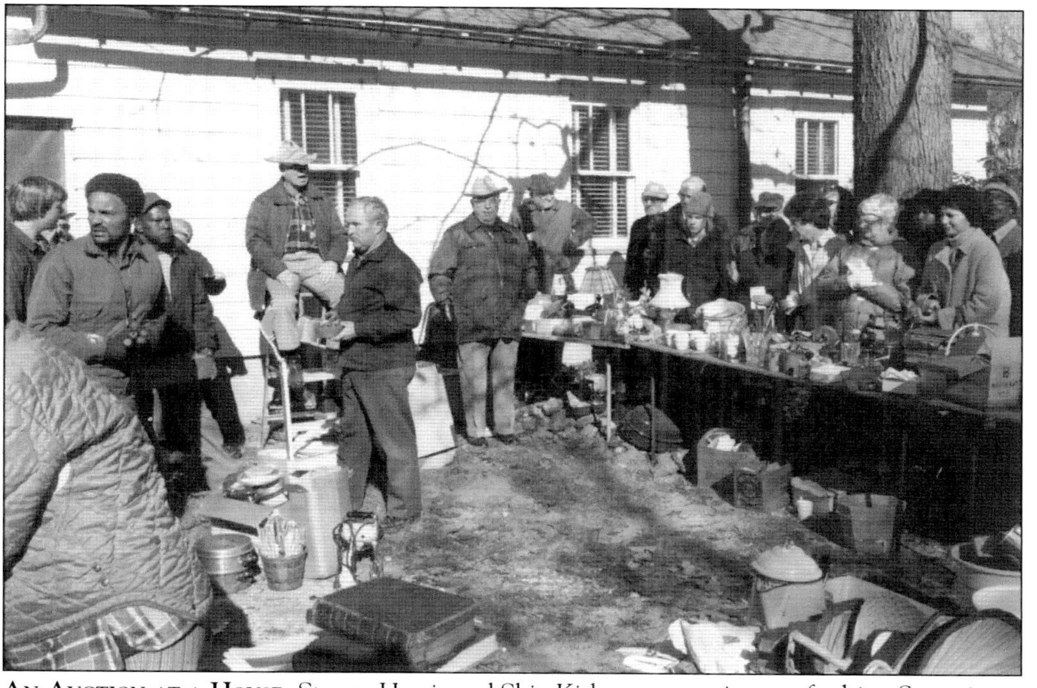

AN AUCTION AT A HOUSE. Stoney Harris and Skip Kirby were auctioneers for hire. Sometimes, they were asked to auction at homes in the South Jersey area. Here, Harris is seated (wearing a cowboy hat) and Kirby is standing in front of him at a home auction. Standing beside Stoney is David Blew (wearing a cowboy hat), who was also an auctioneer that worked with both Stoney and Skip.

HAPPY ANNIVERSARY. Stoney Harris auctioneered for 50 years, spending most of his career as an auctioneer at Cowtown. Each auctioneer develops his or her own style, including choosing the filler words that help build excitement among buyers when presenting incremental dollar increases. This is sometimes referred to as the auction chant, the auction cry, or bid calling. (Courtesy of the Harris family and B.J. Frey.)

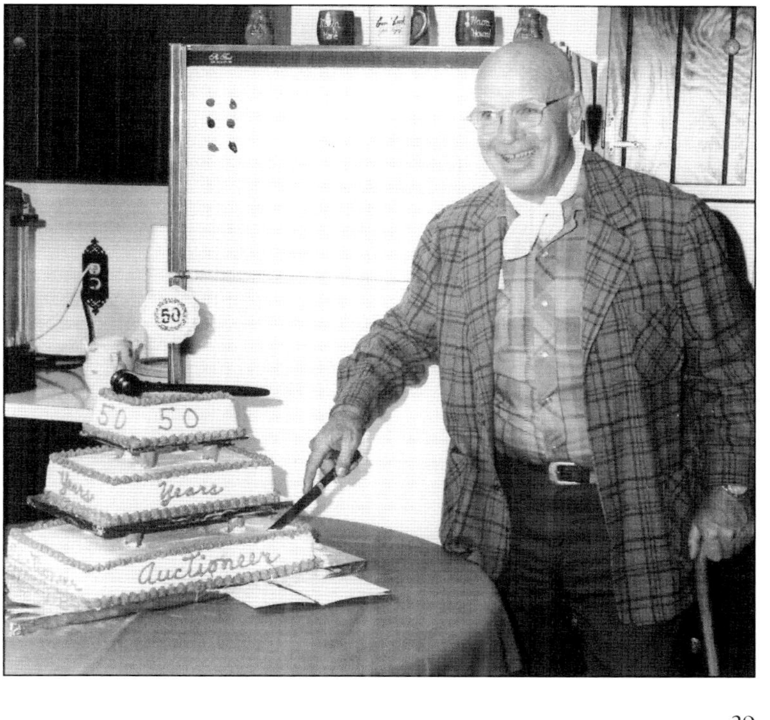

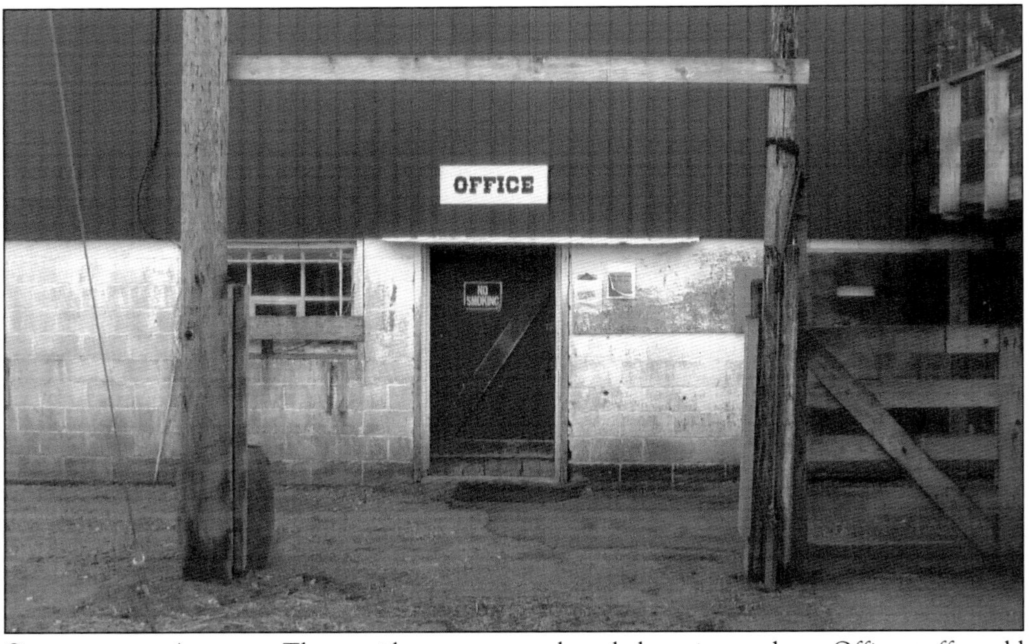

Going to the Auction. The outside entrance to the sale barn is seen here. Office staff would proceed through the office door, while potential buyers and spectators would head to the ramp on the right side and enter the sale ring seating area from that entrance. Auction day, which was always on a Tuesday, had a set schedule of events. Not only did the auction serve a purpose, it was also a source of entertainment for the community.

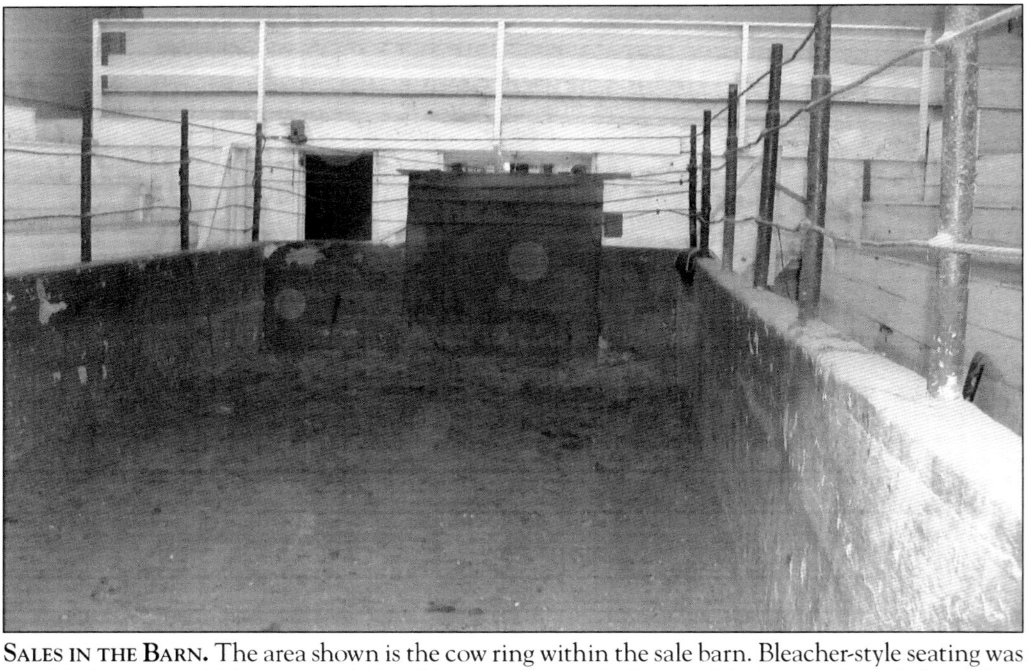

Sales in the Barn. The area shown is the cow ring within the sale barn. Bleacher-style seating was provided so potential buyers would be able to easily see the livestock being auctioned. Attendees would raise their hand or nod to indicate their bid.

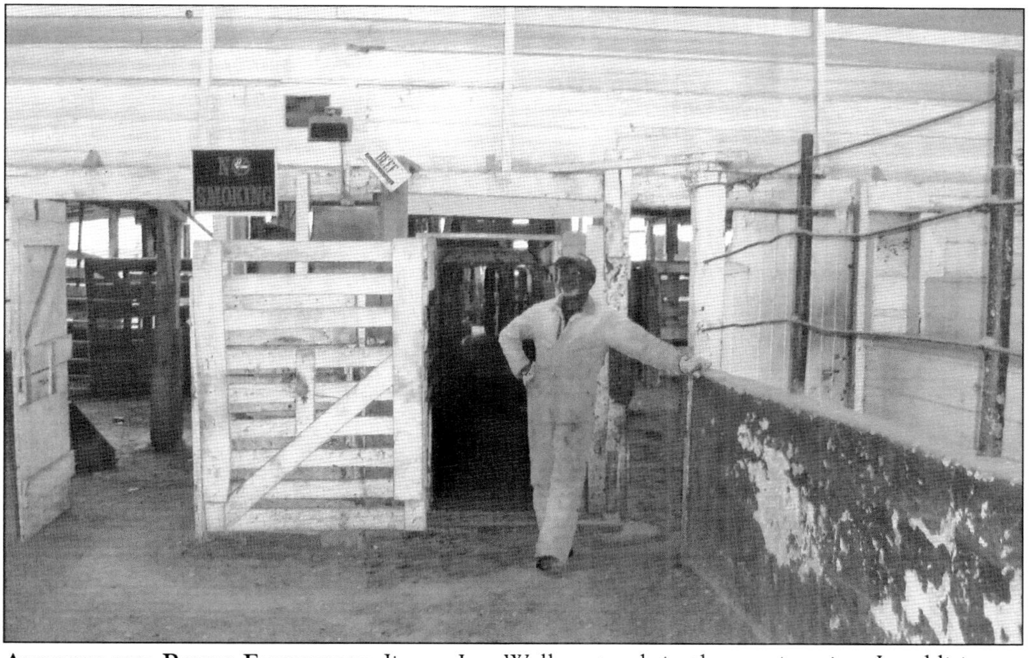

Auction and Rodeo Experience. Jimmy Lee Walker stands in the auction ring. In addition to working at the auction at Cowtown, Walker was also a rodeo competitor and bullfighter. Livestock was brought in through the large doorways and remained in the ring until sold.

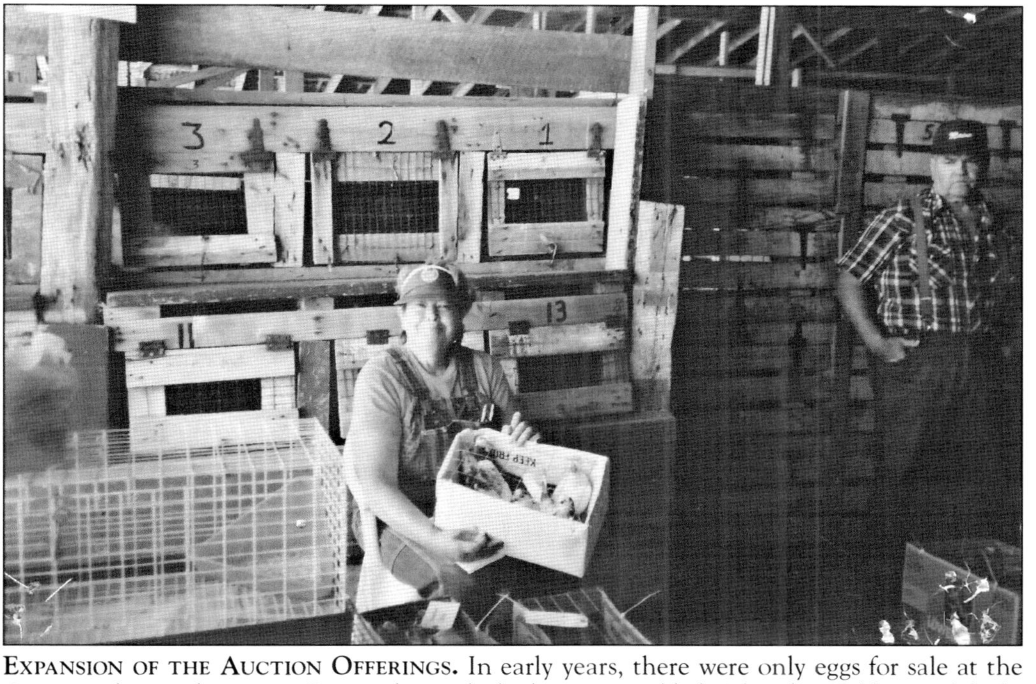

Expansion of the Auction Offerings. In early years, there were only eggs for sale at the Cowtown livestock auction. Due to demand, chickens were added. After that, rabbits and ducks were also added. Pigeons, emus, and the occasional chinchilla have been part of the auction as well. Charlotte Lippincott, seen here, clerked at the egg house for many years.

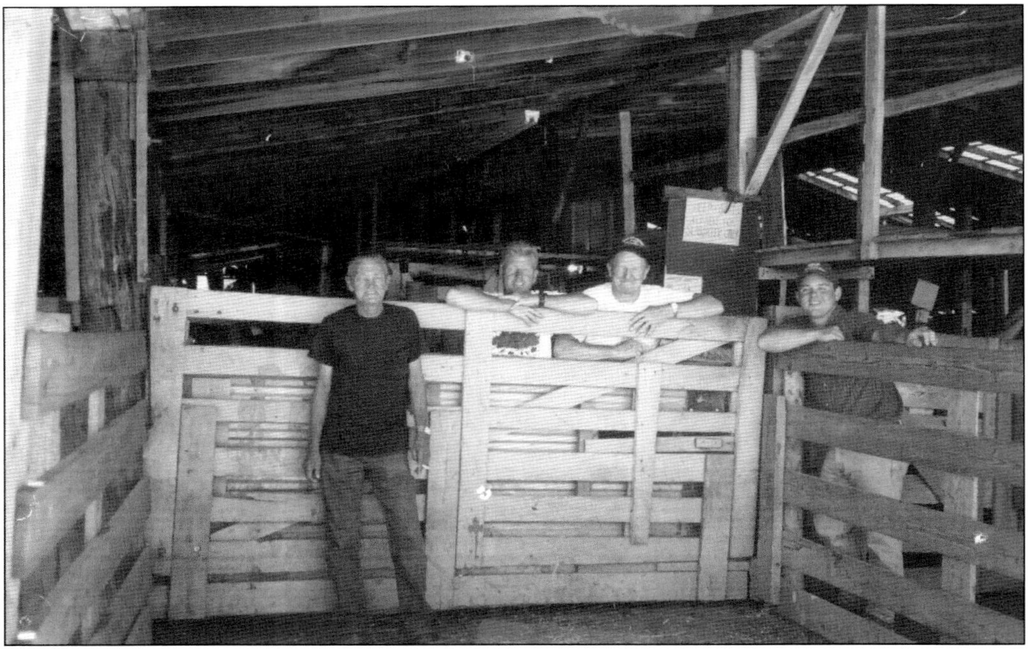

Bidding at the Auction. The auctions were completely open to the public. Initially, anyone could bid, but, eventually, a registration process was put in place, and each potential buyer was assigned a number. During the auctions, if the crowd got too loud, the auctioneer would stop the auction. Live animals and lots of movement made for a noisy event.

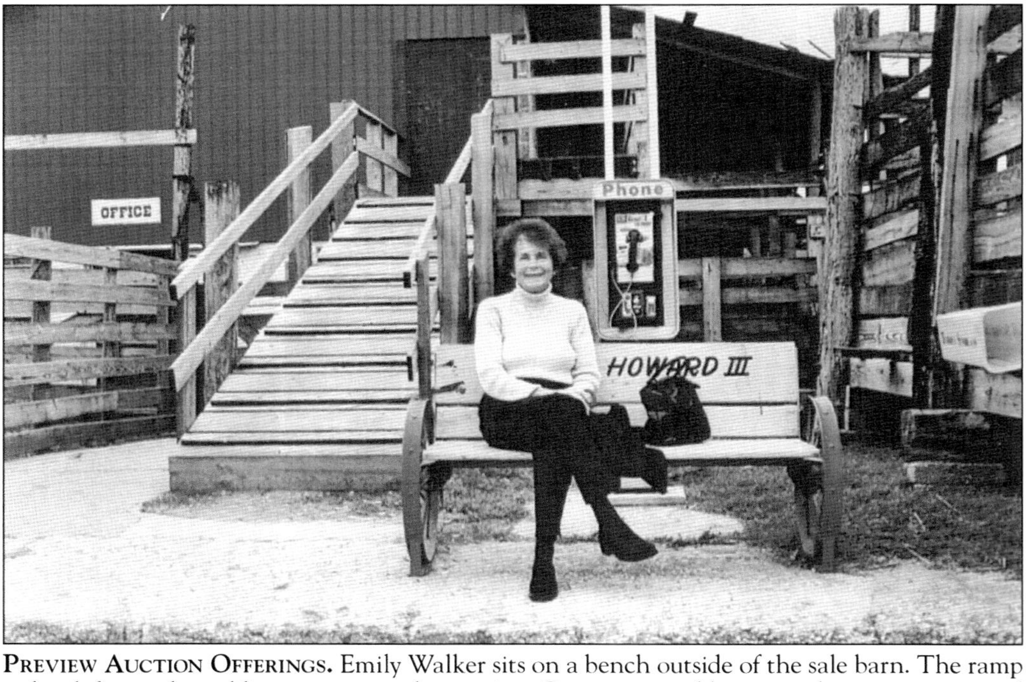

Preview Auction Offerings. Emily Walker sits on a bench outside of the sale barn. The ramp to her left was the public entrance to the auction. Once potential buyers and spectators entered the sale barn, they were able to preview the livestock for sale. (Courtesy of Emily Walker.)

SELLING LIVESTOCK. Cows, calves, lambs, and pigs were sold by the pound. Goats and baby pigs were sold by the head. The dairy cow auctions, which were discontinued in the 1970s, were sold by the head. Horses were also sold by the head. (Photograph by Kate Mondelli.)

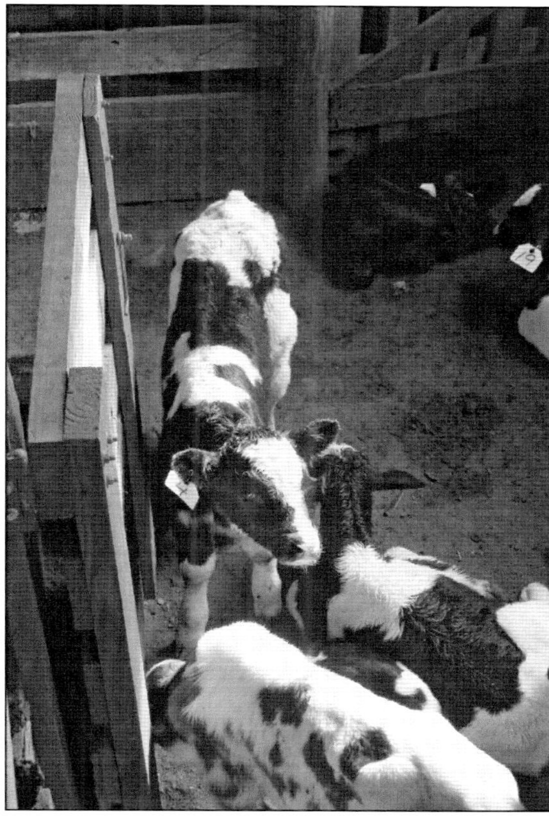

FAMILY BENCH. The bench outside of the sale barn, seen here, was the Harris bench. From left to right, Howard Harris III, Bill Simpkins, and longtime cattle buyer Frank Fillippo wait outside of the sale barn. Carved in the bench were Howard and Irene Harrises' names. Howard and Irene owned the rodeo until 1978. They sold it to their son Grant and his wife, Betsy. Once the sale barn was torn down, the bench was moved to Grant and Betsy's home.

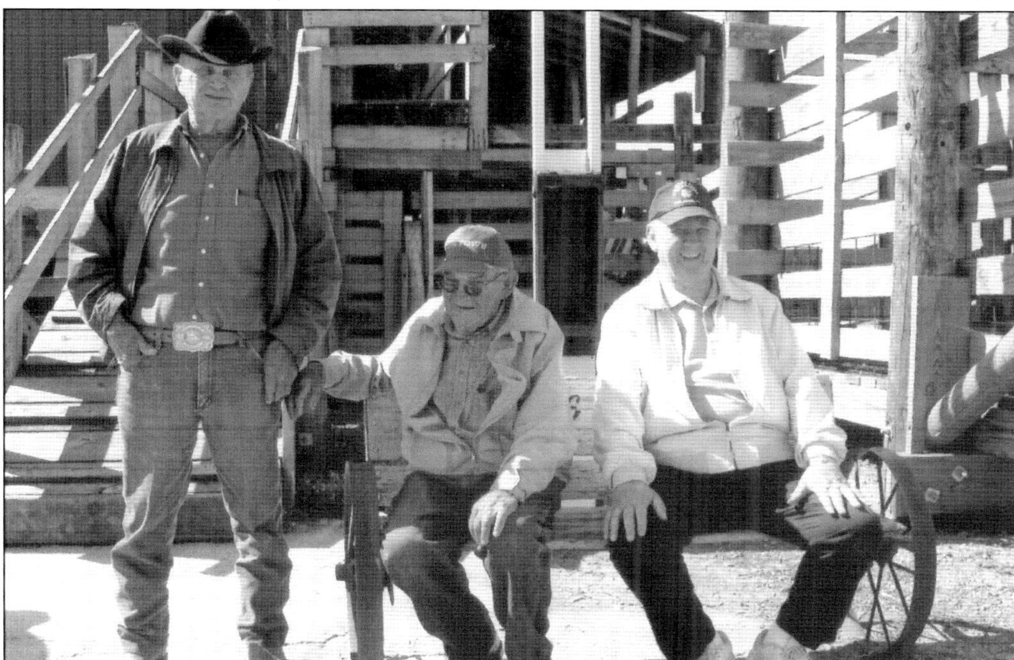

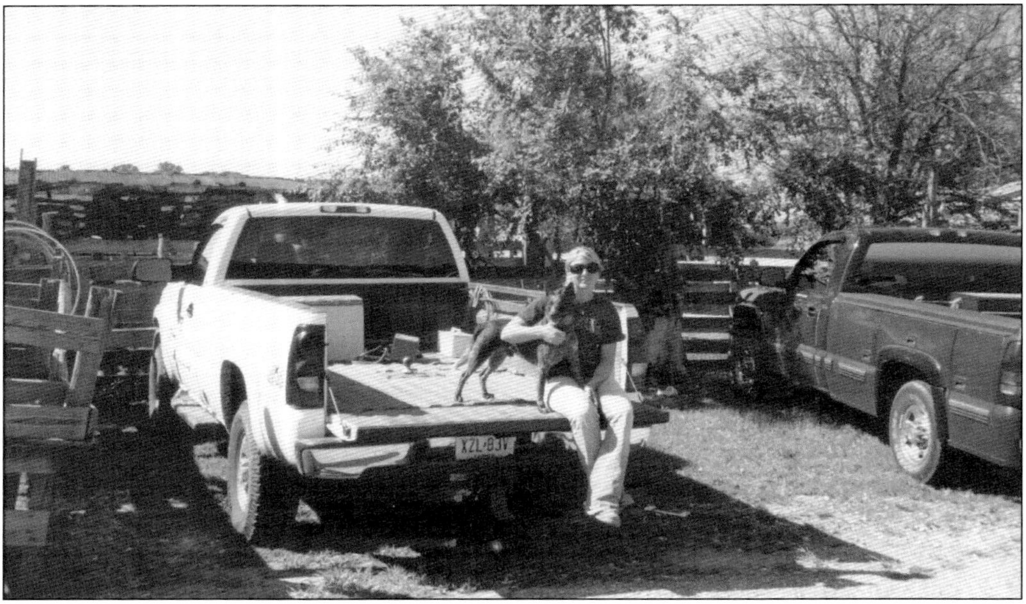

Family Business. Katy Harris Griscom and Cowtown dog Runt rest on the tailgate of a Cowtown pickup truck outside of the sale barn. In keeping the Cowtown tradition going, Katy currently works side by side with her parents at Cowtown. Even though the sale barn auctions are no longer held, the rodeo and the flea market continue to thrive.

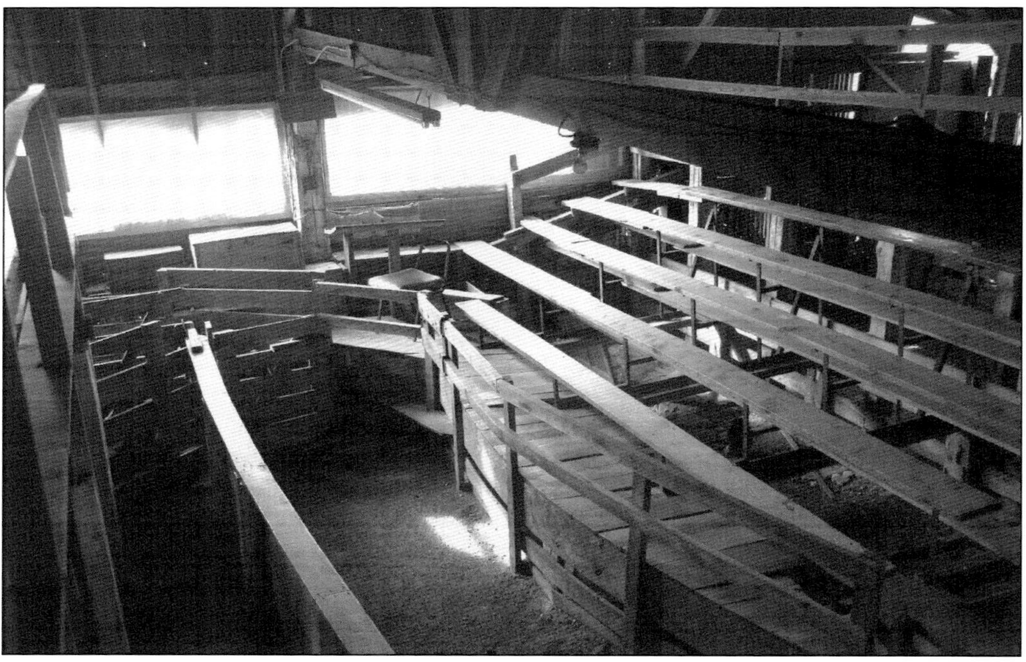

Auction Closes. On Tuesday, December 18, 2007, the Cowtown Sale Barn held its last auction. It was the last remaining livestock auction in South Jersey. At the final sale, Cowtown owner Grant Harris explained that the financial loss had gradually worsened and was just too great. The livestock auction ran from 1926 to 2007. (Photograph by Kate Mondelli.)

Three

The Salem County Fair at Cowtown

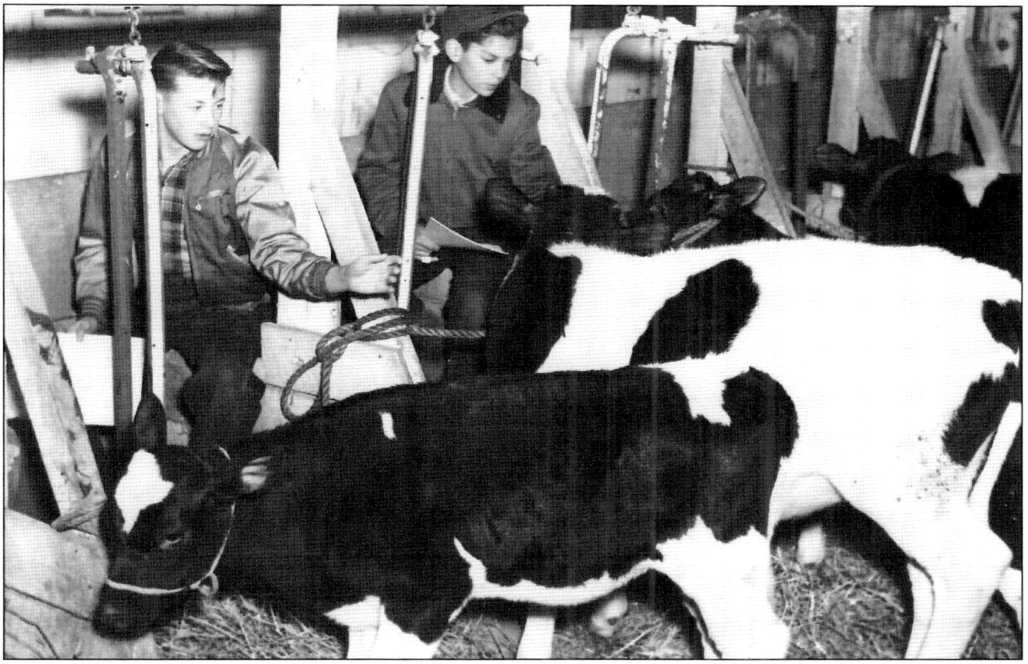

The Best Thing about August. The Salem County Fair is an annual tradition that is still going strong in South Jersey. The Salem County Fair Association works hard each year to provide an opportunity for the Salem County agricultural and farming community to share their hard work and participate in a family-friendly multiday event. Cowtown was integral in reviving the event in the 1920s. (Courtesy of 4-H Rutgers Cooperative Extension.)

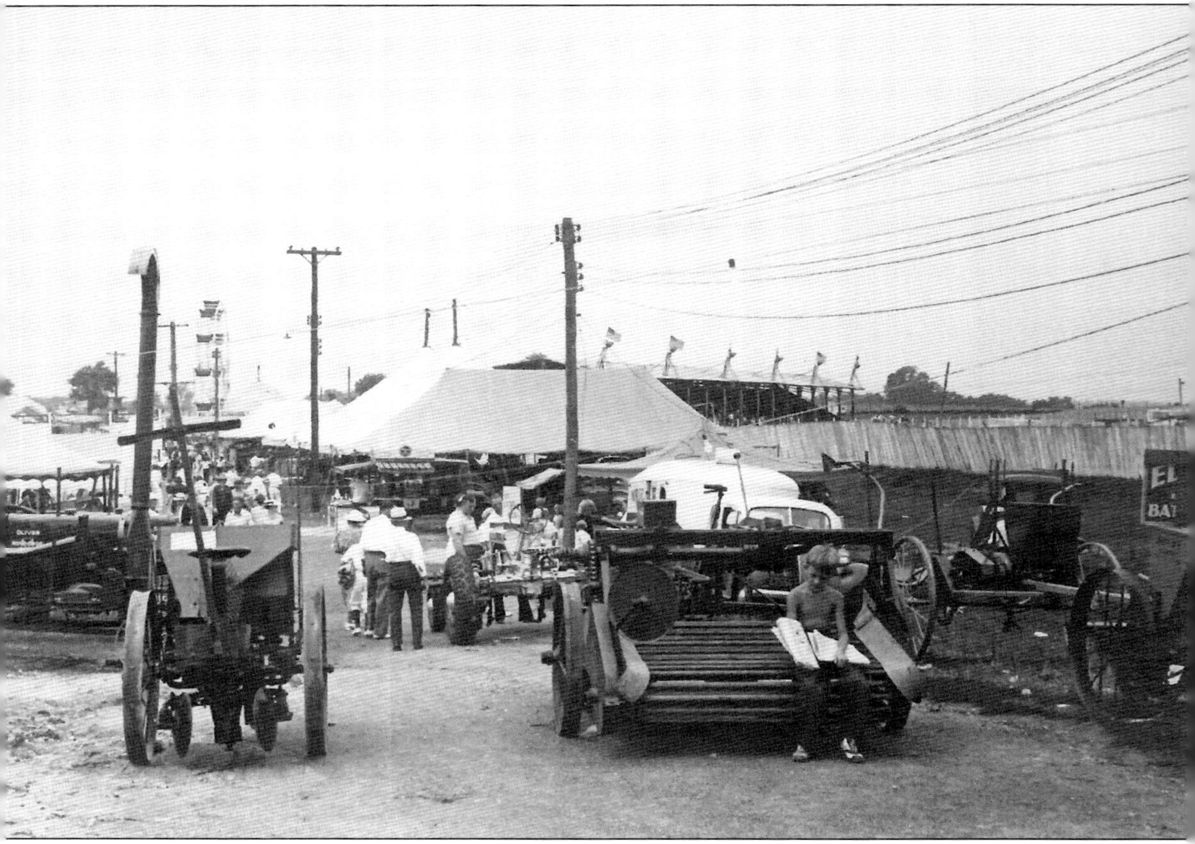

Bringing Back the Fair. The Salem County Fair lost momentum and stopped in the 1920s. Stoney Harris, an influential member of the community, wanted to bring the fair back. Always the entrepreneur, he saw an opportunity to serve the community while bringing some exposure to the Cowtown operation. He teamed up with fair organizers to host the Salem County Fair at Cowtown and helped to sponsor a rodeo. Records indicate that the first fair and rodeo, which was held in Woodstown, was most likely in 1929. The Salem County Fair was held in the center of town in the early years, as pictured here. The fair and rodeo was held at Harris Acres, which is near North Main Street and Auburn Road. Several of the streets around the former Harris property are named after Harris family members.

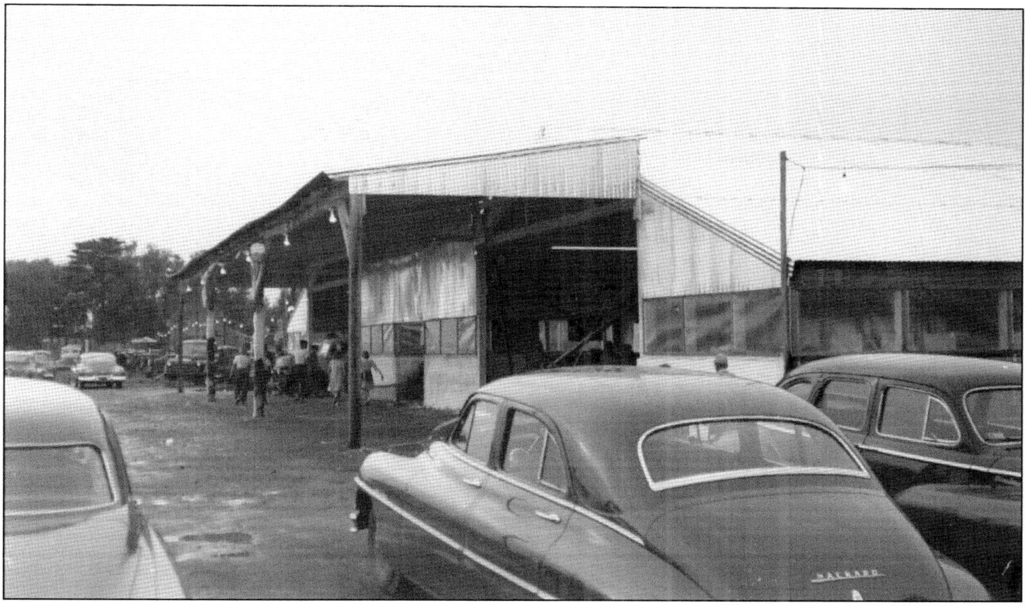

Fair goes to Cowtown. The Salem County Fair was held at the rodeo grounds in Woodstown until World War II, when the annual fair and rodeo event was put on hold until after the war. Once the fair was revived again, fair activities were held on the new Cowtown grounds on Route 40. (Courtesy of 4-H Rutgers Cooperative Extension.)

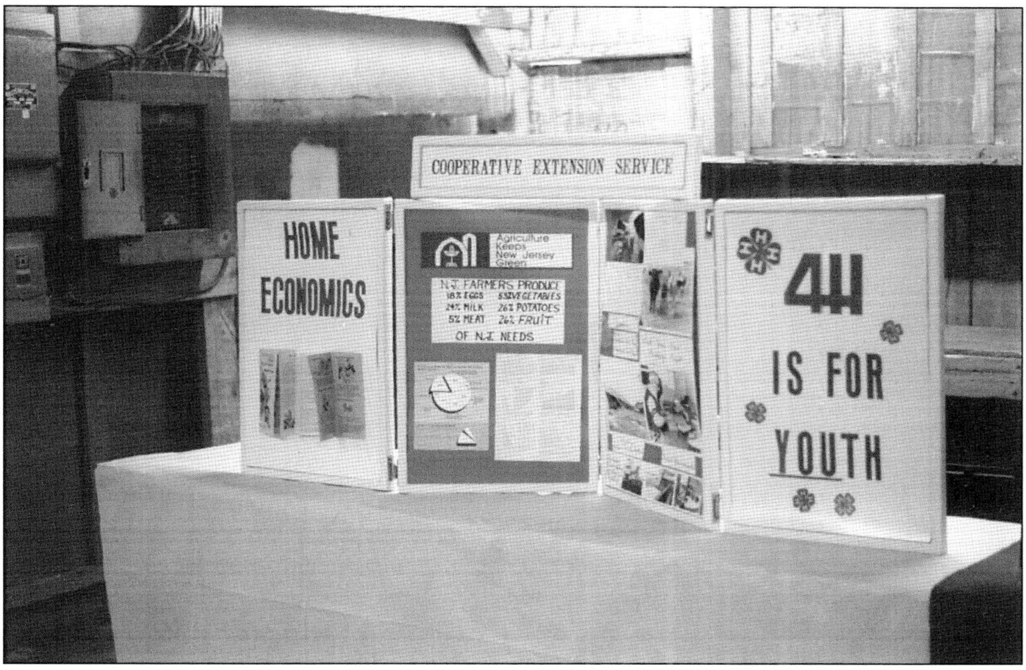

Youth Involvement. 4-H was extremely active in the planning and execution of the fair. Many local students participated in the events. Future Farmers of America (FFA) became involved as well. In this picture, a local Salem County student prepared a display that illustrated their home economics coursework and their 4-H involvement. (Courtesy of 4-H Rutgers Cooperative Extension.)

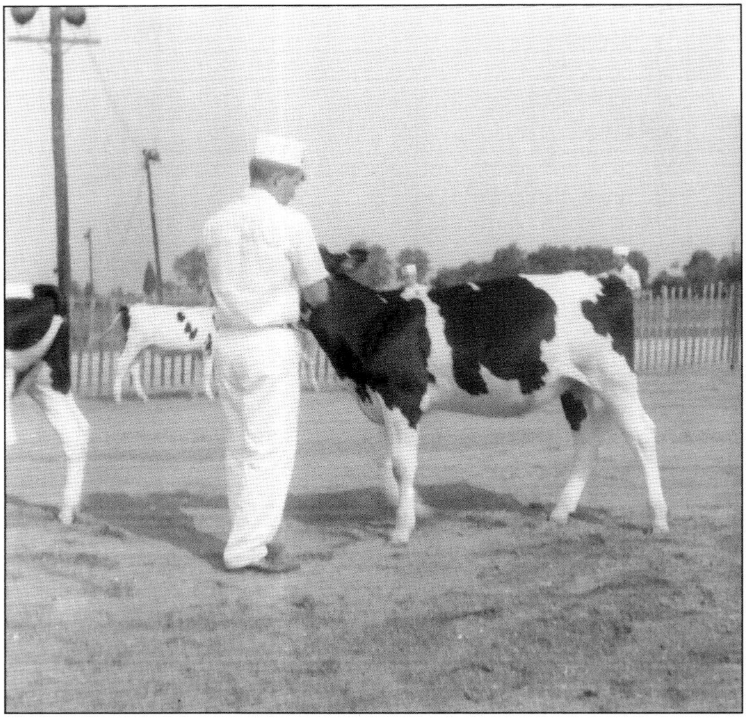

The Fair Organization. The Salem County Fair Association was formed in 1959. The first meeting was held in September 1959. The first executive committee members were Jean Angelo, president; Arthur Jarman, vice president; Amelia Hackett, secretary; and Loren Lounsbury, treasurer. The association was and continues to be responsible for the fair event planning and promotion. (Courtesy of 4-H Rutgers Cooperative Extension.)

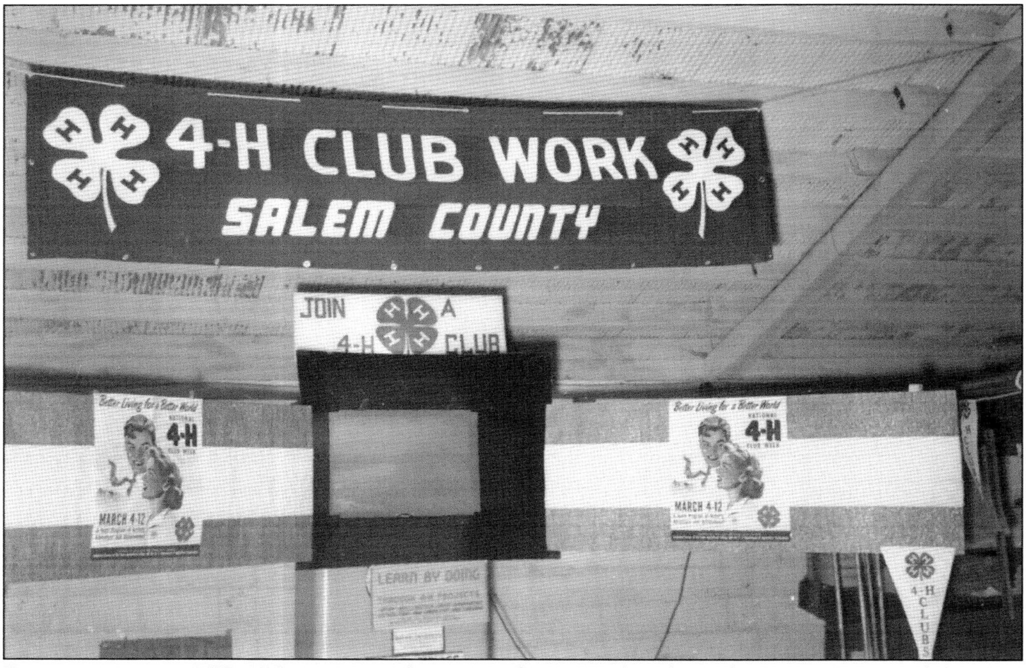

Development of 4-H. 4-H is a national program that started in the early 1900s. Areas with farming communities developed 4-H programs to encourage young people to learn about farming and up-and-coming developments in agriculture. Individual town and county chapters would proudly display their work at fairs across the country. (Courtesy of 4-H Rutgers Cooperative Extension.)

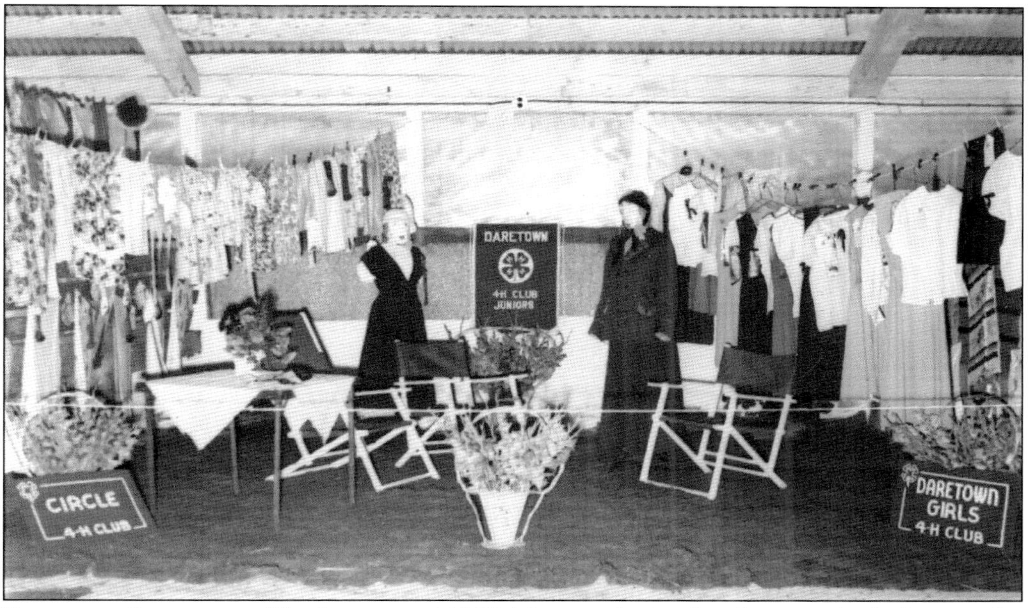

DARETOWN REPRESENTS. The Daretown 4-H Club Juniors display their homemade clothing on the right and the left, as well as on two mannequins in their section. The 4-H club created the scene, complete with an arranged table and chairs and accompanying flower arrangements. Daretown is a small village located outside of Elmer. (Courtesy of 4-H Rutgers Cooperative Extension.)

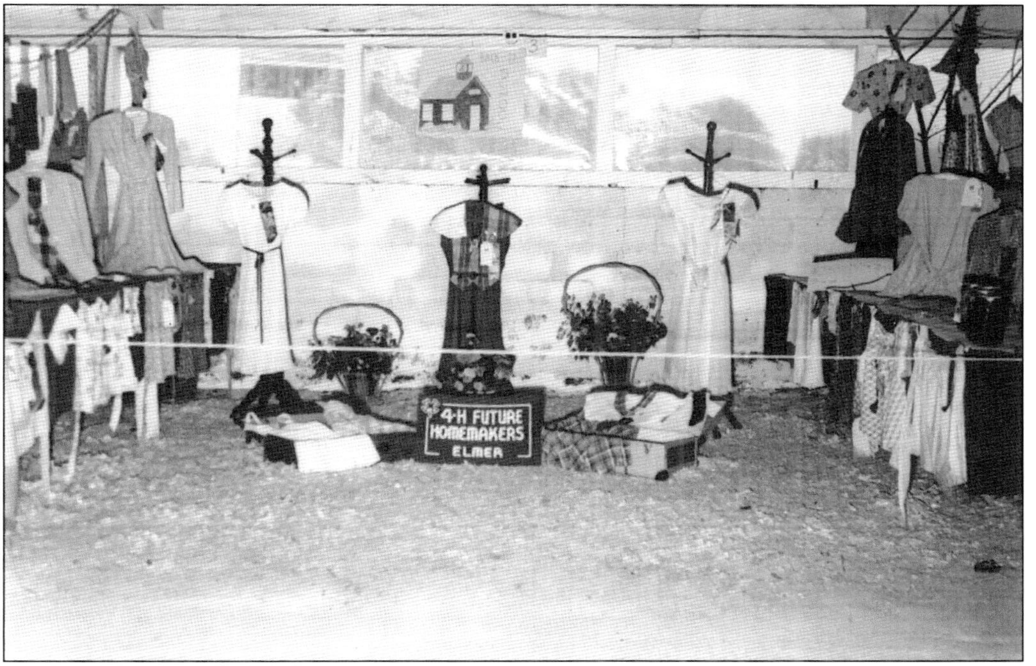

SHOWING THEIR SKILLS. The 4-H Future Homemakers set up this display at the Salem County Fair. By exhibiting clothing that the members made, they demonstrated their sewing and homemaking skills. A key idea that 4-H was founded on was the concept that children can be educated by their environment and learn by doing. (Courtesy of 4-H Rutgers Cooperative Extension.)

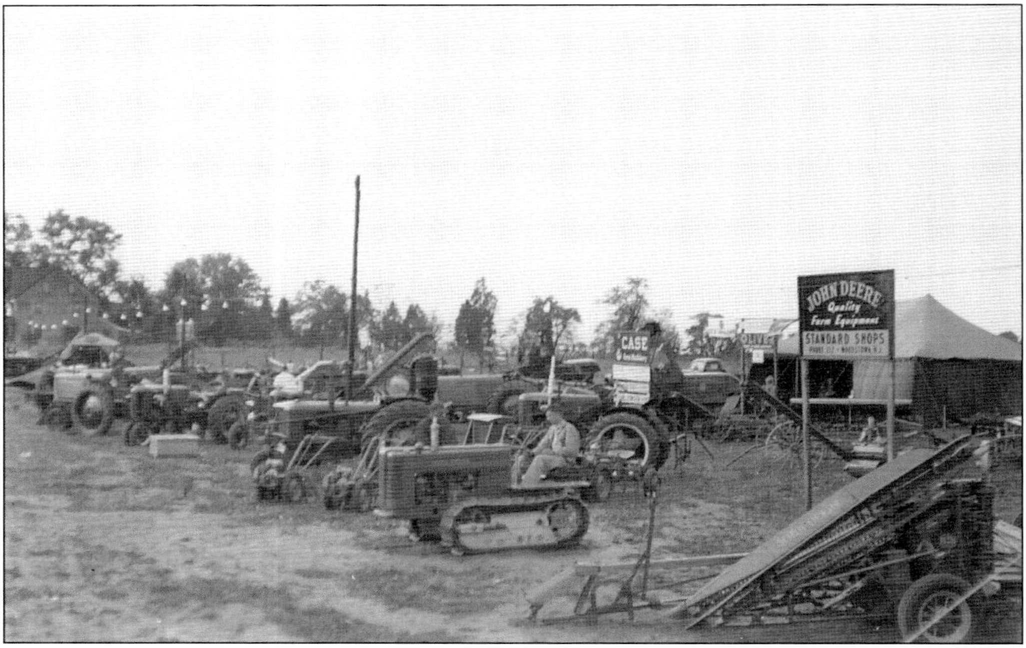

A Fair Staple. Tractors have always been a big part of county and state fairs. John Deere and Case, two of the most well-known tractor manufacturers, display their tractors and other farm equipment. Tractor engines and tractors were developed in the 1800s and revolutionized the agricultural and farming industries. (Courtesy of 4-H Rutgers Cooperative Extension.)

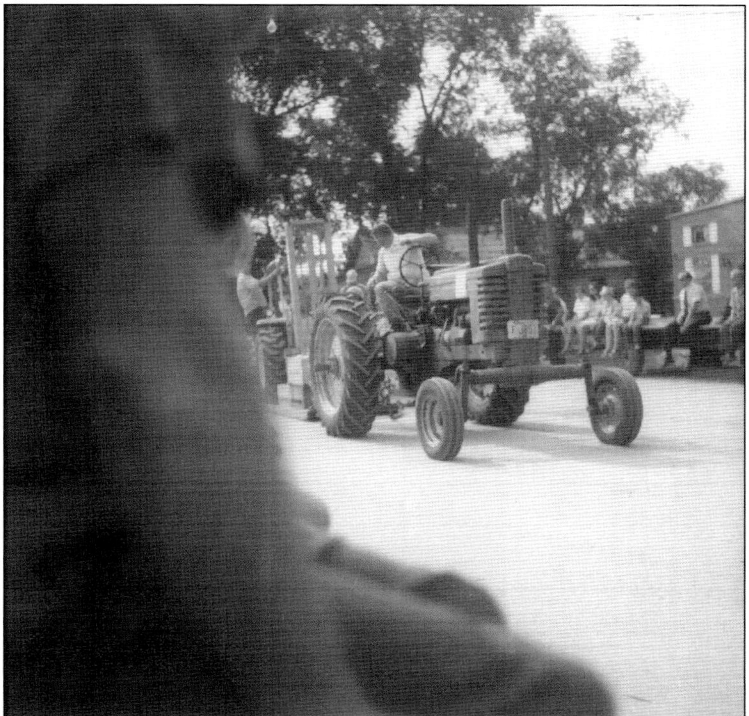

Tractors at the Fair. It is believed that tractor pulling actually stemmed from horse pulling. Farmers would brag about their horses' strength and would challenge neighboring farmers to compete. Horses would drag boards behind them, weight would be added (typically, people would hop on), and the distance the horse dragged the board before stopping would be measured. (Courtesy of 4-H Rutgers Cooperative Extension.)

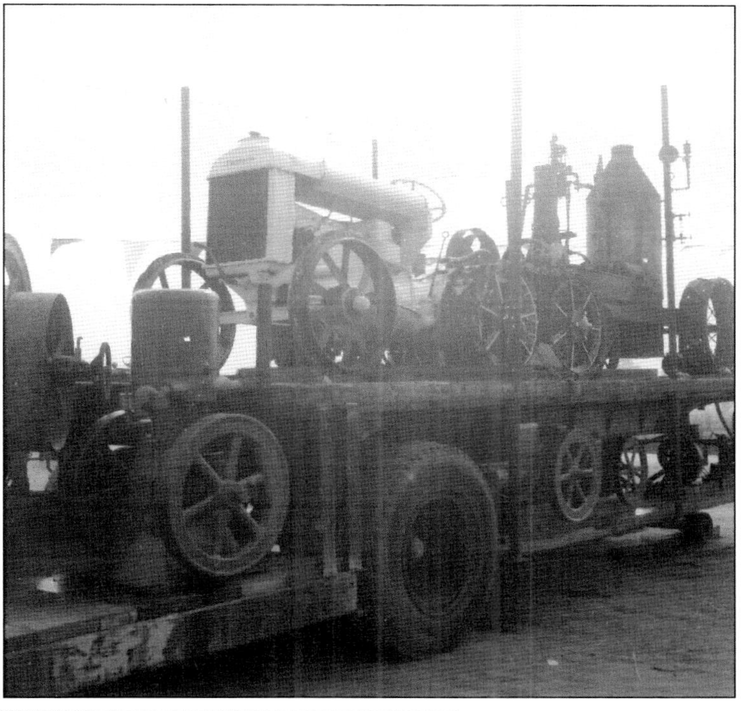

Tractor Pull Popularity Increases. Once the tractor became a staple in farming in the 1900s, horse pulling was replaced by tractor pulling. The first recorded pulling involving an engine goes back to 1929. Records suggest that events were held in both Ohio and Missouri that year. The popularity of the tractor pull continued to grow and surged in the 1950s and 1960s. (Courtesy of 4-H Rutgers Cooperative Extension.)

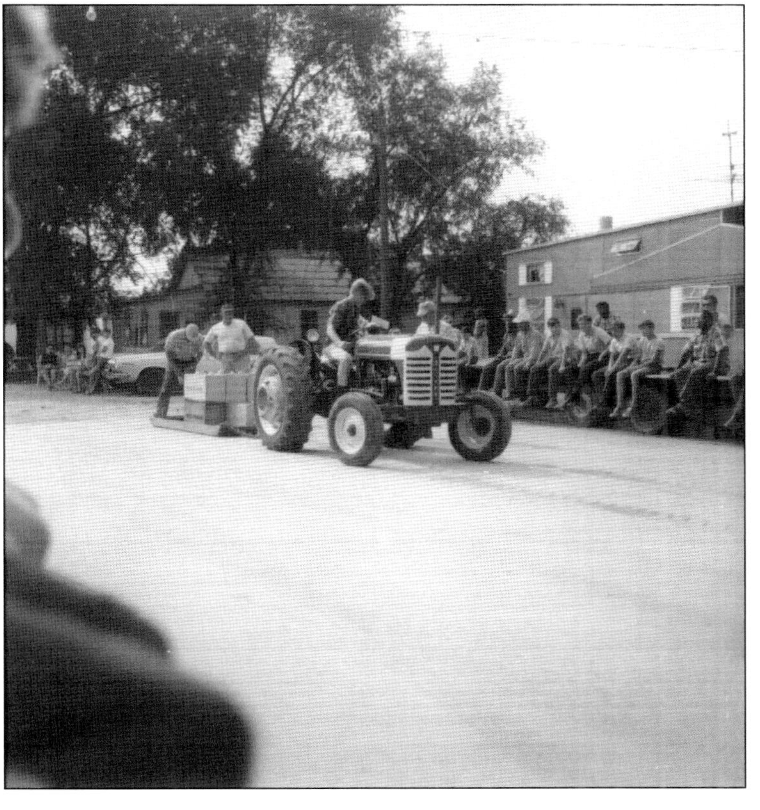

Travel Pull Rules. The National Tractor Pull Association was not formed until 1969. Prior to the formation of the organization, each fair had different rules to govern the pulls. Judges are pictured here next to and behind the tractor. The distance the tractor traveled was recorded during the contest. (Courtesy of 4-H Rutgers Cooperative Extension.)

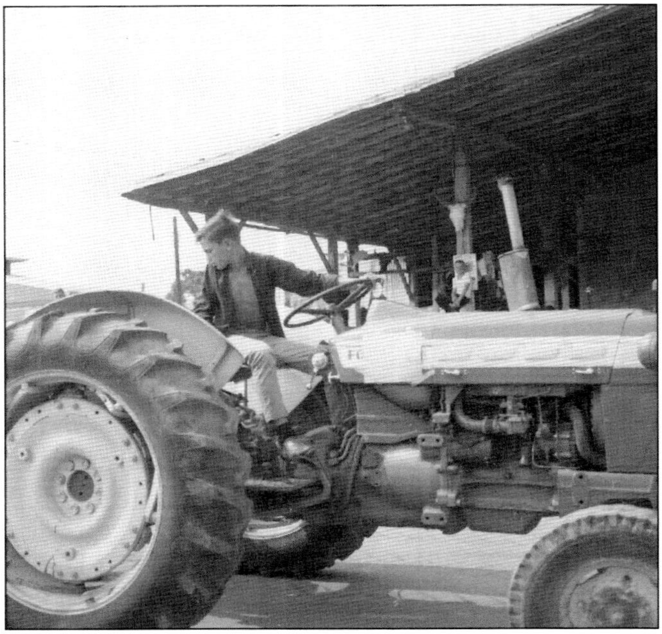

Pulling Surface. The blacktop was laid for the Salem County Fair by Cowtown in 1967. Prior to that, the tractor pull was held on dirt. The surface that the tractors pull on can affect how the tractor performs, so it is important that event participants have uniform circumstances for each pull. (Courtesy of 4-H Rutgers Cooperative Extension.)

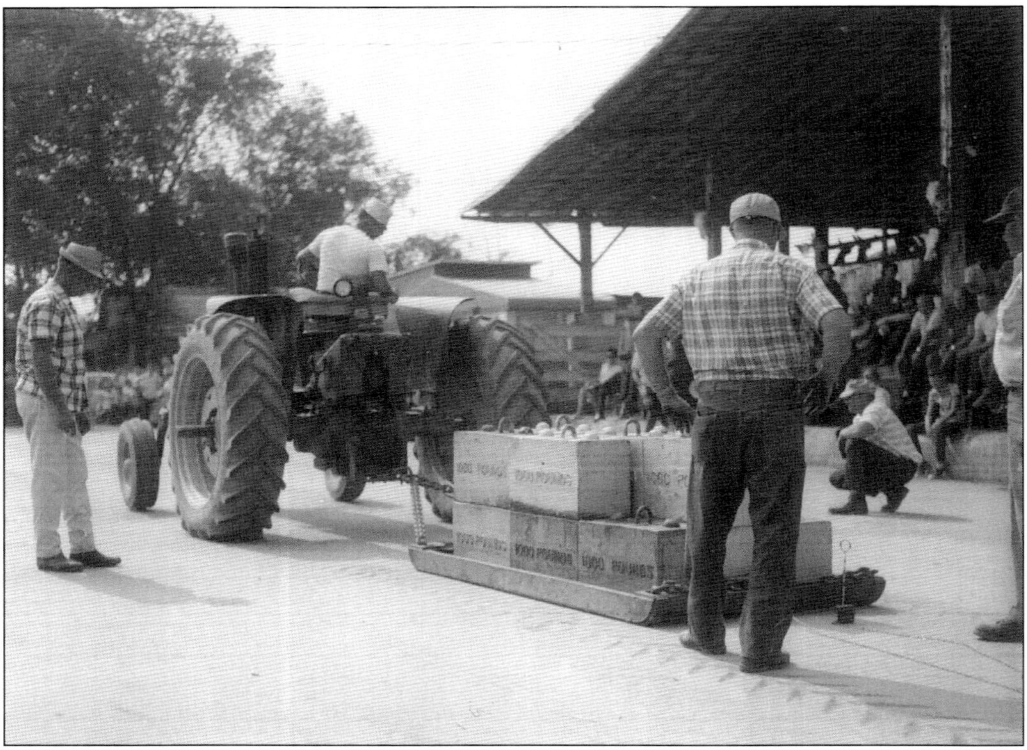

Types of Pulls. Tractor pulls were a traditional and exciting part of the Salem County Fair. Sanctioned tractor pulling had two divisions: stock and modified. Tractor pulls are still held at the Salem County Fair today, although the events have expanded to include modified divisions and trucks. (Courtesy of 4-H Rutgers Cooperative Extension.)

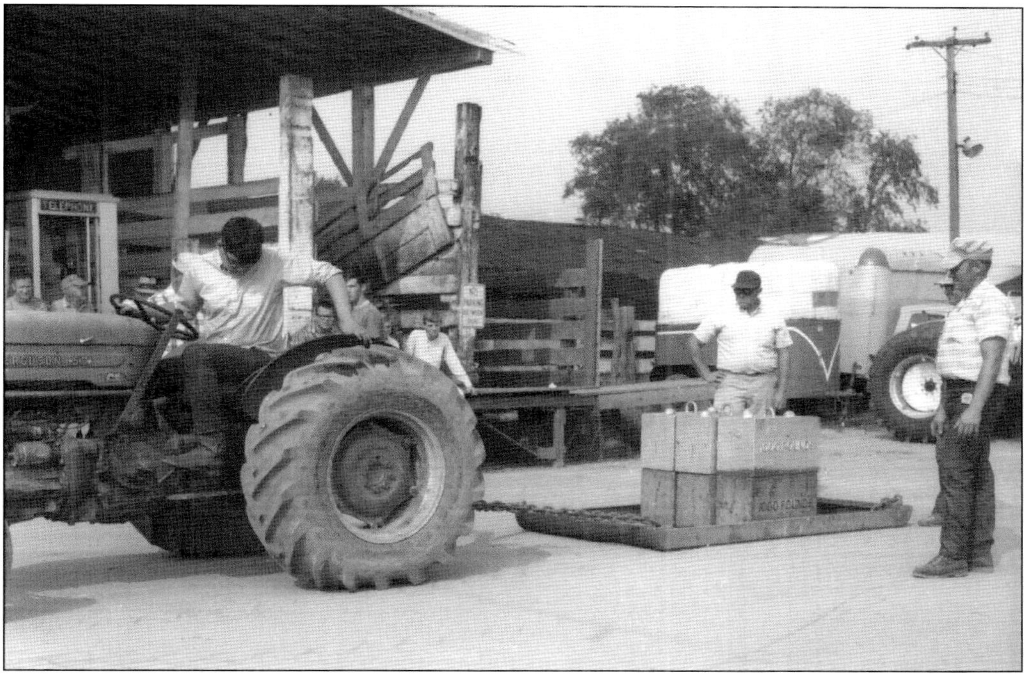

BIG FAIR CROWDS. When the fair and annual rodeo was held at Cowtown, members of the South Jersey community flocked to the Cowtown grounds. During that time, the typically bustling Cowtown office was quiet. Sometimes, staff would even sneak out and watch events like the tractor pull. (Courtesy of 4-H Rutgers Cooperative Extension.)

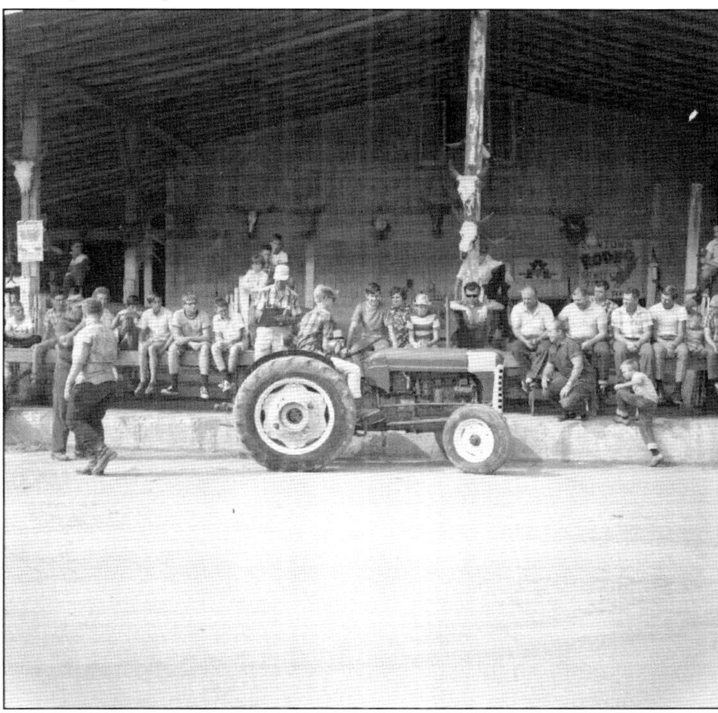

NO FAIR ON AN AUCTION DAY. The annual fair and rodeo, when it was held at Cowtown, was held on Wednesday, Thursday, and Friday. Holding regular Cowtown operations on Tuesdays and Saturdays and hosting the fair events and displays simultaneously was not possible. Posters for the following Saturday night's Cowtown Rodeo can be seen in the background in this photograph. (Courtesy of 4-H Rutgers Cooperative Extension.)

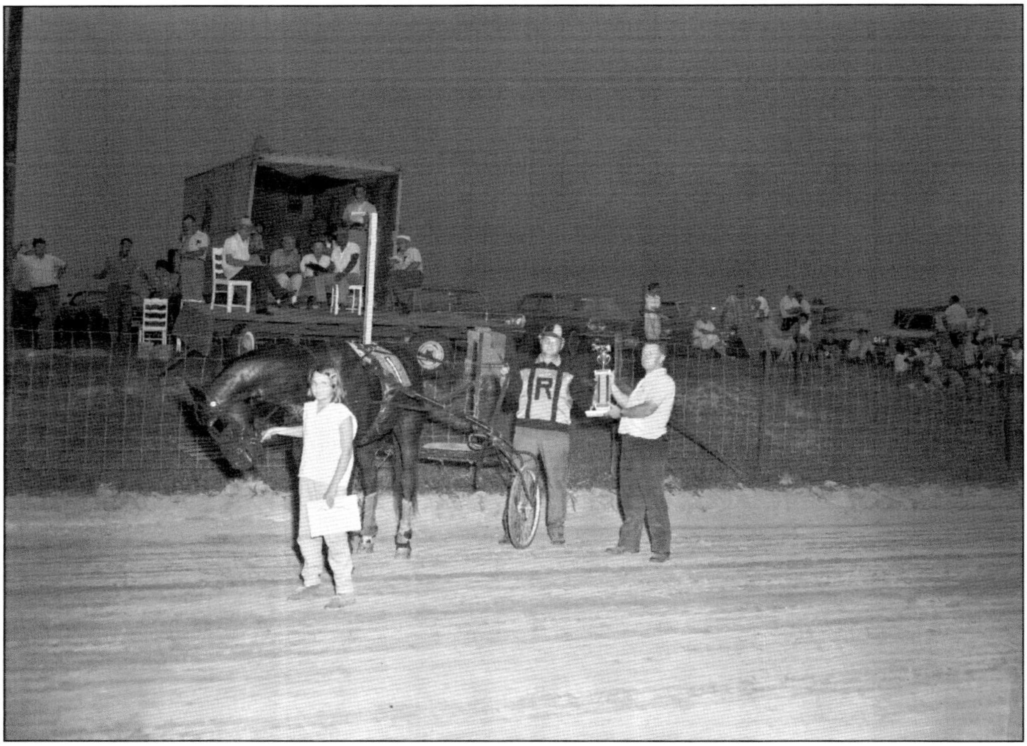

Racing at Cowtown. Harness racing was introduced to the Salem County Fair in 1968. Allen Hart and Marty Craven led the effort to bring it to the fair. The addition of the harness racing events was well received, as matinee harness racing was established in 1969. (Courtesy of 4-H Rutgers Cooperative Extension.)

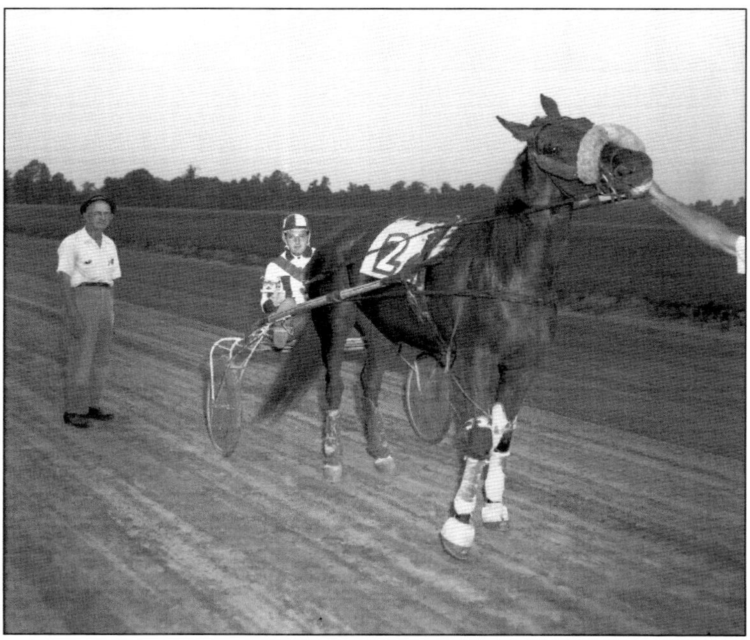

Harness Racing. Harness racing involves a two-wheeled cart, also called a sulky, that is pulled behind the horse. The horse races, which were held on the Cowtown property that sits behind the current New Jersey State Trooper barracks, remained a fair event until the 1980s. (Courtesy of 4-H Rutgers Cooperative Extension.)

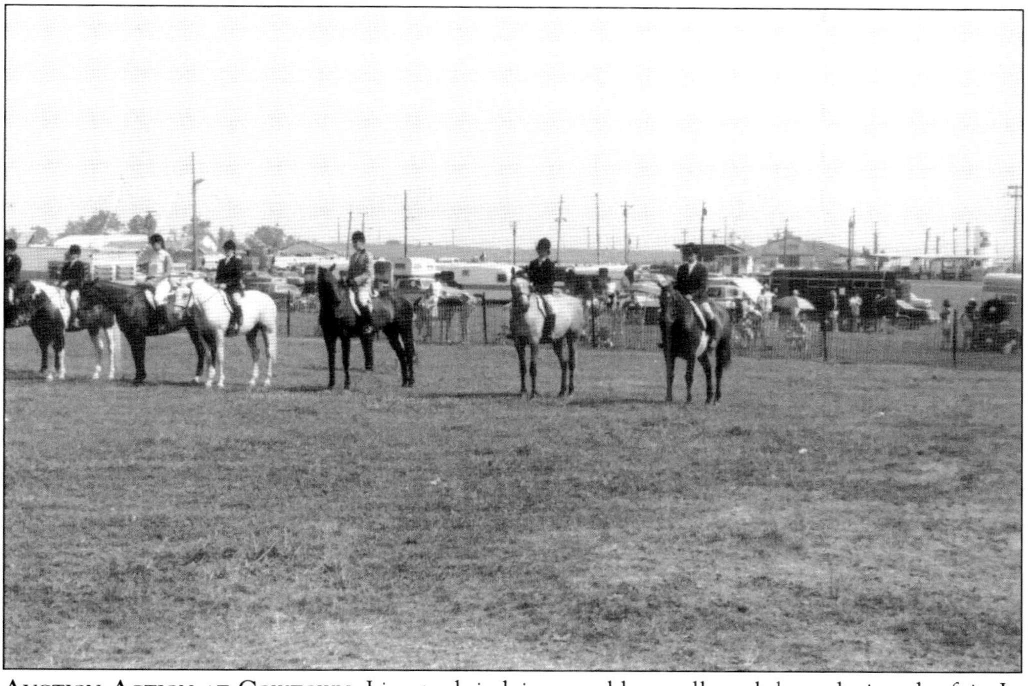

Auction Action at Cowtown. Livestock judging would run all week long during the fair. In addition to the judging, a livestock auction was held on the last day of the fair. Stoney Harris, owner of Cowtown, would act as auctioneer for the fair auctions. (Courtesy of 4-H Rutgers Cooperative Extension.)

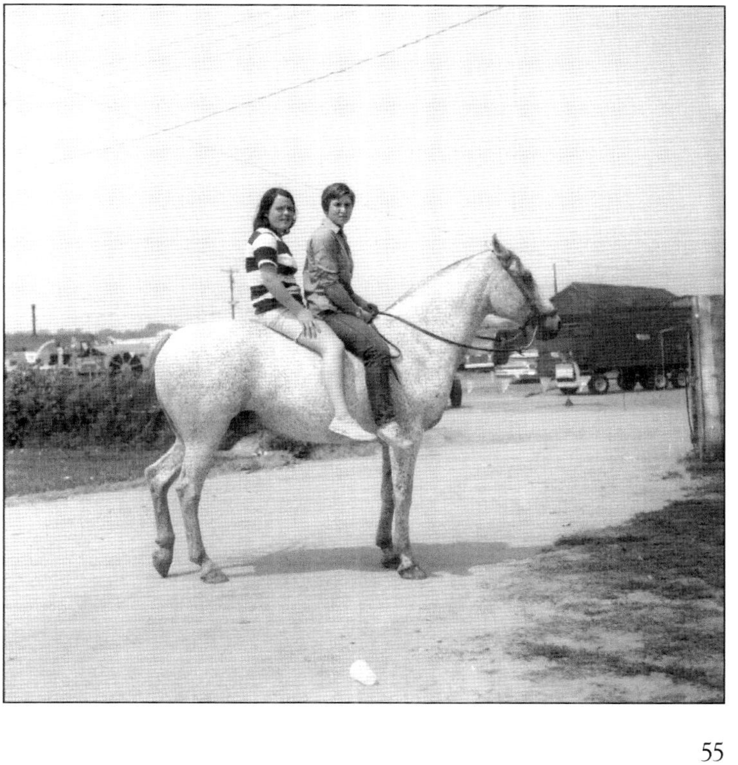

Horses at the Fair. Horse shows were held all week at the fair. The appearance of the horse, the exhibitor, and overall performance were all taken into consideration during judging. Also, when the fair was held in Woodstown in the 1930s, to encourage the local community to attend, a pony would be awarded to one lucky attendee. (Courtesy of 4-H Rutgers Cooperative Extension.)

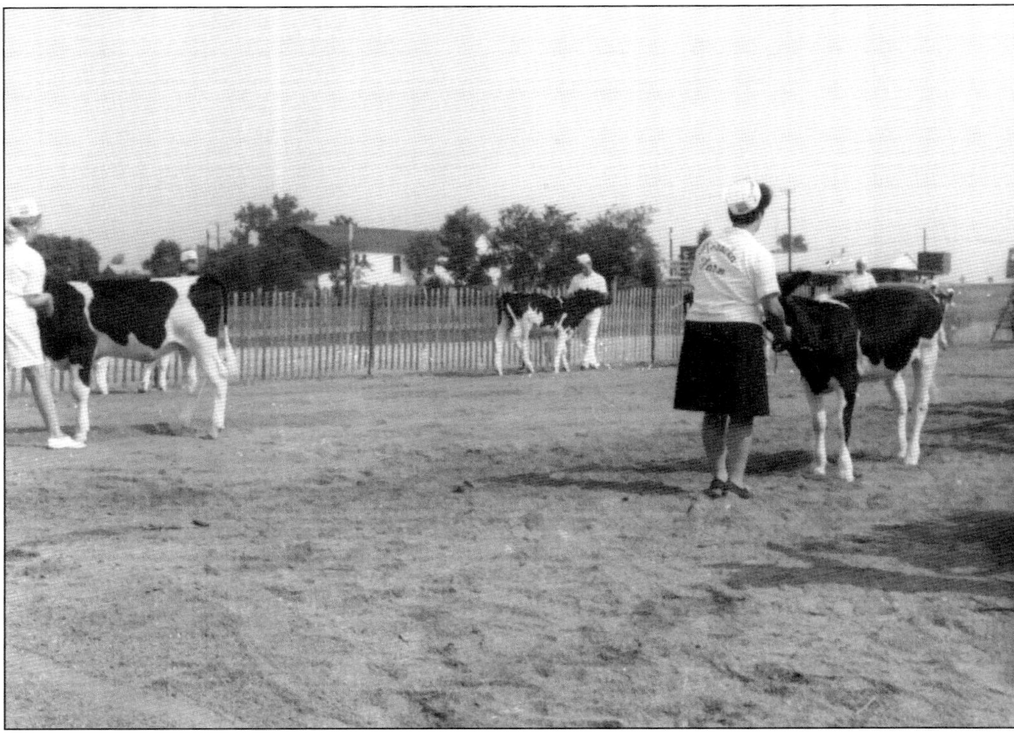

Fair Judging. The Salem County Fair was and continues to be an opportunity for local residents to showcase their livestock. Depending on class, judges follow guidelines to judge entries based on animal appearance, temperament, or presentation. Animals can fall into the showmanship class or the market class. (Courtesy of 4-H Rutgers Cooperative Extension.)

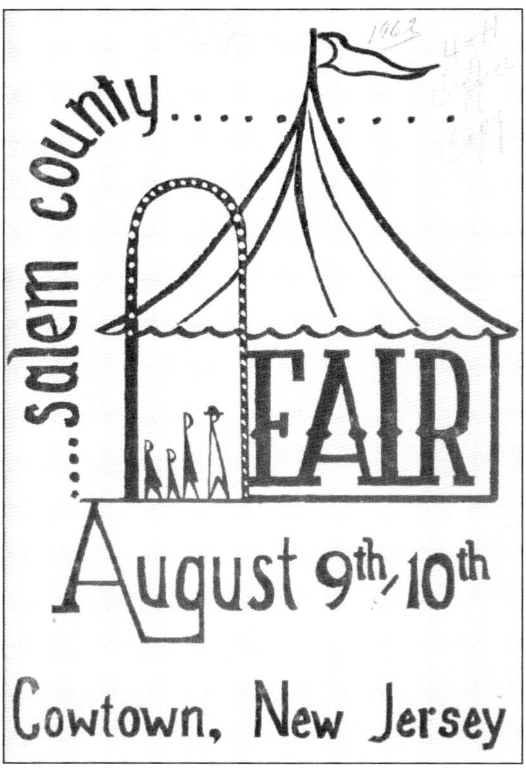

Informative Programs. The Salem County Fair program was distributed each year. The program contained a schedule of events, fair information, and advertisements from local businesses that wanted to show their support of the annual event. Advertisers could promote their business and send best wishes to fair competitors. (Courtesy of 4-H Rutgers Cooperative Extension.)

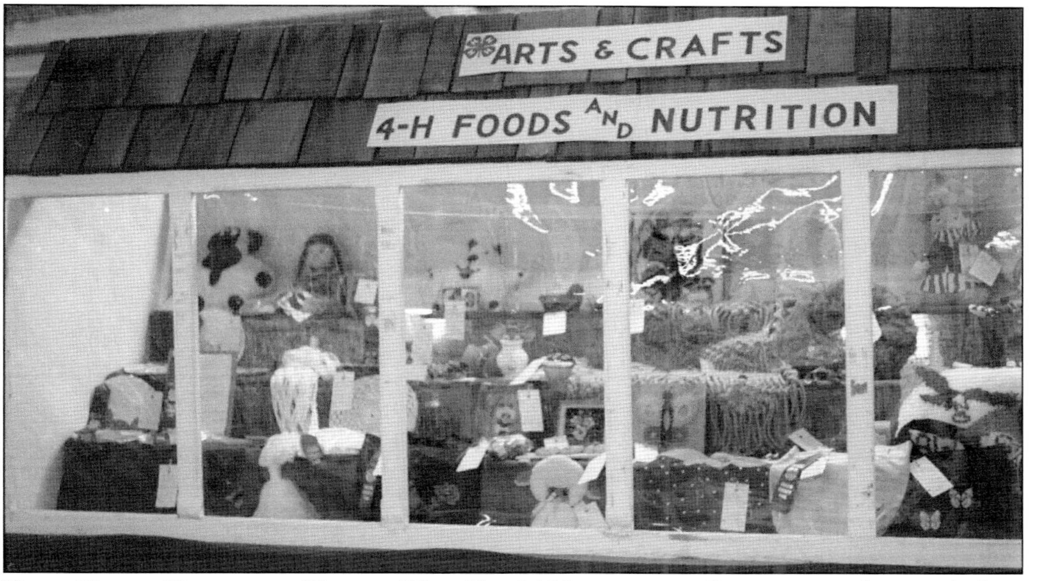

HEAD, HEART, HANDS, AND HEALTH. The official 4-H mission is to "empower youth to reach their full potential working and learning in partnership with caring adults." The 4-H clover was chosen as the national symbol because of the way clover enriches soil. The clover originally had three leaves, but a fourth was eventually added. (Courtesy of 4-H Rutgers Cooperative Extension.)

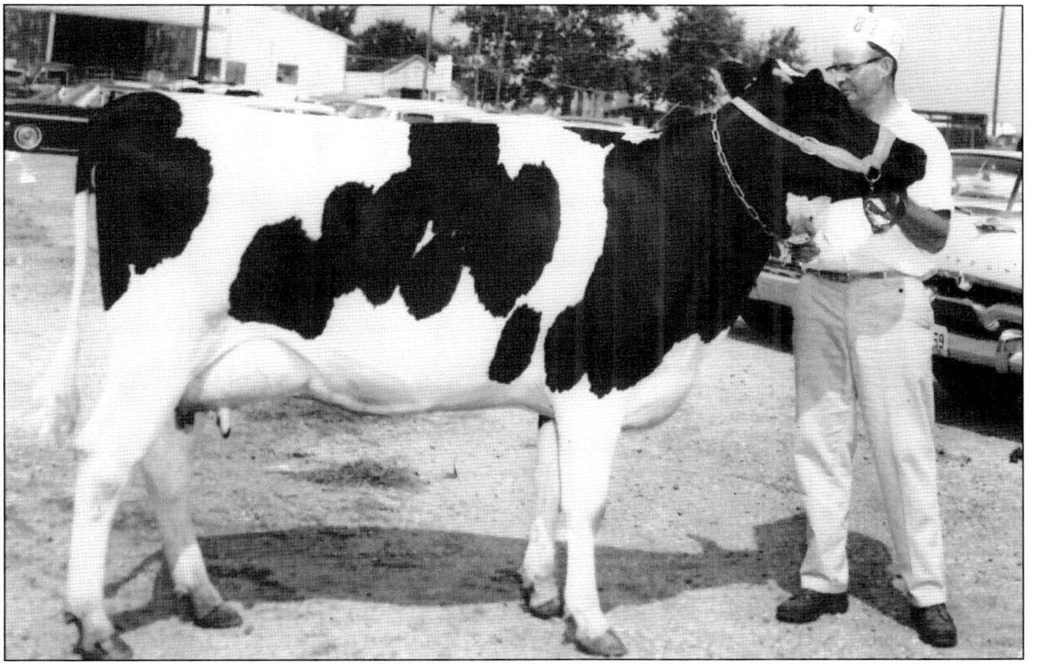

ENTRY IN FAIR COMPETITION. Cream Valley entered this cow, Conquest Marty, in the dairy cow category. Owner Eddie Flitcraft stands with his grand champion Holstein at the Salem County Fair. During the days the fair ran, a schedule of events was followed and programs were distributed to attendees so they could be sure to catch their favorite events. (Courtesy of 4-H Rutgers Cooperative Extension.)

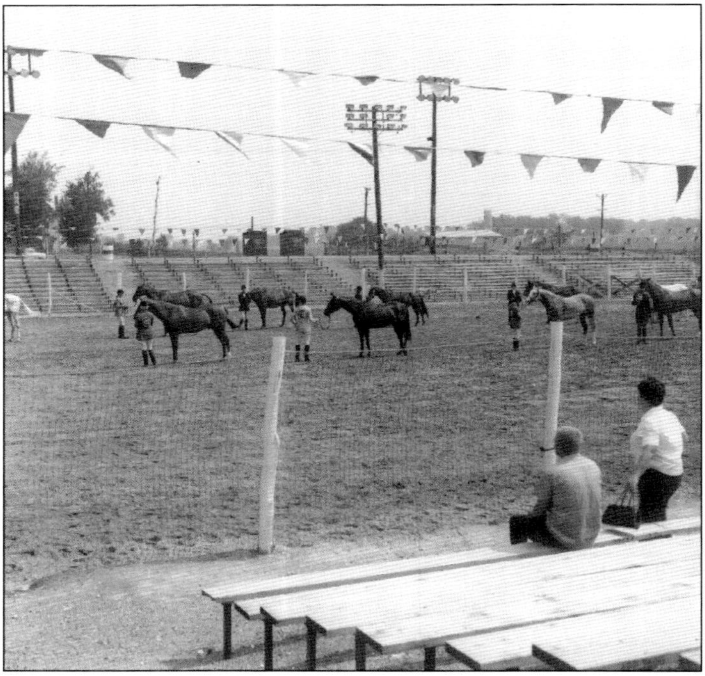

In the Rodeo Arena. This horse show was held in the rodeo arena at Cowtown. In the competitions, the winners of each category receive place ribbons. Participants in the 4-H program learn about animal welfare and the responsibilities that farmers and animal owners have to the animals in their care. (Courtesy of 4-H Rutgers Cooperative Extension.)

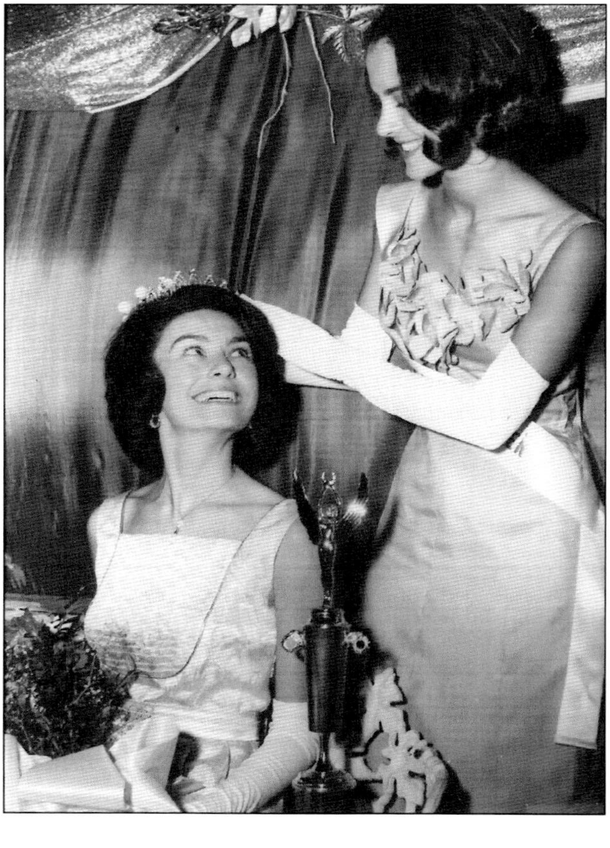

The Fair Queen. The 1965 Salem County Fair queen, Sandra Tweedle, is crowned by the 1964 fair queen, Diana Titus. Today, the Salem County Fair queen must submit an application and be a 16-, 17-, or 18-year-old Salem County resident that is active in 4-H, FFA, Junior Red Cross, Future Homemakers of America, Grange, or the Girl Scouts. (Courtesy of 4-H Rutgers Cooperative Extension.)

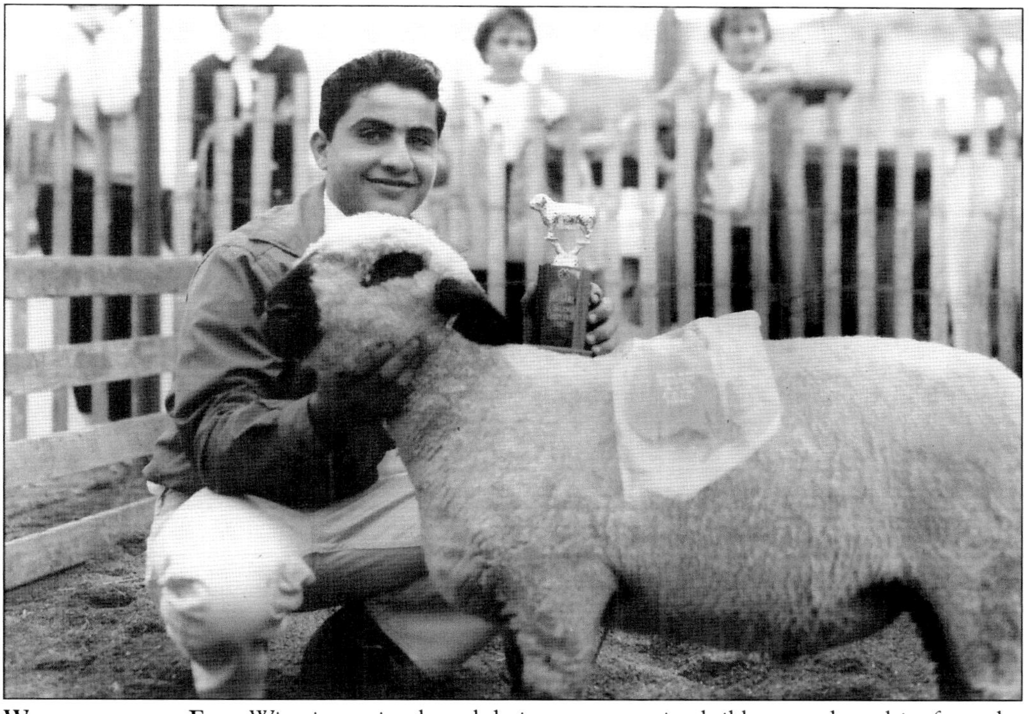

WINNING AT THE FAIR. Winning animals and their owners received ribbons and trophies from the Salem County Fair Association. In 1962, Jim Ragonese received both, and displays them proudly for the camera. Winners were sometimes listed in the local newspapers and in subsequent fair publications and materials. (Courtesy of 4-H Rutgers Cooperative Extension.)

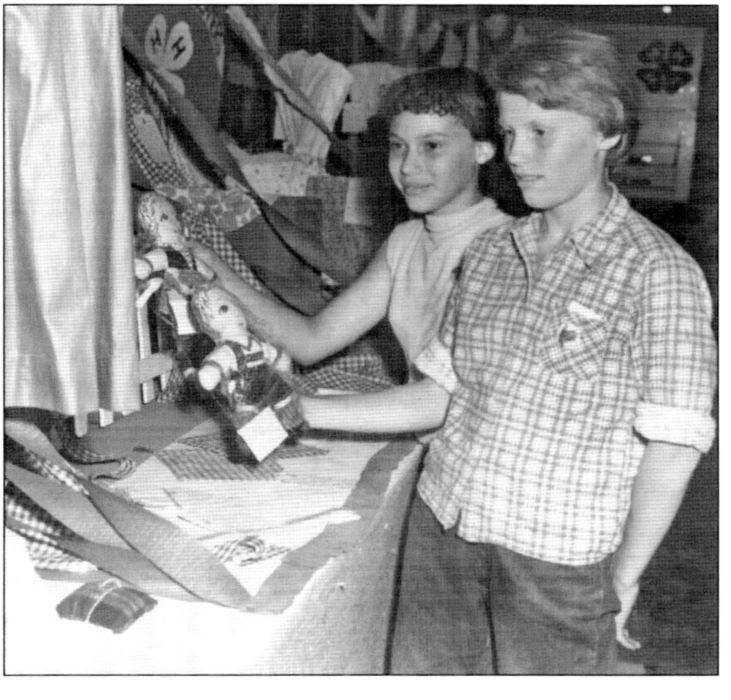

AN EXPERIENCE TO REMEMBER. Many youth that participate in 4-H, FFA, and other educational youth programs that provide practical experience and life skills are very much influenced throughout their formative years by these activities. Those that participate in them often later recognize that their participation was invaluable when it came to learning about responsibility and confidence. (Courtesy of 4-H Rutgers Cooperative Extension.)

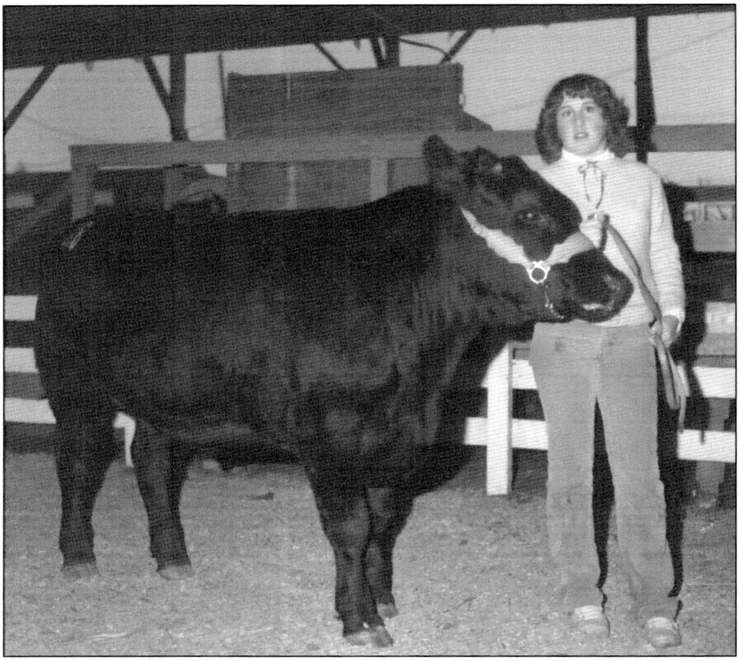

Long Days and Nights. The fair, when it was at Cowtown and even now that it is held at the fairgrounds, is a busy time for participants. Since their animals remain at the fairgrounds for three days, youth and owners spend ample amounts of time caring for and showing their animals. Exhibitors, like Janeen Sickler Hitchner, seen here, can also answer questions from the people attending the fair as they visit the exhibits. (Courtesy of 4-H Rutgers Cooperative Extension.)

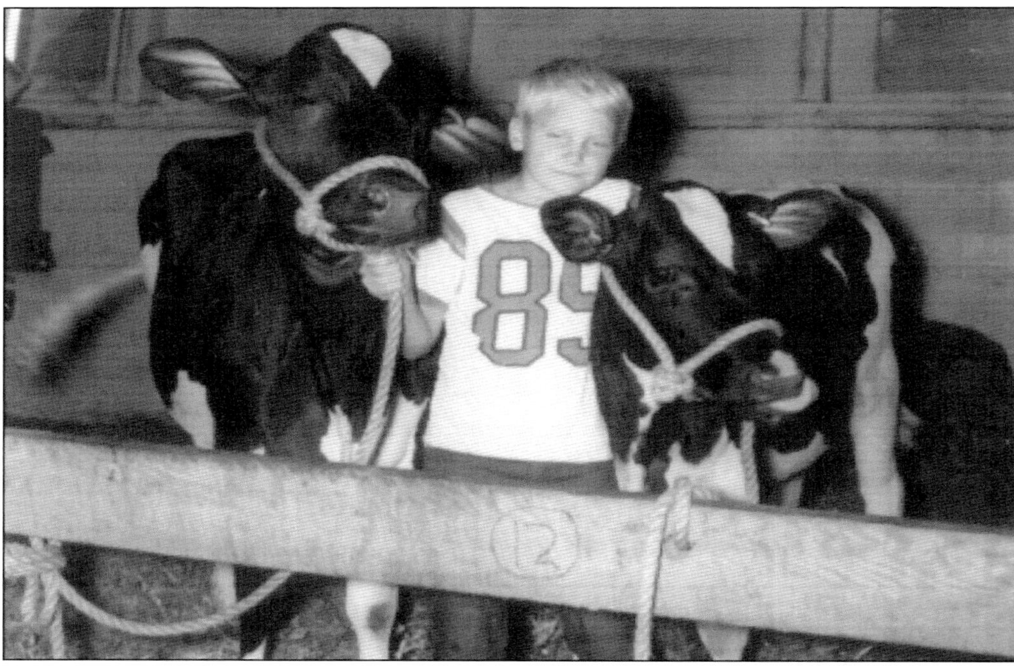

Fair Moves. The Salem County Fair was held at Cowtown until 1985. The fair provided, and continues to provide, the entire county a chance to celebrate local livestock and the farming and agricultural community. Even though the fair moved, the organization still kept ties to Cowtown. In fact, a rodeo event fundraiser was held at the fair in 1985. The fair is now held at the Salem County Fairgrounds, which is within a half mile of Cowtown. (Courtesy of 4-H Rutgers Cooperative Extension.)

Four

Shopping at the Midway Flea Market

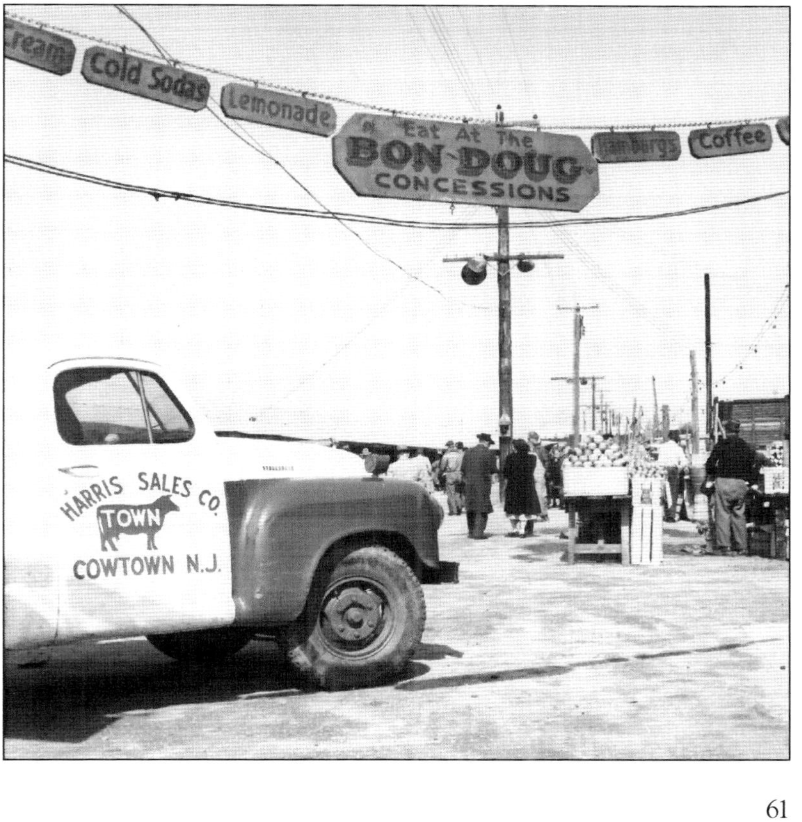

The Auction needs a Market. The Cowtown livestock auction was a growing business in the 1920s. Howard Amos Harris Sr. and his son Stoney began allowing local merchants to sell their goods at the auction. The very first vendor to do this was a horse tack salesman. This was the beginning of the flea market.

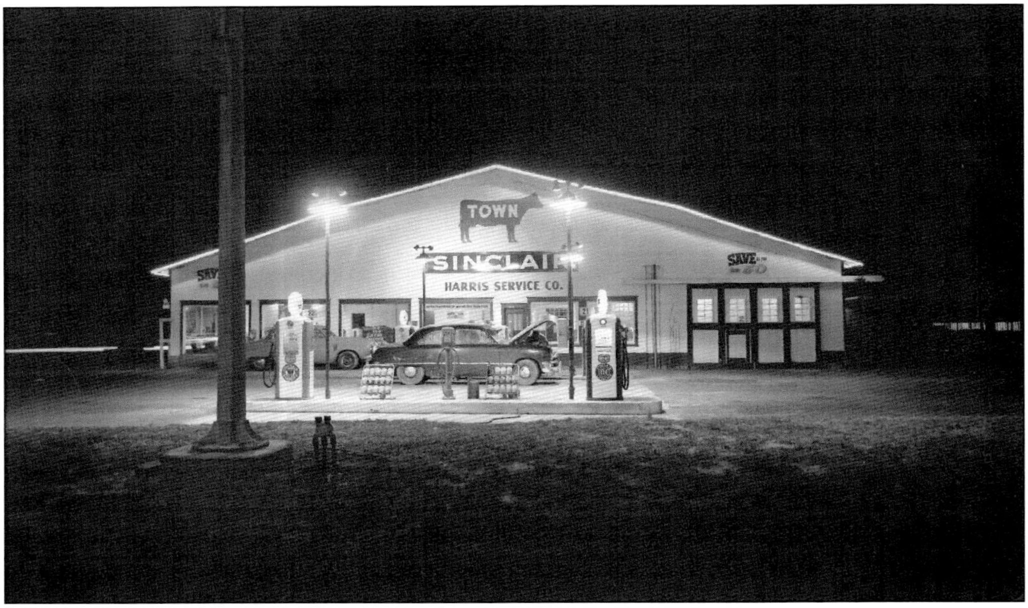

SELLING CARS. Cowtown moved to its current location in the 1940s. The service station was built a couple of years after the auction operation started. A showroom was included that featured cars such as Nashes and Studebakers. The steakhouse opened in 1947, replacing the showroom.

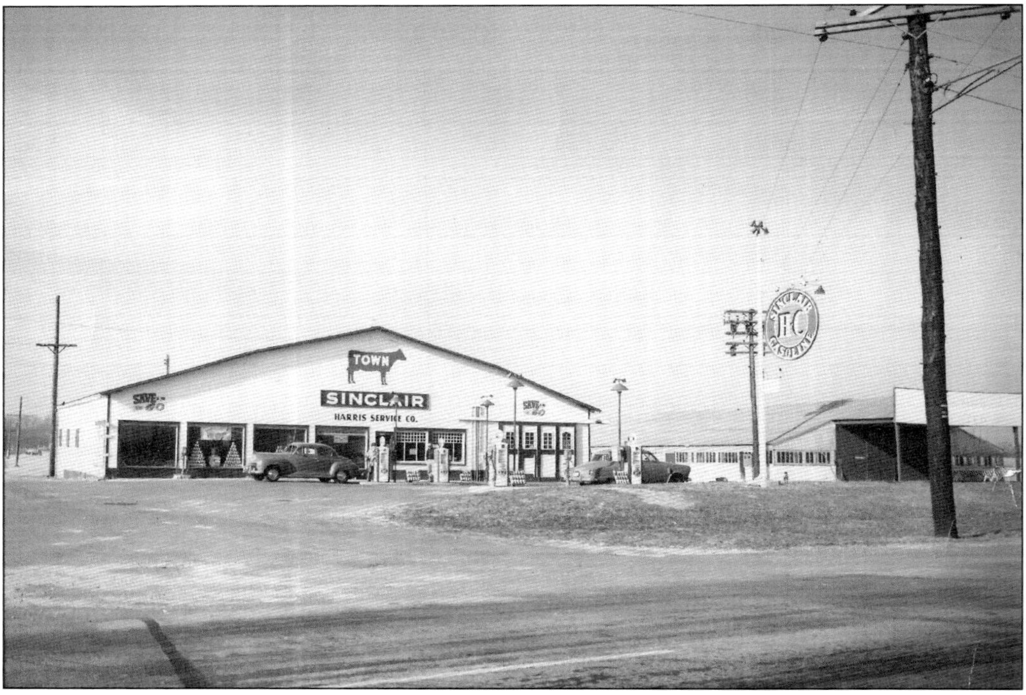

THE COW IS IN THE SHOWROOM. The automobile showroom was certainly Cowtown themed. Rodeo scenes were painted on the oversized showroom windows, and the Cowtown cow was located inside. Once the car showroom was no longer needed, the original Cowtown cow was moved from the showroom. Joe Back of DuBois, Wyoming, built the cow to display at Cowtown.

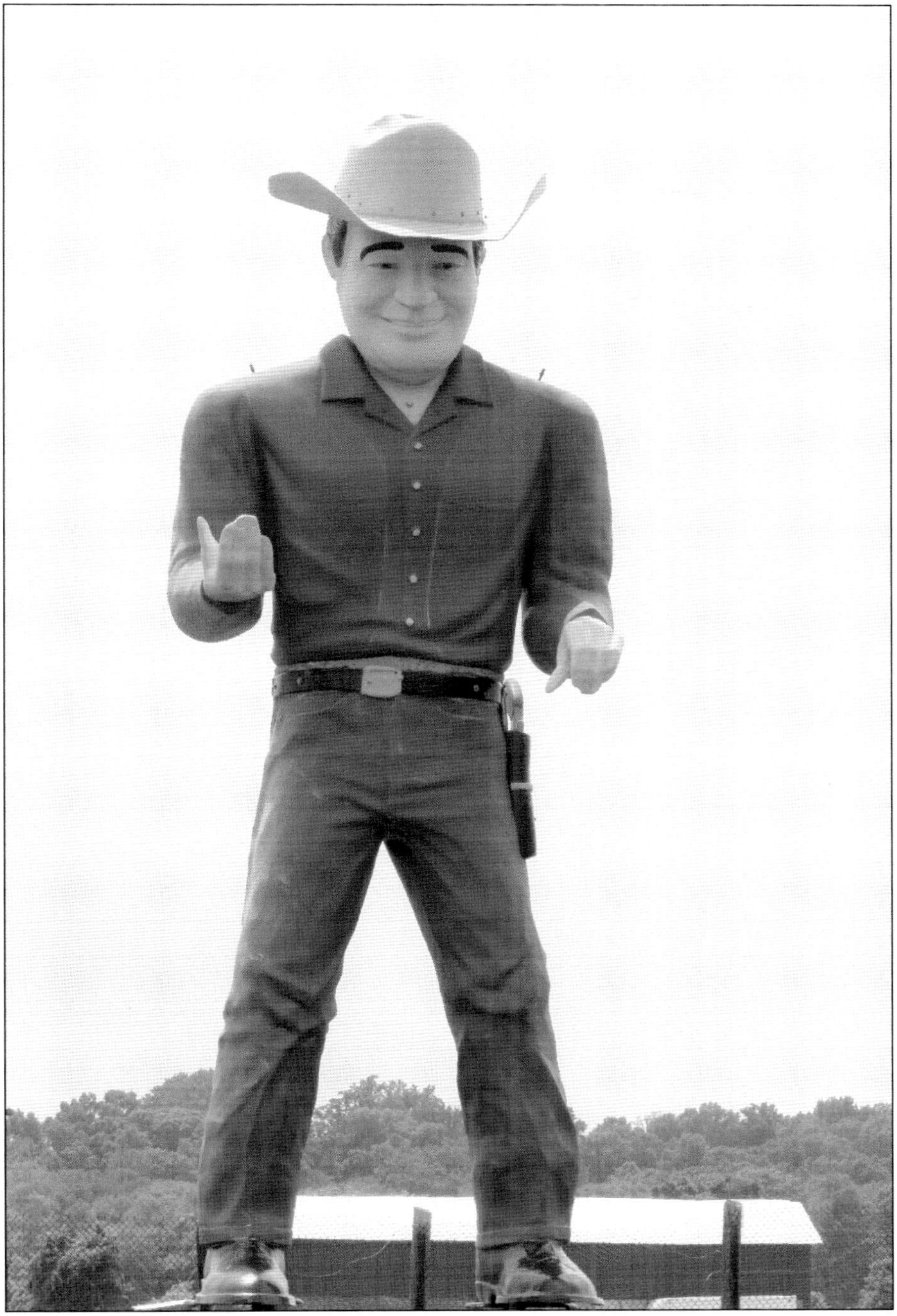

Howdy Cowtown Visitors. The cowboy, a muffler man, arrived from a nearby Dodge dealer that went out of business. Muffler men were fiberglass sculptures that were used as advertising and/or decoration throughout the United States. The cowboy stands over 20 feet high and arrived at Cowtown in the 1970s. The cowboy has been accessorized over the years for holidays and special occasions and even needed a major repair in 2005 when severe wind gusts broke his torso. (Photography by Lisa Soltner.)

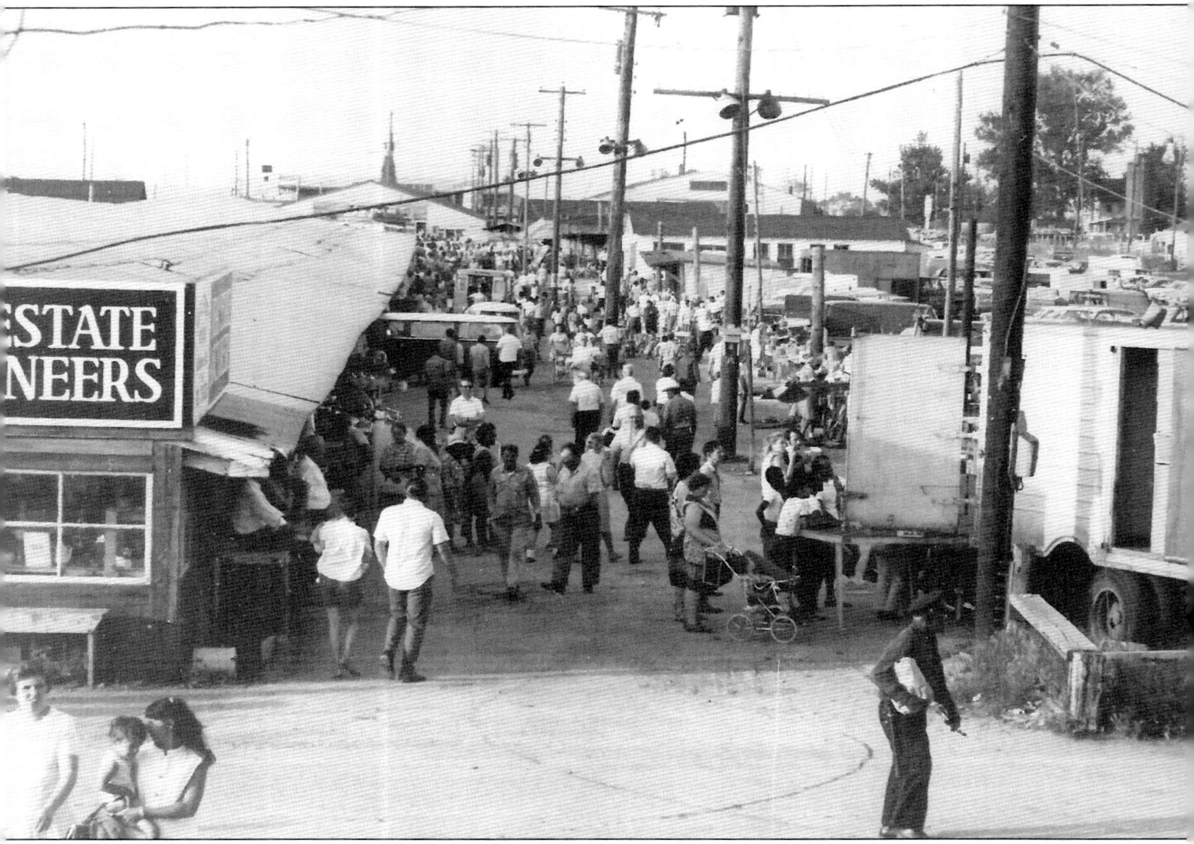

Harris Sales Co. Stoney Harris and Skip Kirby, Stoney's nephew, were estate auctioneers in addition to running the livestock auction. Their storefront, seen here on the left, was located at the market. Harris Sales Co. was what the business and marketplace was known as until Stoney bought the sale barn back from his son Howard in the late 1950s. Soon after, the entire operation—not just the location—began to be called Cowtown. (Courtesy of Emily Walker.)

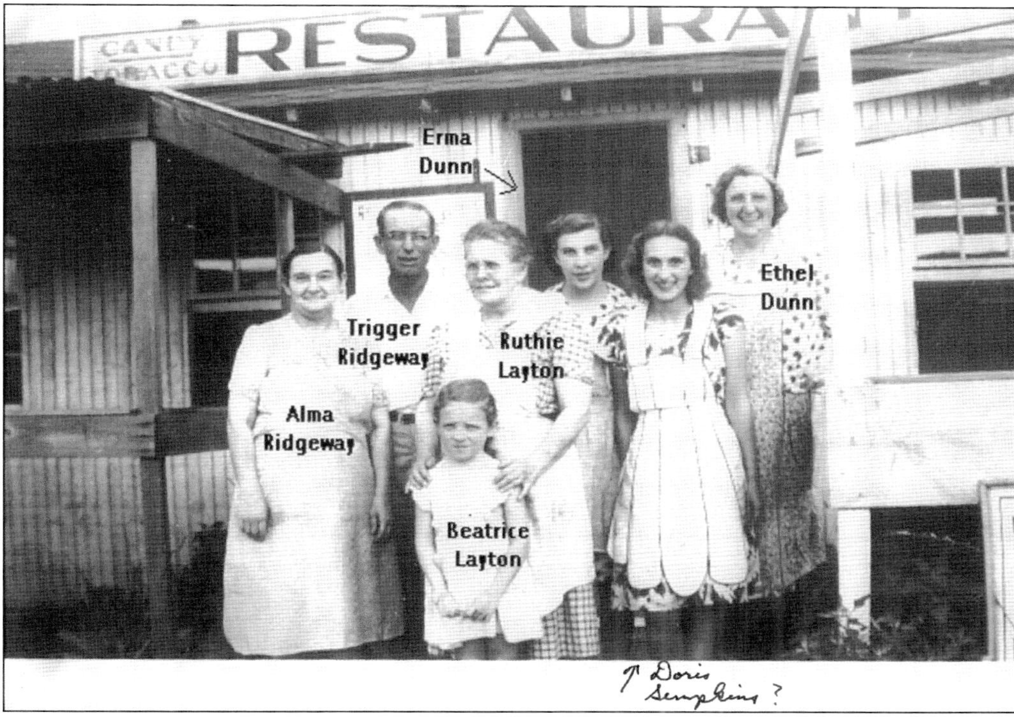

EAT AT THE MIDWAY. The Midway Restaurant was a popular eatery at the Cowtown Market. From left to right, Alma Ridgeway, Trigger Ridgeway, Beatrice Layton, Ruthie Layton, Erma Dunn, Doris Simpkins, and Ethel Dunn pose in front of the restaurant in the 1950s. The restaurant was run by women of the Sharptown Church for many years to raise money for the church. (Courtesy of Bob and Maxine Brown.)

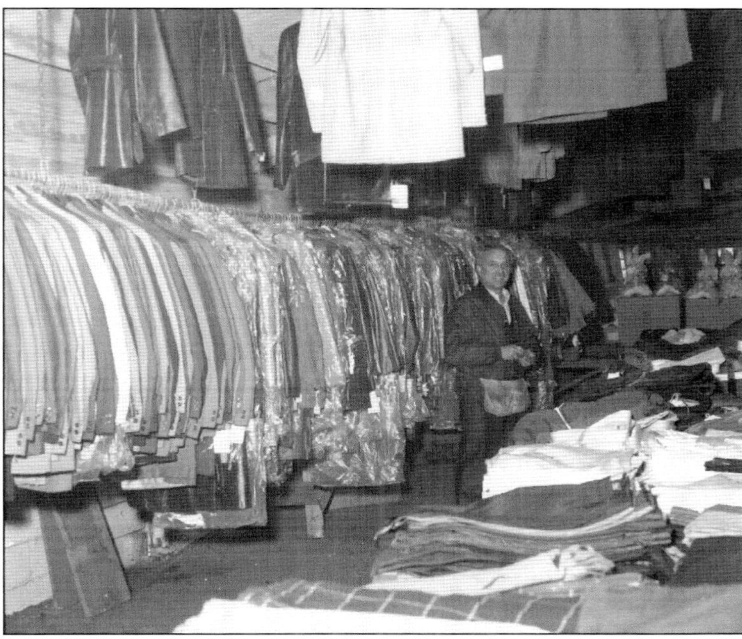

VENDORS. Joe Lamberg, pictured here, was a regular vendor at the market and a popular source of menswear in Salem County for nearly 50 years. The vendor spots at the market were open to anyone as long as the merchant paid the rental fee. Some vendors had long-term spots, while others would rent space for a week or two. Short-term rentals were sought out by people cleaning out homes to sell random household items.

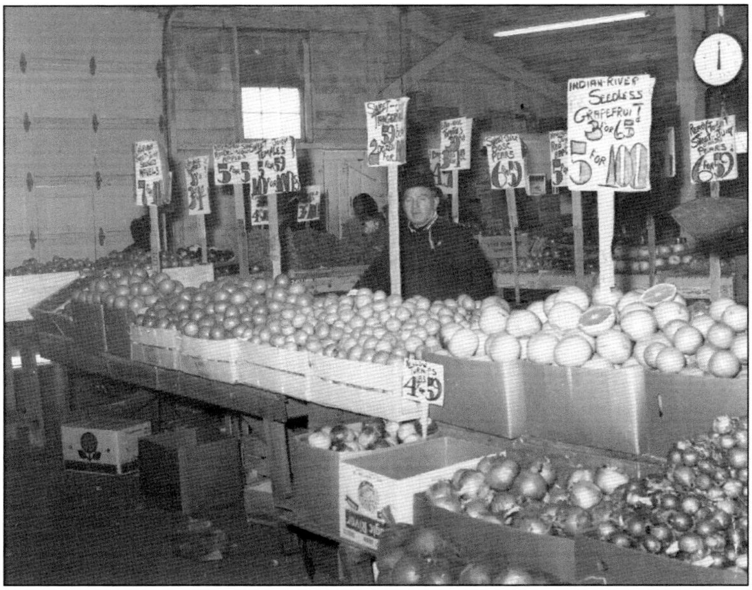

Everything is There. Some have said over the years (and some still do) that a shopper could find anything at the Cowtown Midway flea market. For years, fresh produce vendors have been selling fruits and vegetables at Cowtown. Clothing, housewares, books, electronics, and many other items have also been available.

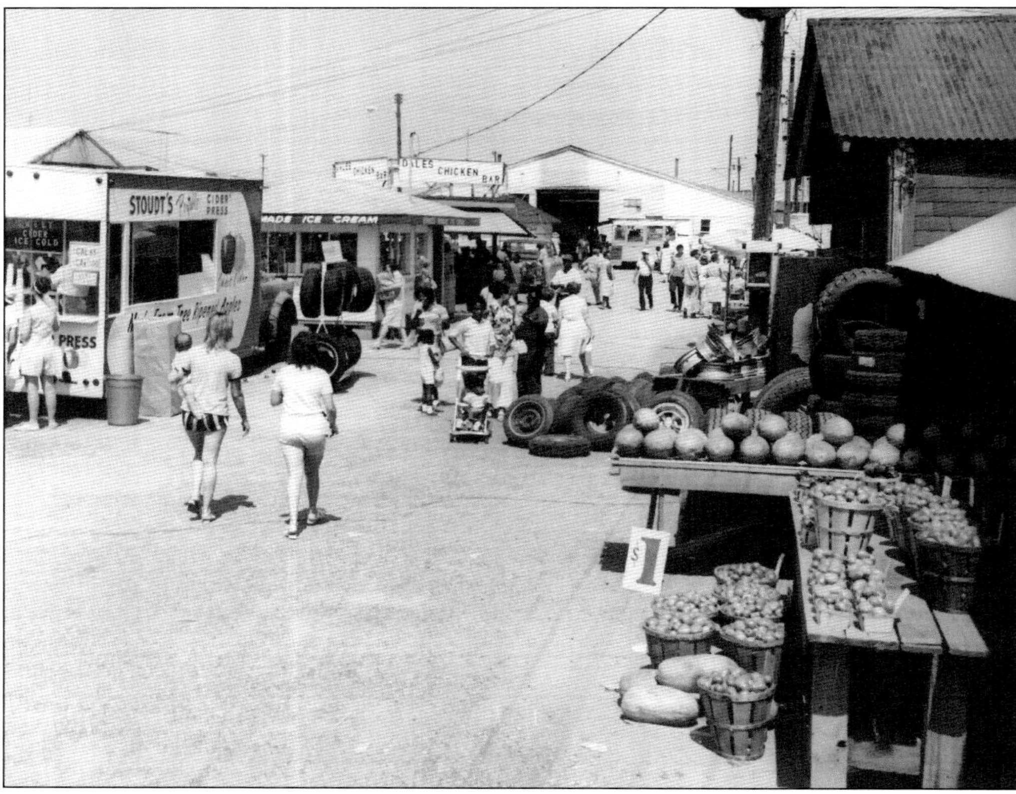

Space for each Vendor. Vendors at the market set up in either inside or outside booths. Booth space is assigned by the Cowtown office. The midway is often referred to as a flea market. These types of markets probably originated in the 1800s and often attract crowds with highly variable shopping needs. (Courtesy of Emily Walker.)

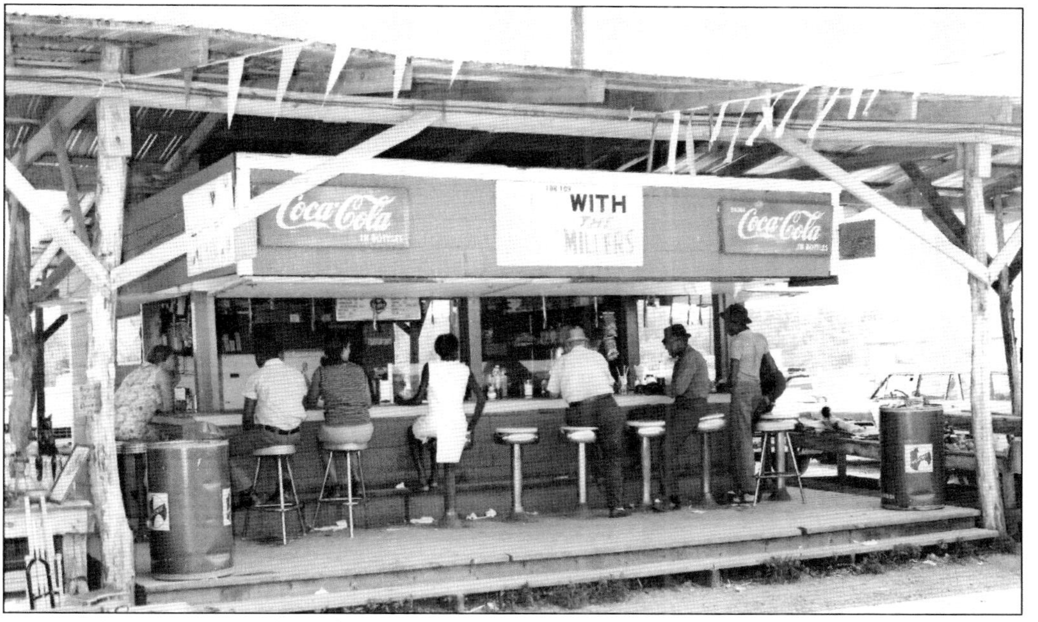

EAT AT COWTOWN. Food vendors are an important part of any market, and the midway flea market is no exception. One of the most well-known food vendors is Miller's restaurant. There were both inside and outside Miller's eateries. Pictured is a group of diners in the 1970s sitting at the counter at Miller's. The restaurant remains at Cowtown today. (Photograph by David Turnbull; courtesy of Emily Walker.)

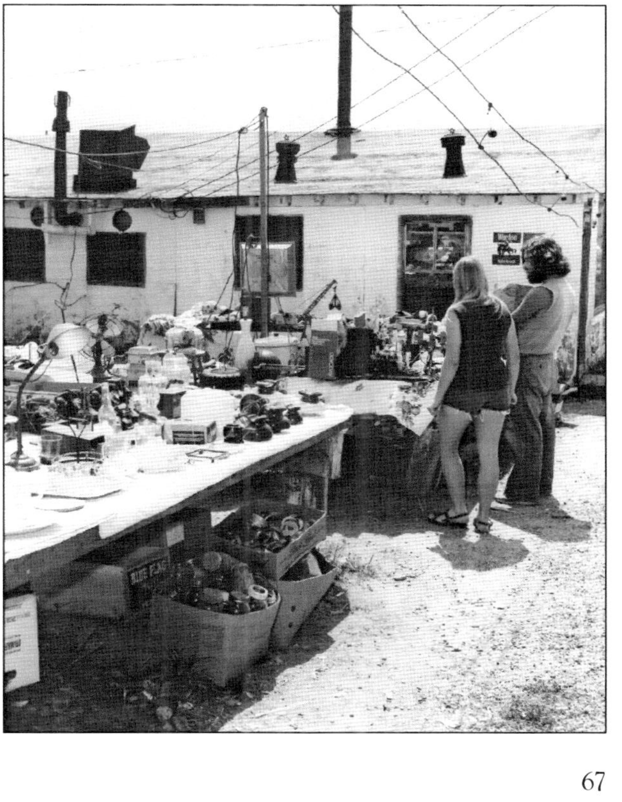

ADDING A SHOPPING DAY. The market attracted and continues to attract shoppers from the Mid-Atlantic region on Tuesdays and Saturdays. Originally, the market was only open on Tuesdays. Stoney tried to add Saturdays in the 1970s, but it was not well received by the community. He tried again in the mid-1970s without success. Saturdays were finally added to the sale days in the 1980s, and, eventually, there was enough business to warrant being open for two days a week. (Photograph by David Turnbull; courtesy of Emily Walker.)

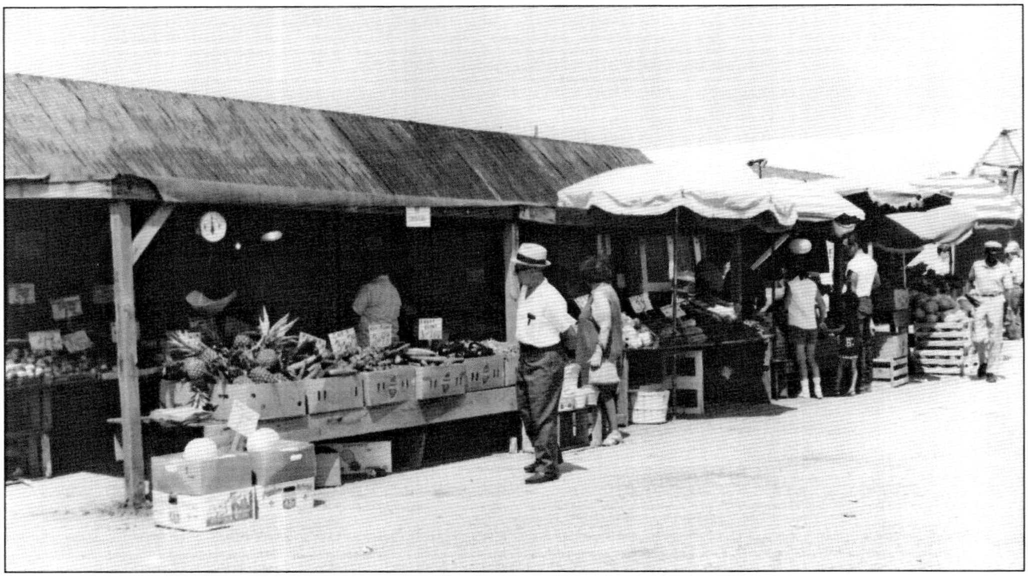

Looking for a Deal. In the 1940s, merchants at the Cowtown market did not open until 8:00 a.m. Over the years, merchants have gradually made the start time earlier. Today, shoppers can swing by as early as 6:30 a.m., when some vendors are setting up tables and booths. Bargain hunters typically try to get there early to get the first look at the merchandise. (Photograph by David Turnbull; courtesy of Emily Walker.)

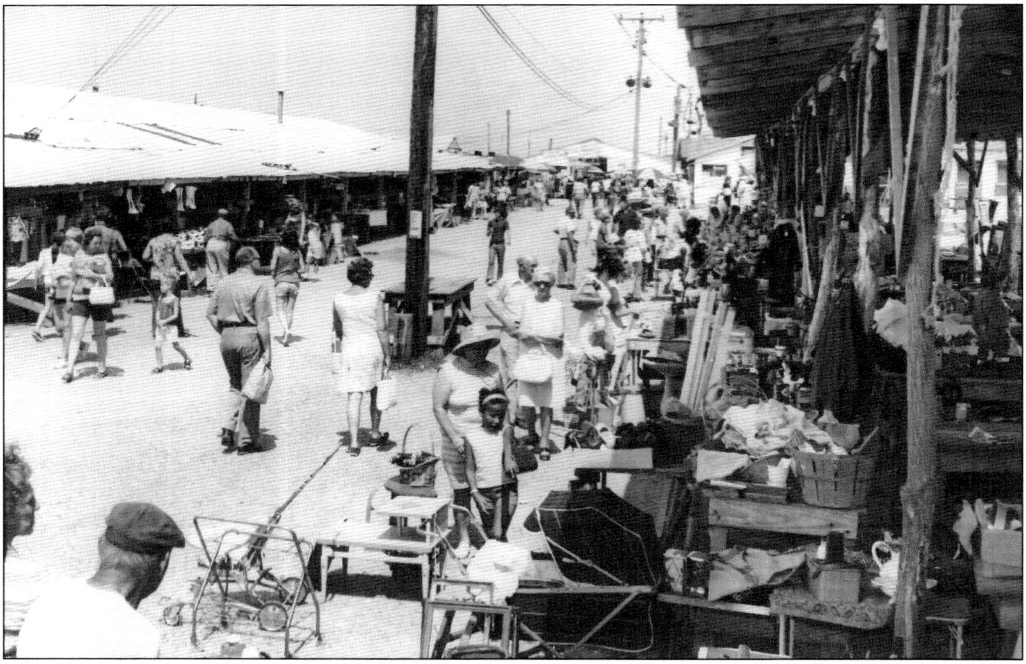

No Vendor Restrictions. Stoney and Howard Harris believed in the concept of a competitive market and did not restrict vendors, even if the same or similar products were being sold by multiple vendors. More vendors provide more choice for the shoppers at the market. (Photograph by David Turnbull; courtesy of Emily Walker.)

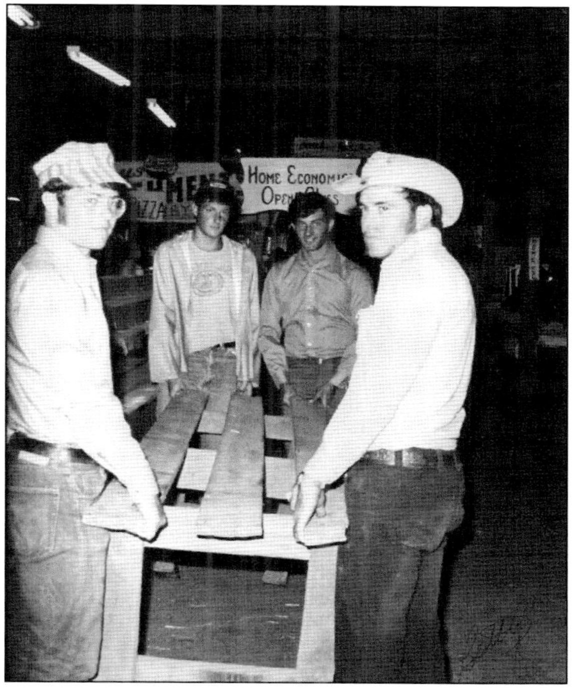

The Fair at the Midway. Before the Salem County Fair moved to the official fairgrounds, the fair was held at Cowtown. On Tuesday nights, after the auction and market had ended, the tables would be moved aside for fair displays. All of the tables would be moved back after the fair ended. Here, from left to right, Jim Boland, Jeff Allen, Dr. Mickey Ostrum, and Ed Flitcraft Jr. help prep Cowtown for the fair.

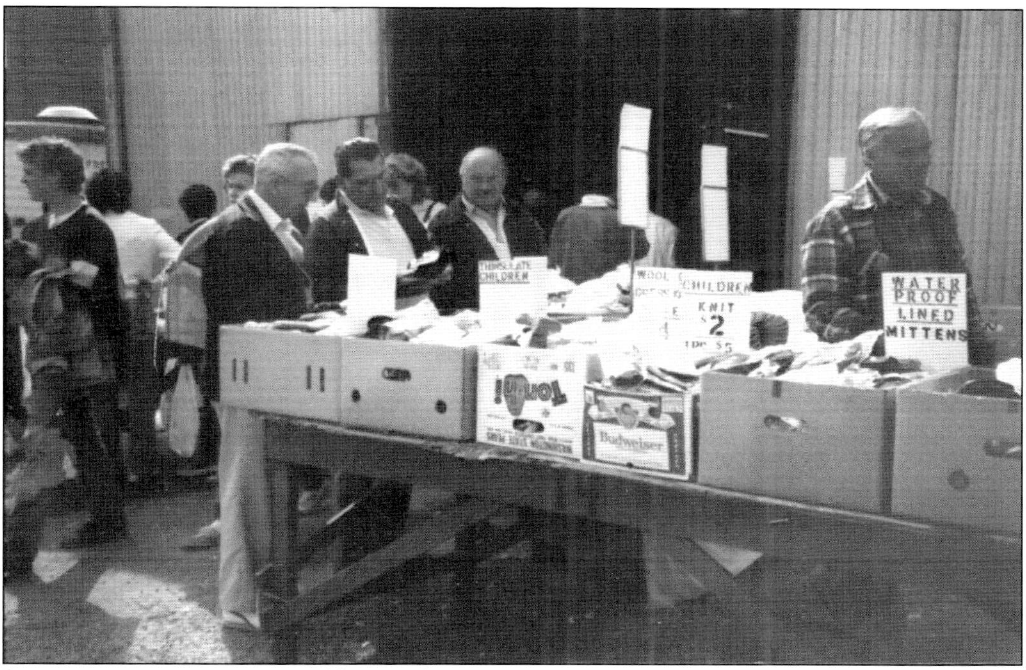

Shopping at the Mall. Just like any department store, the offerings change with the seasons. In this photograph, mittens and other cold-weather apparel are offered to meet the needs of the shoppers. Over the years, some people have referred to Cowtown as the Sharptown Mall, since it has been and continues to be one of the largest shopping areas in the region. (Courtesy of Cliff and Dot Jones.)

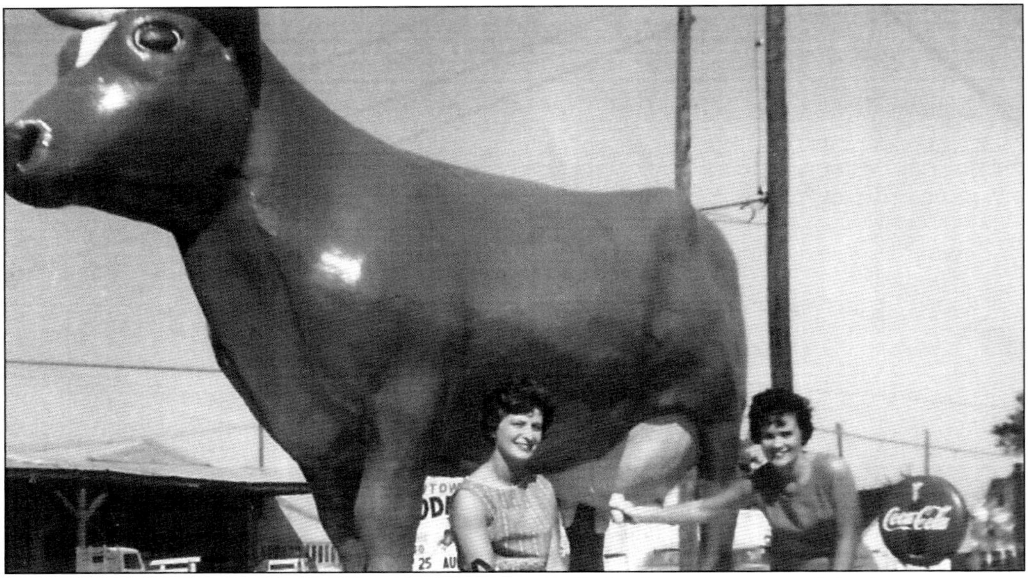

Everything is Red. The first Cowtown cow, originally built in the automobile showroom, was eventually moved to the front of Cowtown when the showroom was converted to a restaurant. The cow was red, which is Cowtown's signature color. Helen Jones and Mary Brady of Danville, Pennsylvania, are pictured here with the cow. (Courtesy of Helen Jones.)

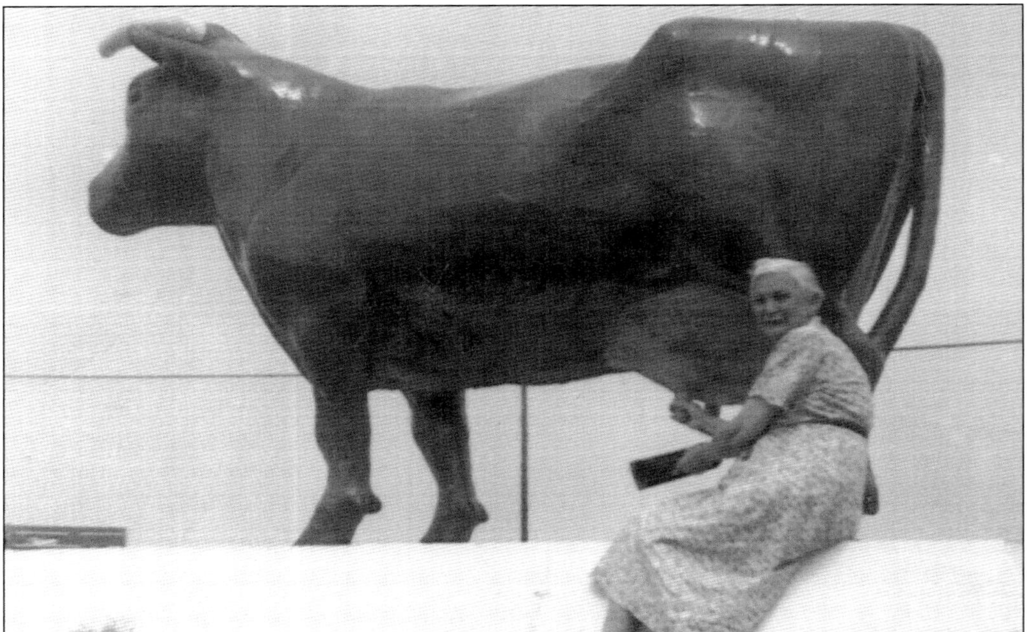

Pose for a Cow Picture. The original Cowtown cow started to deteriorate approximately 40 years after it was built, so a new cow was ordered to replace it. The replacement cow was positioned in front of Cowtown in the mid-1980s. At age 80, Mary Best, seen here, playfully poses with the cow, pretending to milk it. Over the years, Cowtown staff have seen thousands of people stop at the cow and pose for a picture. (Courtesy of Cliff and Dot Jones.)

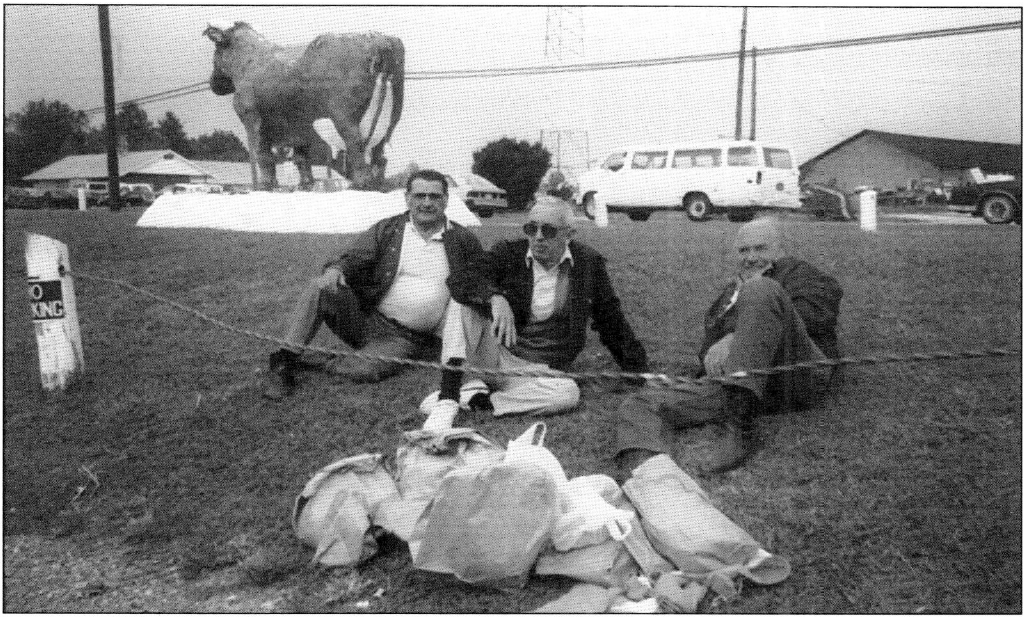

RELAXING AFTER SHOPPING. These men lounge in front of Cowtown while their wives presumably continue to shop. The iconic cow and Route 40 are seen here behind, from left to right, Emmet Reefer, Earl Scholl, and Cliff Jones. Cowtown is an often-referenced landmark in South Jersey because of the cow and cowboy statues. (Courtesy of Cliff and Dot Jones.)

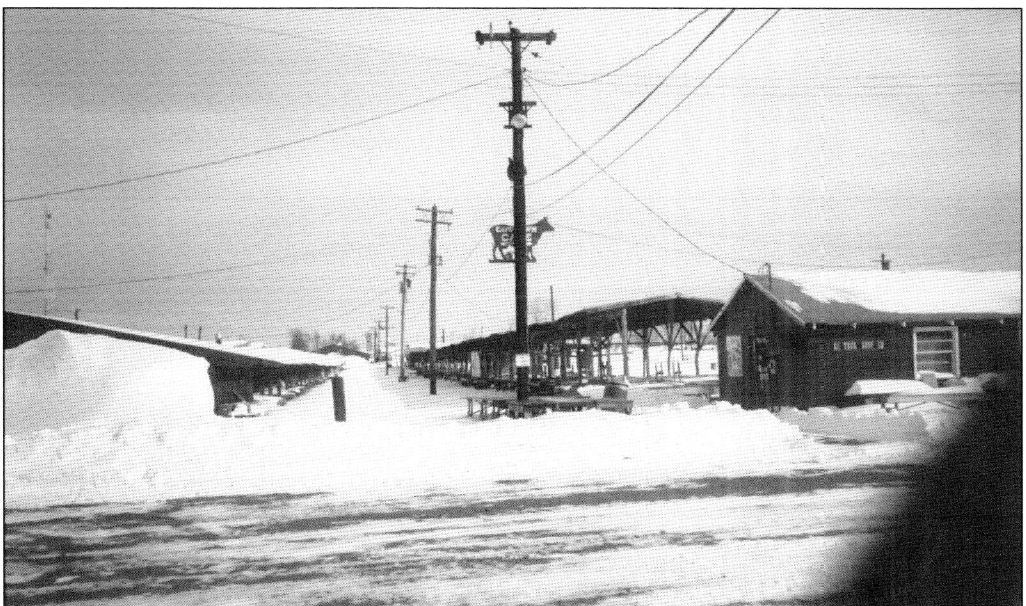

SNOWY DAY. The Cowtown market is open on Tuesdays and Saturdays rain or shine. Since the 1920s, Cowtown has provided a unique shopping experience for Mid-Atlantic consumers; however, the market is not the only large-scale shopping experience that Cowtown offered. An early version of a supermarket was also accessible to shoppers in the 1960s at Cowtown, before Acme Market was available in Woodstown.

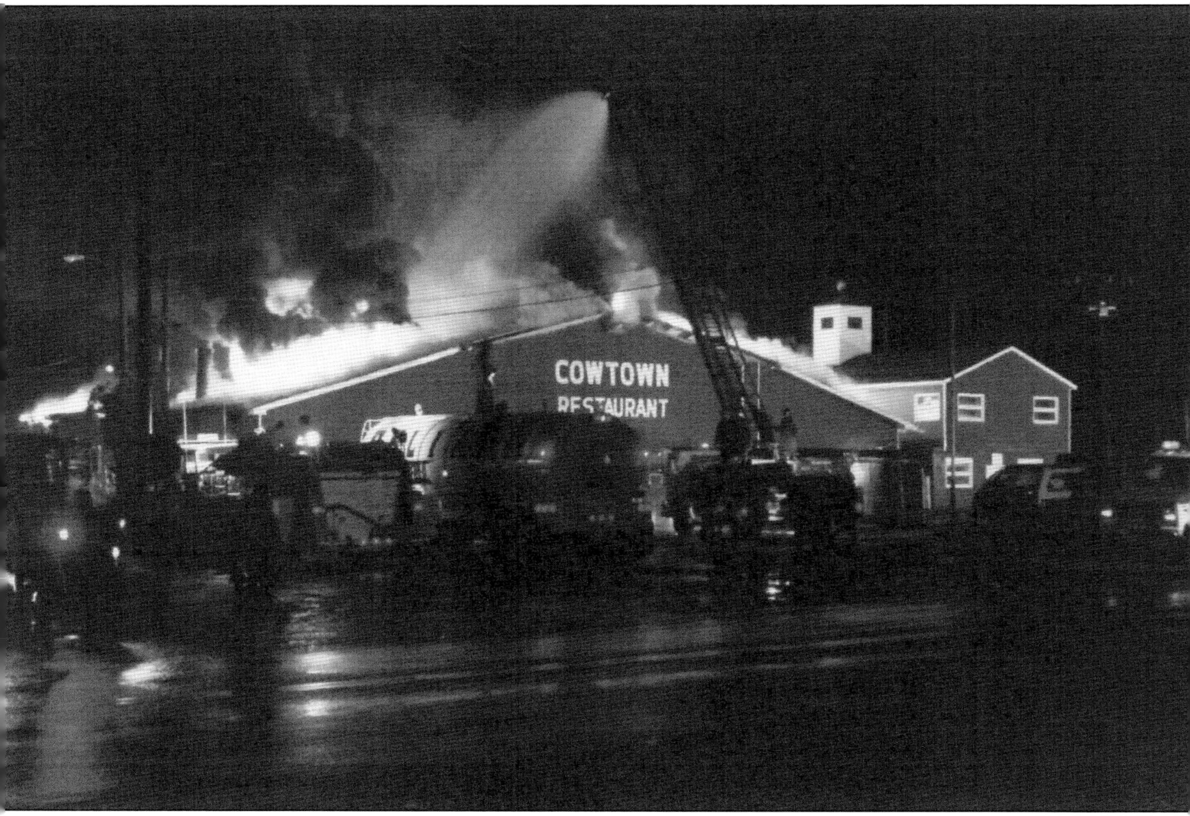

COWTOWN RESTAURANT FIRE. There was a fire at the Cowtown Restaurant in November 1985. The restaurant had served meals to members of the local community, visitors of Cowtown, and travelers passing by for many years. No one was injured in the blaze, but the structure was burned beyond repair.

Five

Clowning around at the Rodeo

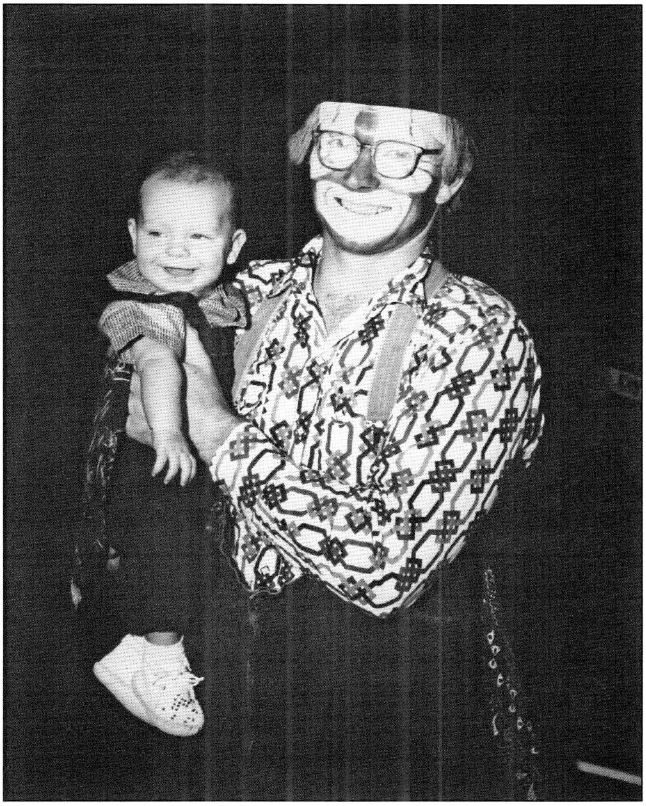

Everyone Loves a Clown. Rodeo clowns, or bullfighters, as they are also sometimes called, provide comic relief during the rodeo and also ensure that cowboys remain safe after their rides. Many rodeo clowns wear wigs and brightly colored clothes to match their antics in the arena. Here, George Doak holds a baby before beginning his performance in the arena. (Courtesy of George Doak.)

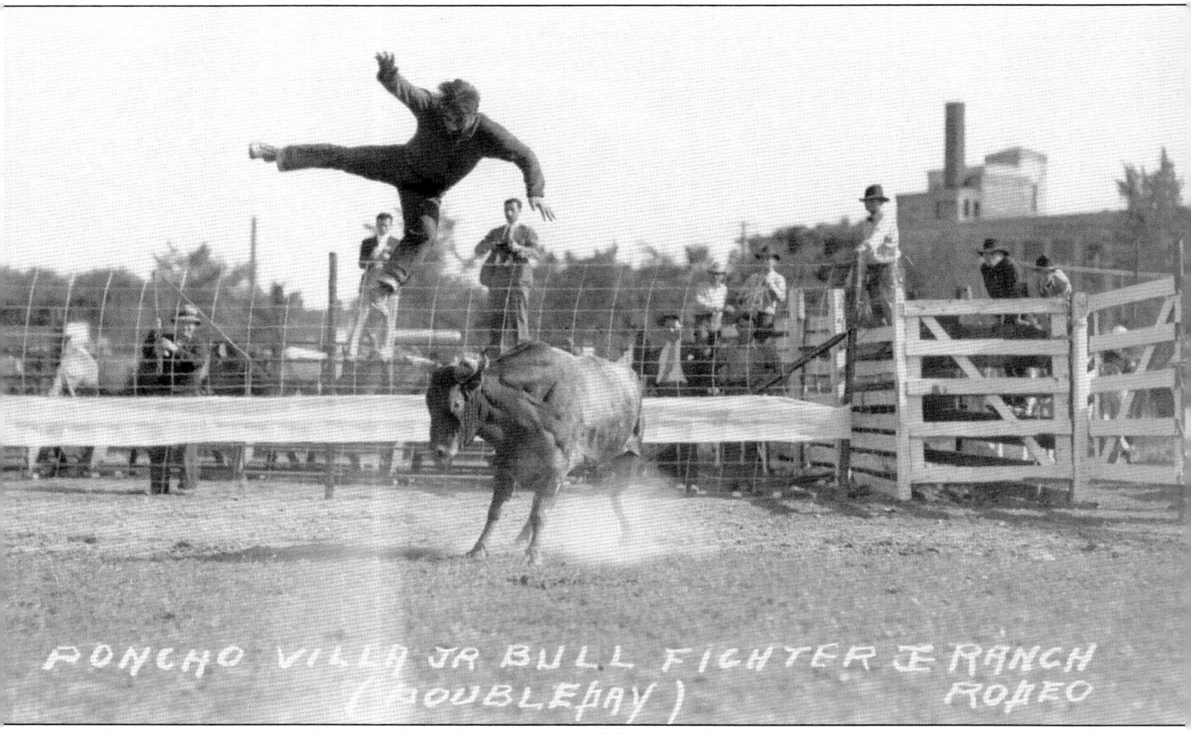

PLAYING WITH THE BULLS. One of the most well-known clowns in the history of rodeo is Poncho Villa, seen here on a postcard of a photograph that was also featured in the 1938 Cowtown Rodeo program. Pancho Villa would not only entertain the crowd, but also provide help for the bull rider. Poncho Villa performed from the late 1910s to the 1940s. He would march into the arena and let the bull chase him, hit him, and attempt to gore him. When he performed, he did not appear fearful. He entertained the crowds and helped distract the bulls with his antics. Allegedly, moonshine was an important part of his rodeo prep ritual.

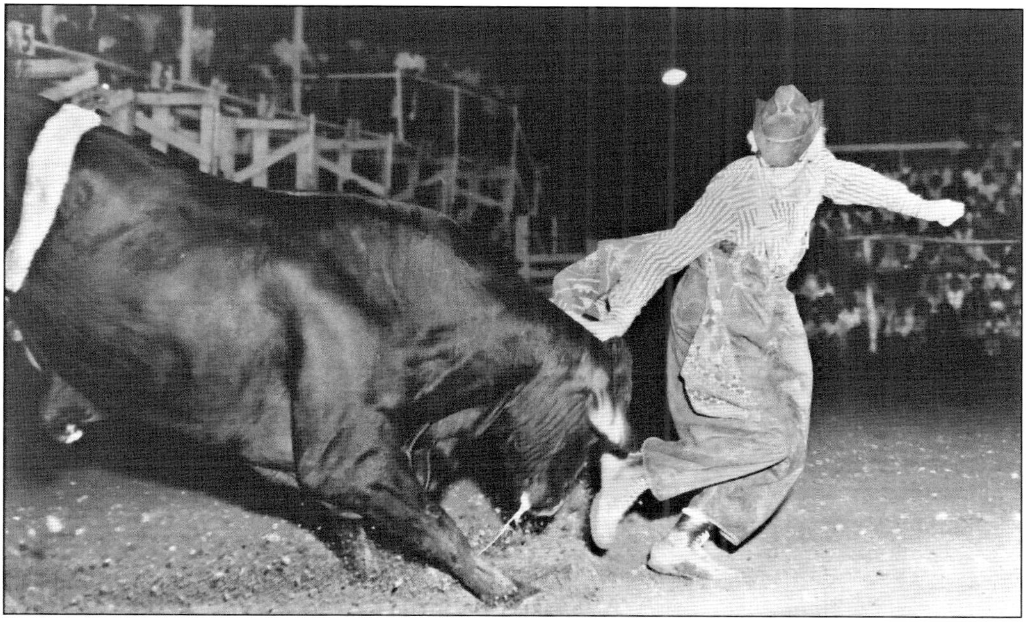

Shifting Sides. If a rider is bucked, then the clown distracts the bull so the cowboy can quickly get to a safe location. The terms *rodeo clown* and *bullfighter* are sometimes used interchangeably. George Doak, a well-known rodeo clown at Cowtown, is seen here shifting to the other side of the bull. (Courtesy of George Doak.)

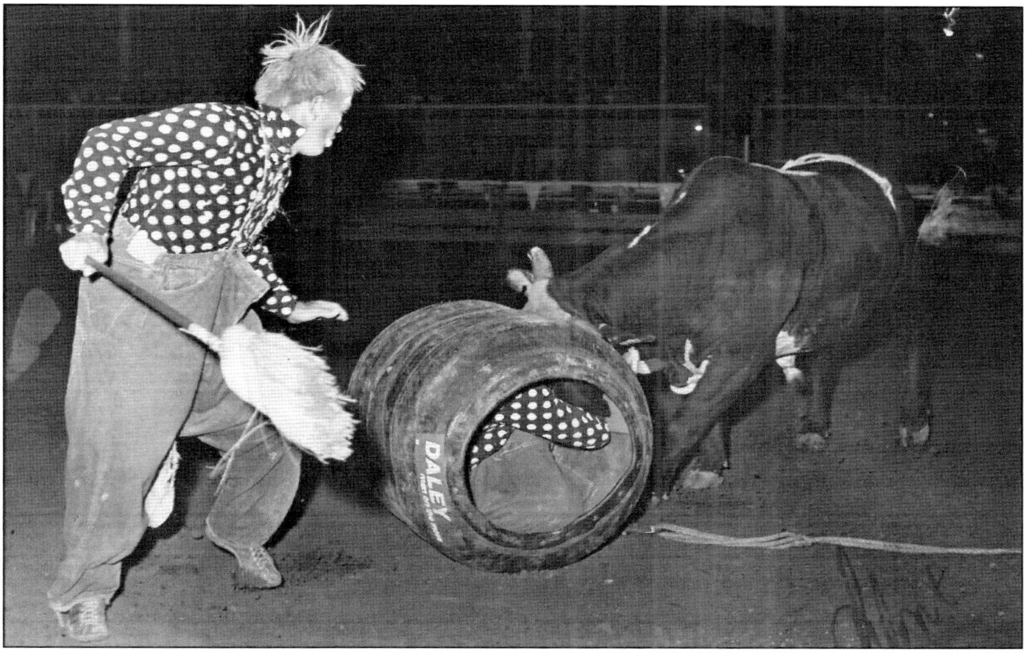

Use of the Barrel. Sometimes, when rodeo clowns are performing, especially when two clowns have partnered, one will assume the role of the barrel man. The barrel man may hop in and out of the reinforced barrel to help both the cowboy and the fellow clown. Howard Harris III (left) was a clown for the rodeo, but not necessarily a barrel man.

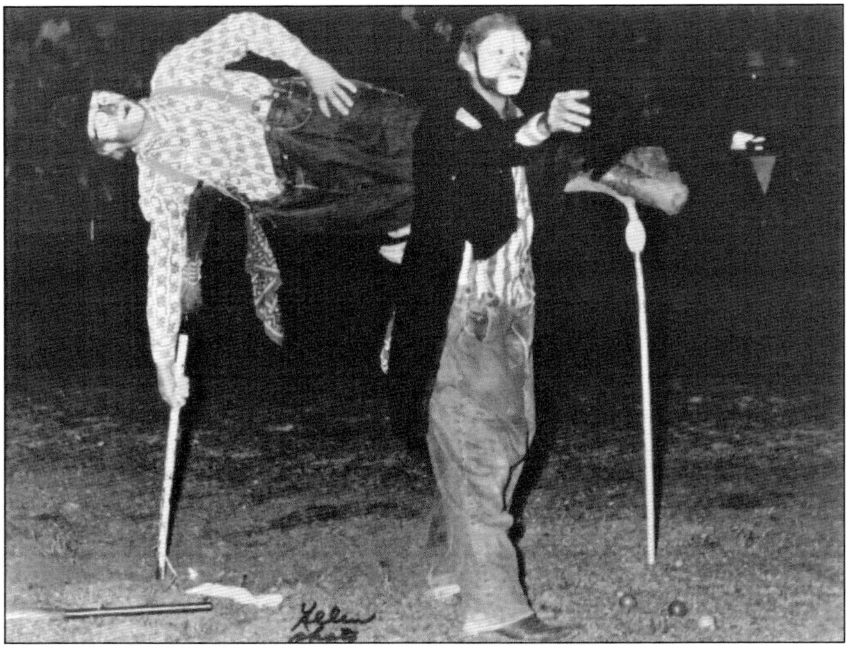

CLOWN TRICKS. George Doak, a rodeo clown and bullfighter, began his career at the Cowtown Rodeo in 1957. Doak traveled around the country as a clown and was called the "fearless funnyman." In these two images, Doak and his clowning partner wow the crowd with a trick. Doak appears to be resting in midair on two thin poles. His clowning partner removes the pole that keeps his feet propped up, and Doak remains horizontal four feet above the ground. In between rides, clowns keep the audience entertained. They tell jokes and use props to keep the crowd laughing. But when the cowboys begin the ride, it is back to business to keep the cowboy from harm's way. (Both courtesy of George Doak.)

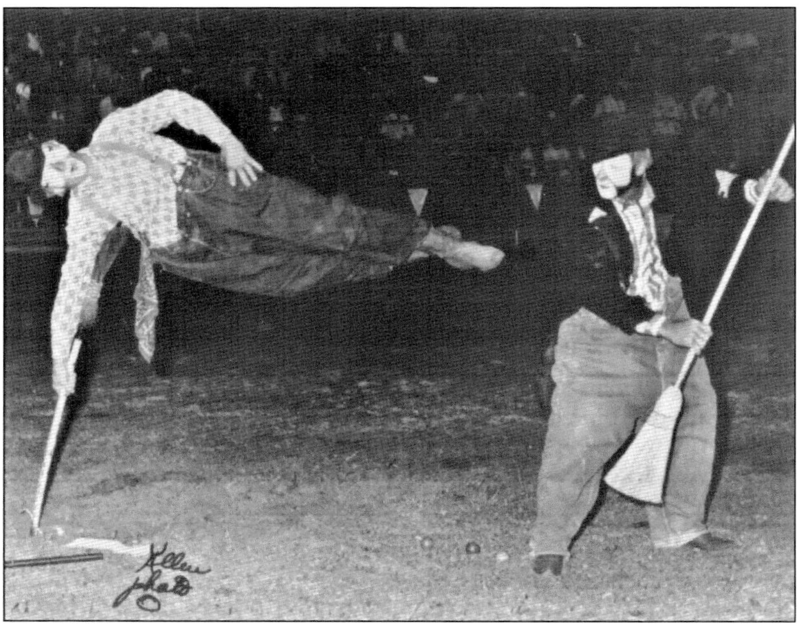

Road Show. George Doak and Junior Meek take a ride around an arena on a road show. Doak (left) rides a mule, while Meek swings his lasso in the air. Cowtown would put on rodeos up and down the East Coast, literally taking the show on the road. Both Doak and Meek were inducted into the Cowboy Hall of Fame.

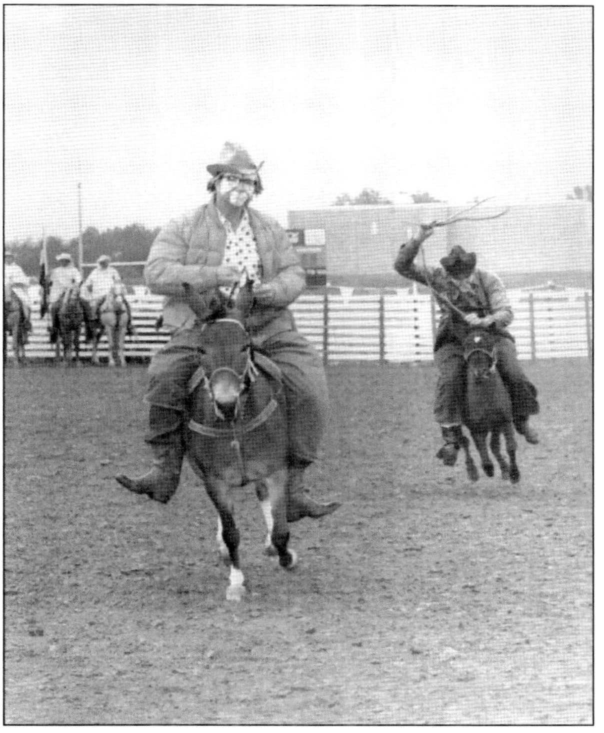

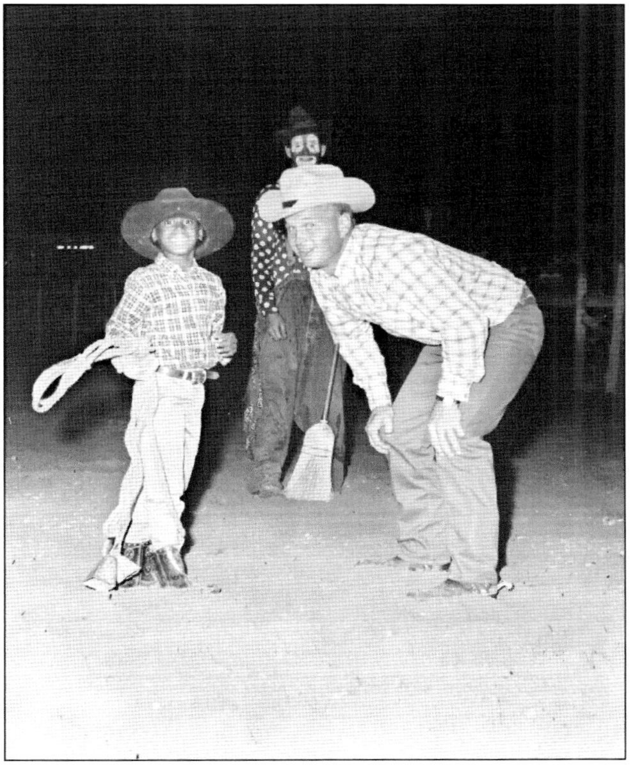

Kids Love Clowns. Clowns are a favorite part of the rodeo show for many kids. Howard Harris III, owner of Cowtown, leans over for a photo opportunity with a young rodeo-goer while Cowtown rodeo clown George Doak looks on. (Courtesy of George Doak.)

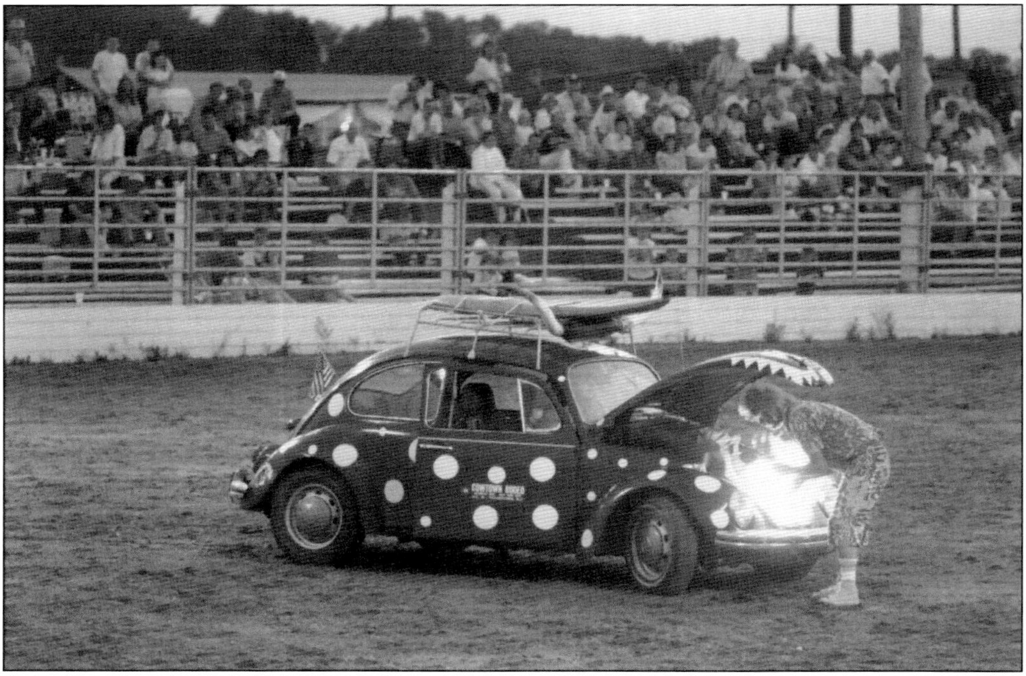

Creative Props get Laughs. Good clowns can make or break the show. Clowns keep things exciting and light while the next contestant gets situated in the bucking shoot. T.J. Hawkins, pictured here, would appear with his Volkswagen bug and elicit laughter by shooting at it and setting it on fire. Sometimes, he would even jump on top of it and be driven around the arena. The car was painted red, the Cowtown signature color, with polka dots, a rooftop surfboard, and teeth cutouts around the front hood. (Both courtesy of T.J. Hawkins and Sharon Sunderland.)

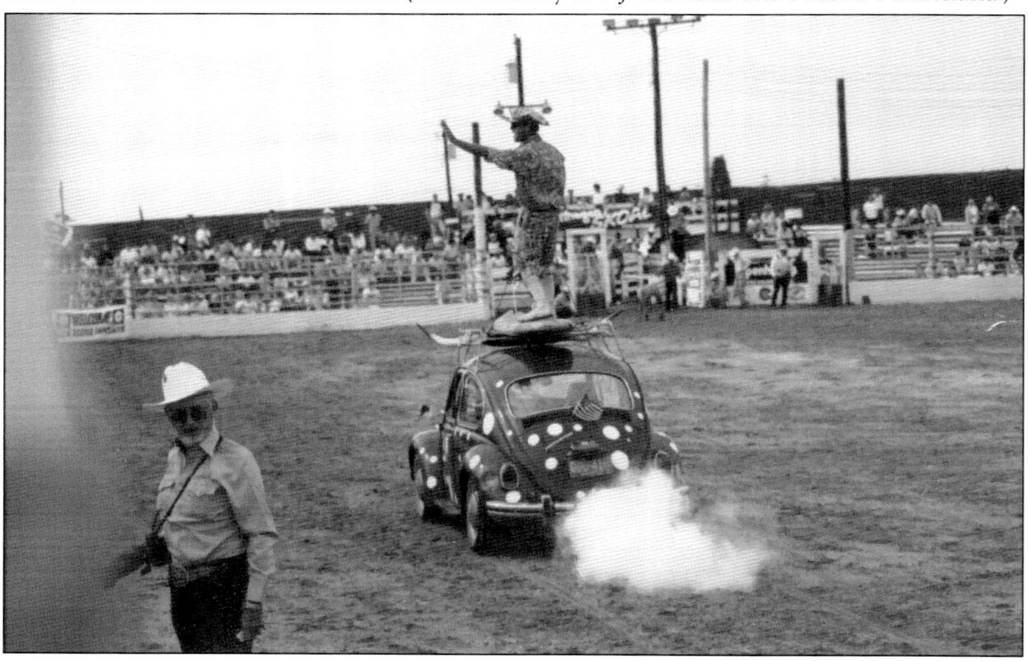

Injured and Performing. Nothing could stop Hawkins's dedication to clowning. Even when injured, he would bound into the arena and perform, crutches and all. Here, Hawkins hops up on the fence to charm the crowd. The injury was likely rodeo-related, as rodeo clowns in general end up with bumps, bruises, and breaks. (Photograph by Bob Hill; courtesy of Jimmy Lee Walker.)

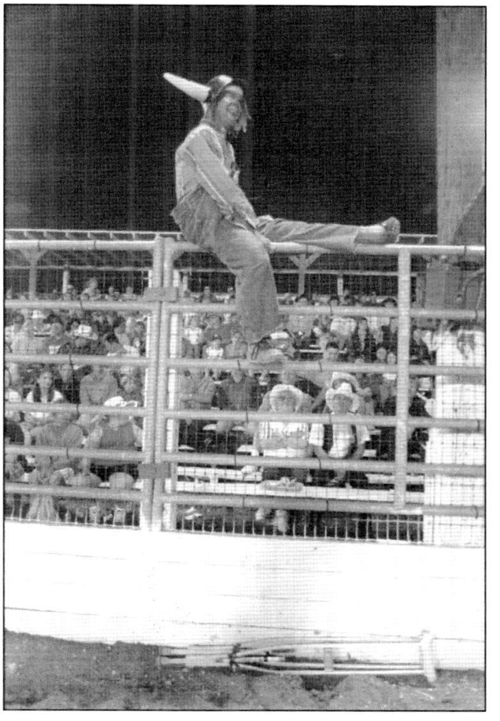

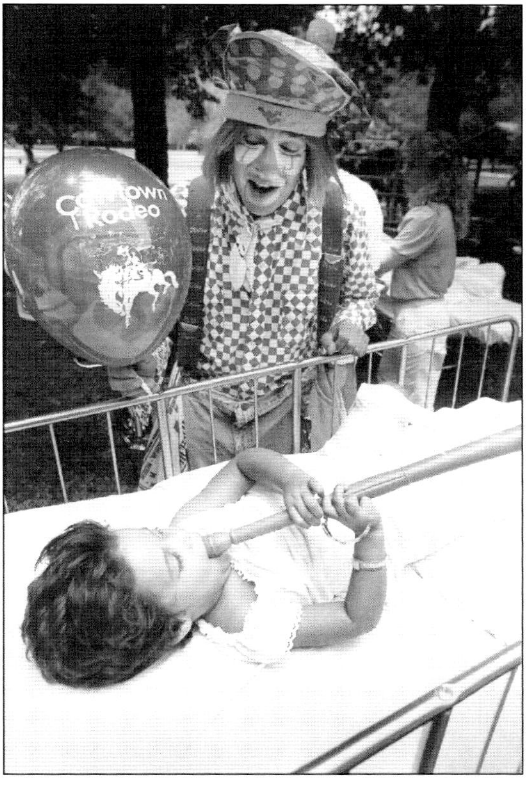

Laughs at the Hospital. Hawkins, a well-known clown and bullfighter that performed often at the Cowtown Rodeo, was not just a funnyman in the rodeo arena. He would also visit children at the Shriners Hospital and tell jokes. The patients enjoyed his tricks and laughed a lot when Hawkins was around. (Courtesy of T.J. Hawkins and Sharon Sunderland.)

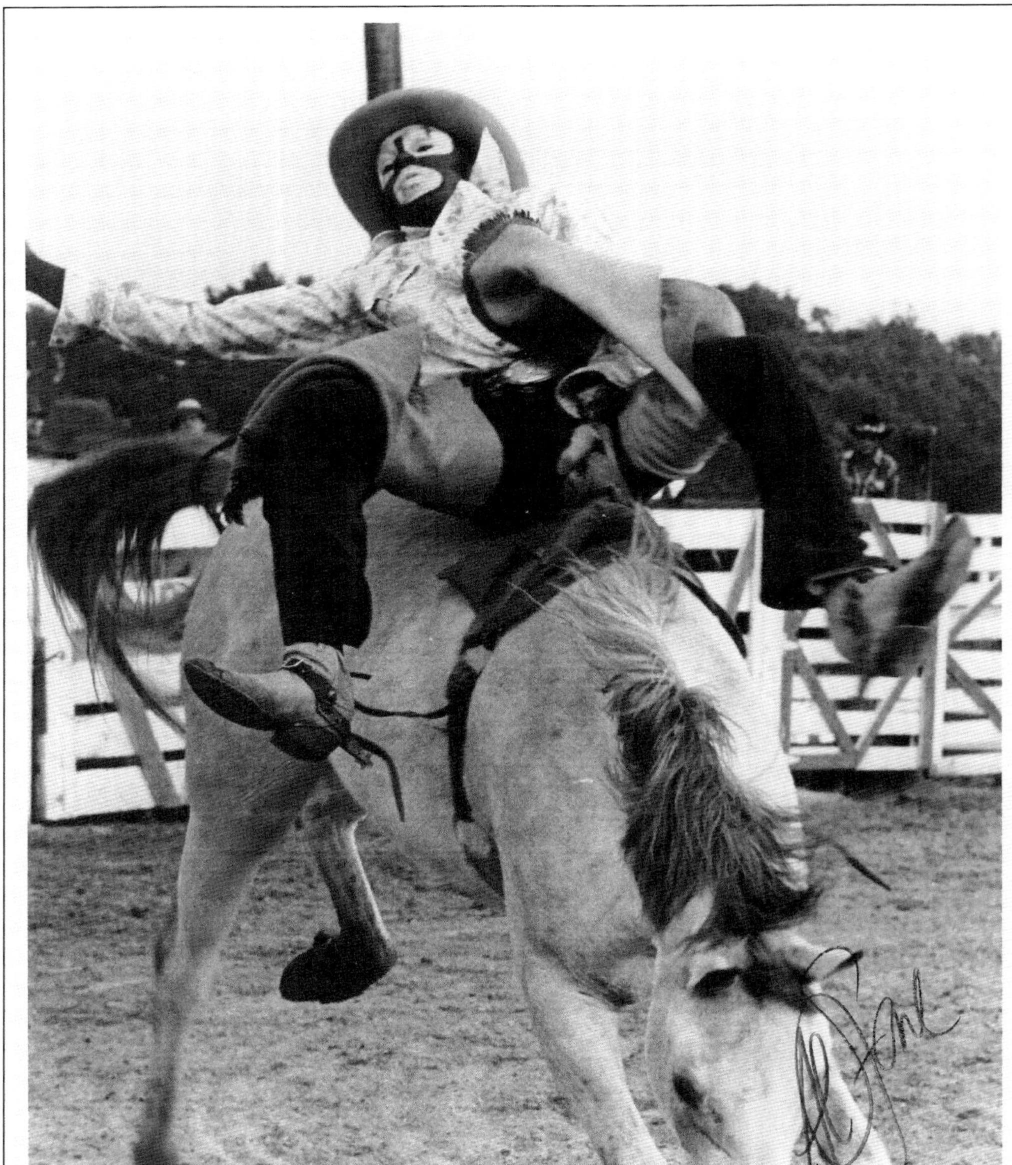

Double Duty. Jimmy Lee Walker, an accomplished bullfighter, started his rodeo clowning in 1969 at Cowtown. Walker was not only a bullfighter, but also a bareback and bull rider too. Sometimes, he would ride in his clown costume and makeup, as seen here. Walker was able to live both sides of the experience. (Courtesy of Jimmy Lee Walker.)

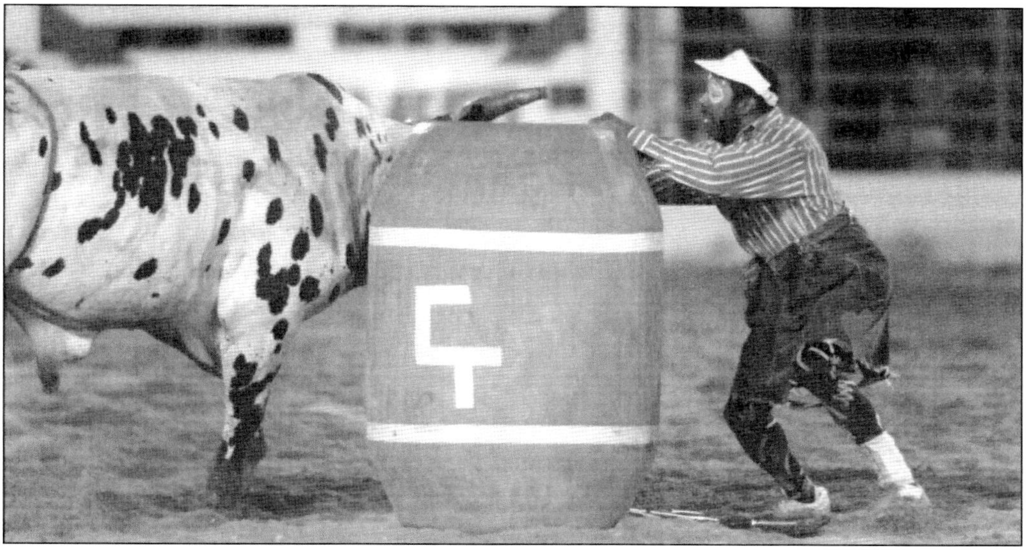

Jalapeno. The bull seen here is the infamous Jalapeno, a particularly intimidating bull that only the bravest riders and fighters faced at Cowtown. Average bucking bulls weigh 1,700–1,800 pounds and are bred to buck. Jalapeno tested the athletic abilities of every rider and fighter he encountered. (Courtesy of Jimmy Lee Walker and Bob Hill.)

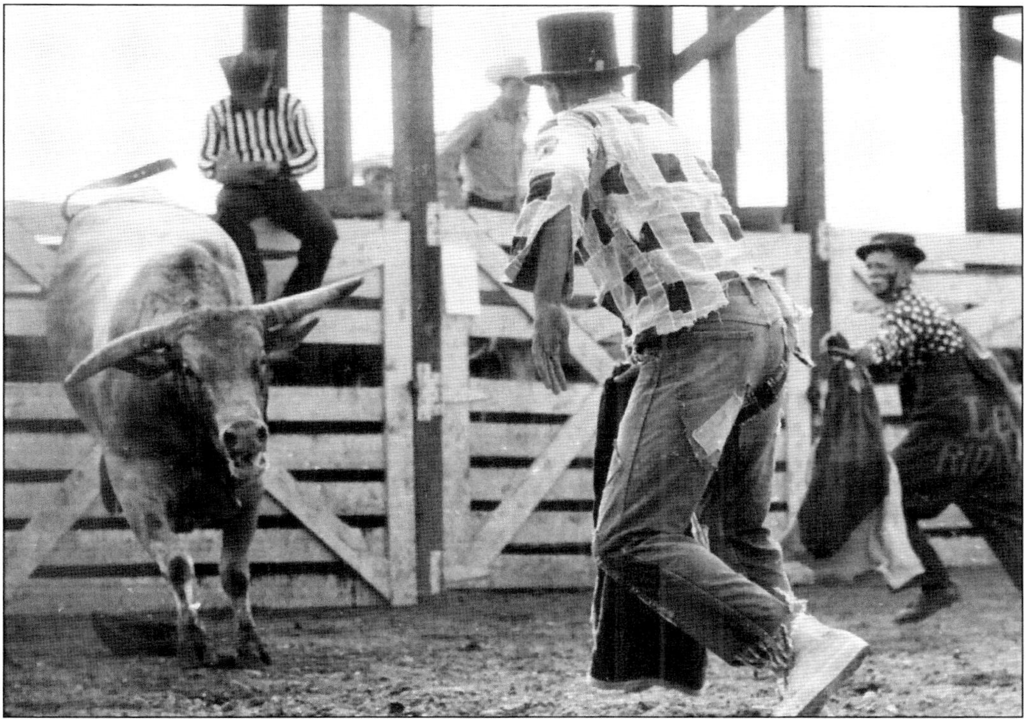

Brave Men. Rodeo clowns are sometimes within inches of aggressive bulls and must constantly be aware and on their toes while in the arena. The more a bullfighter gets in the arena, the better he gets at anticipating how the bull will move. Practice makes perfect. (Courtesy of Jimmy Lee Walker.)

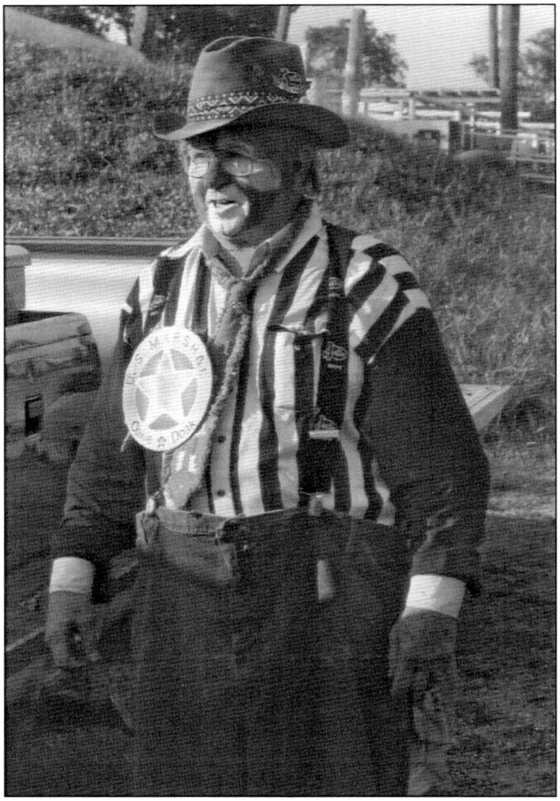

Doak Returns. In 2007, George Doak came out of retirement to perform at the Cowtown Rodeo once again. Earlier in his career as a rodeo clown, Doak and his family would come to Cowtown for the summer, and he would bullfight for the rodeo season. After that, he would travel around the country on road shows. His return to Cowtown to clown brought him out of his 1981 retirement.

Hanging out in a Barrel. Cowtown clown and bullfighter Marvin Nash, pictured here, peeks out of a barrel during a show. Nash used his reach as a performer to promote a "No 'Bull'ying" message both in and out of the arena. He utilized an image of a bull in his campaign to emphasize his message. (Photograph by Don Pivonka.)

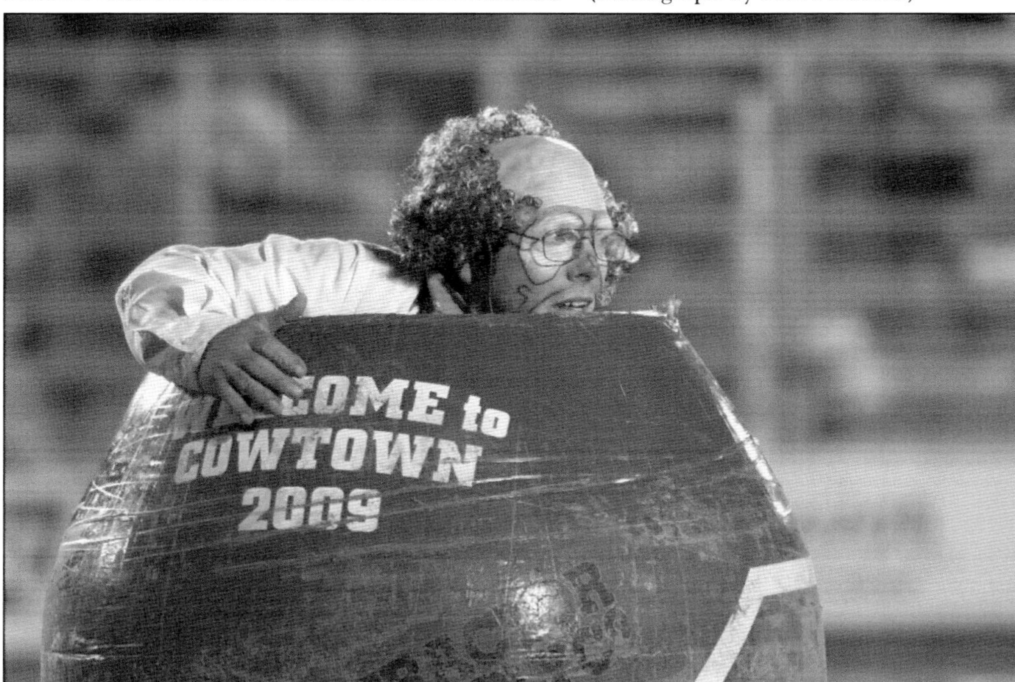

Six

Happy Trails at the Cowtown Rodeo

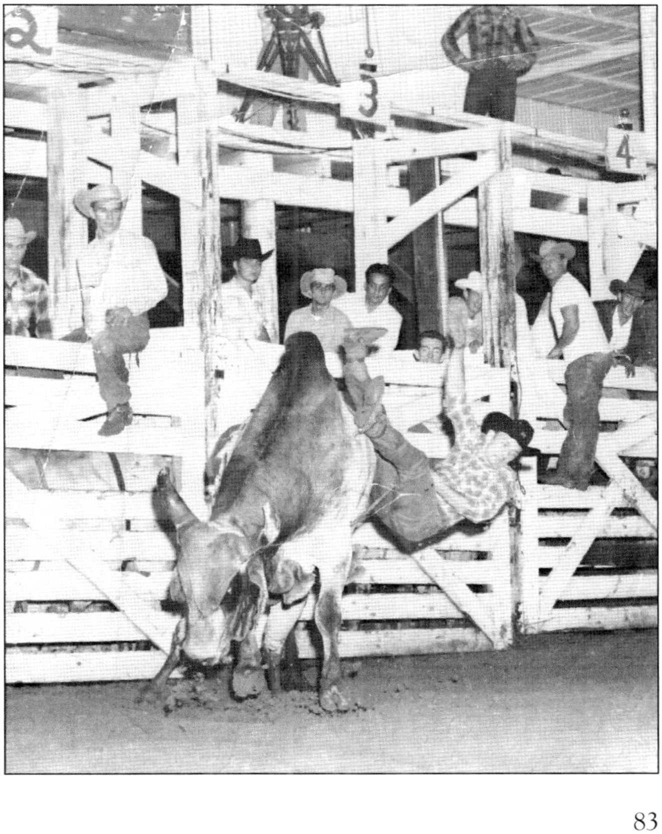

Rodeo in Salem County. The term *rodeo* comes from the Spanish verb *rodear*, meaning "to go around" or "to surround." Rodeo is a competitive sport with events that involve bulls, horses, and calves. The Salem County Fair had sponsored a rodeo during the fair, but after World War I, the entire event fizzled. Cowtown helped bring the fair and the rodeo back to Salem County in the late 1920s. (Courtesy of Lee and Lorraine Curry.)

OFFICIAL DAILY PROGRAM

First Annual County

FAIR and RODEO

Salem County Fair Grounds

Direction of
Howard Harris Sr. and Howard Harris Jr.

Music furnished for the Rodeo by Swedesboro Kiwanis Boy Band

Pete Adams, Announcer

Judges

Auvil Gilliam .... Waco, Texas
Shorty McCrory .... Marland, Oklahoma
Red Thompson .... Ft. Worth, Texas

Officials

Howard Harris Sr., Director — Howard Harris Jr., Arena Director
Candy Hammer, Ass't Arena Director — Hexlow Coates, Arena Sec.

Woodstown, N. J., September 1931

THE FAIR AND RODEO RETURN. Cowtown hosted the first rodeo in conjunction with the fair, most likely in 1929 or 1930. This event sheet for the "First Annual County Fair and Rodeo" is from 1931, but other sources indicate that a rodeo and fair event may have been hosted prior to that. Events were organized and promoted by Howard Amos Harris Sr. and Stoney Harris.

Official Racing Program

Friday Afternoon September 4, 1931

Starter, H. K. Kneeder, Philadelphia, Pa.
Judge, Charles Lippincott, Sr., Woodstown, N. J.
Clerk of Course, Harvey Hartman, Quakertown, N. J.

Free For All Purse $200.00

No.	Horse	Sire	Driver
1.	Gwyn Wortly, b g. Owner, Harris, Woodstown, N. J.	Guy Axwortly	Wilgus
2.	Al B., b g. Owner, Dennis, Doylestown, Pa.	Hal B.	Yelland
3.	Robert Dale, b g. Owner, Sparks, Phila.		Peacock
4.	Director Guy, b g. Barrett Stables, Merchantville	Guy Axwortly	Barett
5.	Daylight, blk s. Myers & Sons, Bridgeville, Del.	Drystar	Myers
			Time

Official Rodeo Program

Event No. 1
Grand Entry and Introduction

Event No. 2
Cowboy and Cowgirl Quadrille on Horseback

Event No. 3
Wild Brahma Steer Riding

Frank Daniels, Jack Bowen, Slim Welsh, Nelson Benn, Pete Forrester, Tommy Horner, Elmer Sutterly, Earl Sutton, Bill McBride, Frank Scott, Don Trieweiler, Everett Vassar

Event No. 4
Trick and Fancy Roping

Frank Biron, Auvil Gilliam

Event No. 5
Cowgirl Bronc Riding

Madge Runyan, Alice Adams, Rose Herlin, Alice Sisty, Clara Thompson

Event No. 6
Wild Cow Milking

Event No. 7
Bob Roebuck and his educated horse

Billie Keene and his high jumping Roman Team jumping an automobile

Event No. 8
Cowgirl Trick and Fancy Riding

Clara Belcher, Ruth Frazier, Madge Runyan, Alice Sisty, Mary Keene, Clara Thompson, Rose Herlin, Alice Adams

Event No. 9
Cowboy Bronc Riding

Tommy Horner, Ken Insley, Lou Weir, Jack Bowen, Jack Chapman, Slim Welsh, Dallas Conley, Bill McBride, Earl Sutton, Red Parker, Nelson Benn, Bert Peters, Pete Forrester, Don Trieweiler, Frank Scott, Blackie Russell, Al Allen

Event No. 10
Cowboy Trick and Fancy Riding

Frank Biron, Frank Scott, Elmer Sutterly, Donal Biron, Tommy Horner, Frank Donald, Bill Keene, Everett Vasser

Event No. 11
Wild Steer Bulldogging

Lou Weir, Bert Peters, Ken Insley, Jack Chapman, Jack Bowen, Earl Sutton, Shorty McCrory, Blackie Russell, Al Allen, Lou Weir, Bert Peters, Jack Chapman

Event No. 12
Bulldogging a wild steer from running board of an automobile.

Special Features

Stack Lee in an exhibition of rifle shooting
Tom Hunt and his educated and dancing mule
Juvenile Cowboy Burro Riders

SATURDAY AFTERNOON

Stock Parade, Pulling Contest and complete Rodeo Program

OFFICIAL RACING PROGRAM. A total of 12 events were scheduled, and events kicked off with Grand Entry. Some of the events listed differ from rodeo events today. For instance, today, contestants compete in bull riding, not steer riding, and trick riding and fancy riding are not scheduled as regular rodeo events. Also, the last bulldogging event on this program included an automobile, which does not happen today.

THE RULES. Stoney Harris hosted the third annual rodeo in conjunction with the county fair in Woodstown in August 1932. At that time, Harris Sales Co. was located on North Main Street in Woodstown. The cover of the program features Stoney on horseback. The first page of the program was "How to Play the Rodeo Games" (below). In the description, Stoney wrote, "Because there are still quiet folk who believe in the Old American ideals, I will try to treat succinctly with some of the innocent sports of the cow-gentlemen and cow-ladies with hope that some of these innocent sports may yet find their way into South Jersey homes, and exert their bucolic influence against the dark menace of tiddle-winks and ping-pong. To that end, I shall try to describe these sports, giving their rules, either for ladies or gents."

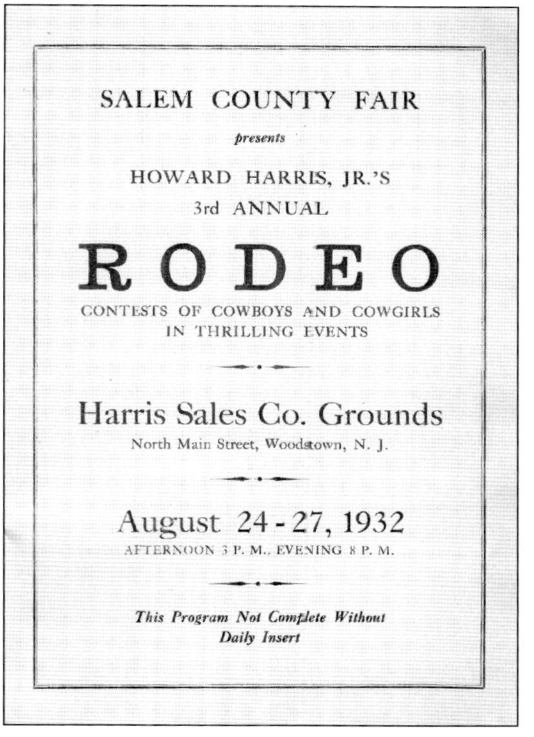

SALEM COUNTY FAIR

presents

HOWARD HARRIS, JR.'S

3rd ANNUAL

RODEO

CONTESTS OF COWBOYS AND COWGIRLS
IN THRILLING EVENTS

Harris Sales Co. Grounds

North Main Street, Woodstown, N. J.

August 24 - 27, 1932

AFTERNOON 3 P. M., EVENING 8 P. M.

This Program Not Complete Without Daily Insert

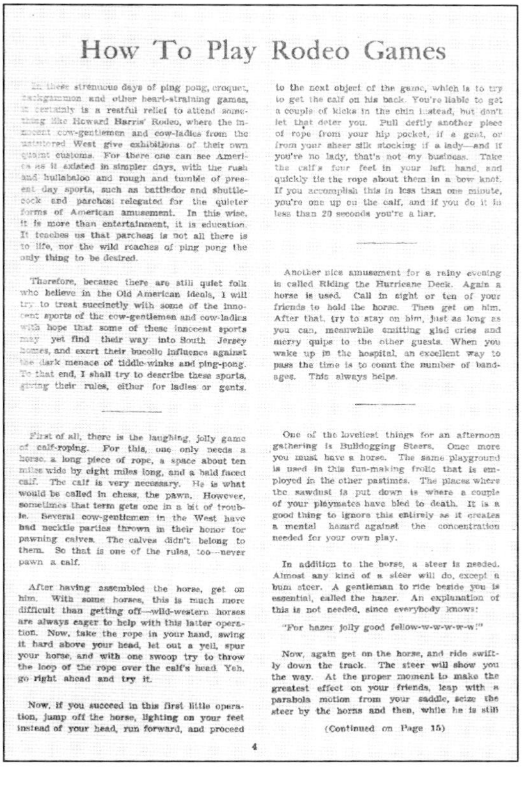

How To Play Rodeo Games

In these strenuous days of ping pong, croquet, backgammon and other heart-straining games, it certainly is a restful relief to attend something like Howard Harris' Rodeo, where the innocent cow-gentlemen and cow-ladies from the untutored West give exhibitions of their own quaint customs. For there one can see America as it existed in simpler days, with the rush and hullabaloo and rough and tumble of present day sports, such as battledor and shuttlecock and parchesi relegated for the quieter forms of American amusement. In this wise, it is more than entertainment, it is education. It teaches us that parchesi is not all there is to life, nor the wild reaches of ping pong the only thing to be desired.

Therefore, because there are still quiet folk who believe in the Old American ideals, I will try to treat succinctly with some of the innocent sports of the cow-gentlemen and cow-ladies with hope that some of these innocent sports may yet find their way into South Jersey homes, and exert their bucolic influence against the dark menace of tiddle-winks and ping-pong. To that end, I shall try to describe these sports, giving their rules, either for ladies or gents.

First of all, there is the laughing, jolly game of calf-roping. For this, one only needs a horse, a long piece of rope, a space about ten miles wide by eight miles long, and a bald faced calf. The calf is very necessary. He is what would be called in chess, the pawn. However, sometimes that term gets one in a bit of trouble. Several cow-gentlemen in the West have had necktie parties thrown in their honor for pawning calves. The calves didn't belong to them. So that is one of the rules, too—never pawn a calf.

After having assembled the horse, get on him. With some horses, this is much more difficult than getting off—wild-western horses are always eager to help with this latter operation. Now, take the rope in your hand, swing it hard above your head, let out a yell, spur your horse, and with one swoop try to throw the loop of the rope over the calf's head. Yeh, go right ahead and try it.

Now, if you succeed in this first little operation, jump off the horse, lighting on your feet instead of your head, run forward, and proceed to the next object of the game, which is to try to get the calf on his back. You're liable to get a couple of kicks in the chin instead, but don't let that deter you. Pull deftly another piece of rope from your hip pocket, if a gent, or from your sheer silk stocking if a lady—and if you're no lady, that's not my business. Take the calf's four feet in your left hand, and quickly tie the rope about them in a bow knot. If you accomplish this in less than one minute, you're one up on the calf, and if you do it in less than 20 seconds you're a liar.

Another nice amusement for a rainy evening is called Riding the Hurricane Deck. Again a horse is used. Call in eight or ten of your friends to hold the horse. Then get on him. After that, try to stay on him, just as long as you can, meanwhile emitting glad cries and merry quips to the other guests. When you wake up in the hospital, an excellent way to pass the time is to count the number of bandages. This always helps.

One of the loveliest things for an afternoon gathering is Bulldogging Steers. Once more you must have a horse. The same playground is used in this fun-making frolic that is employed in the other pastimes. The places where the sawdust is put down is where a couple of your playmates have bled to death. It is a good thing to ignore this entirely as it creates a mental hazard against the concentration needed for your own play.

In addition to the horse, a steer is needed. Almost any kind of a steer will do, except a bum steer. A gentleman to ride beside you is essential, called the hazer. An explanation of this is not needed, since everybody knows:

"For hazer jolly good fellow-w-w-w-w-w!"

Now, again get on the horse, and ride swiftly down the track. The steer will show you the way. At the proper moment to make the greatest effect on your friends, leap with a parabola motion from your saddle, seize the steer by the horns and then, while he is still

(Continued on Page 15)

4

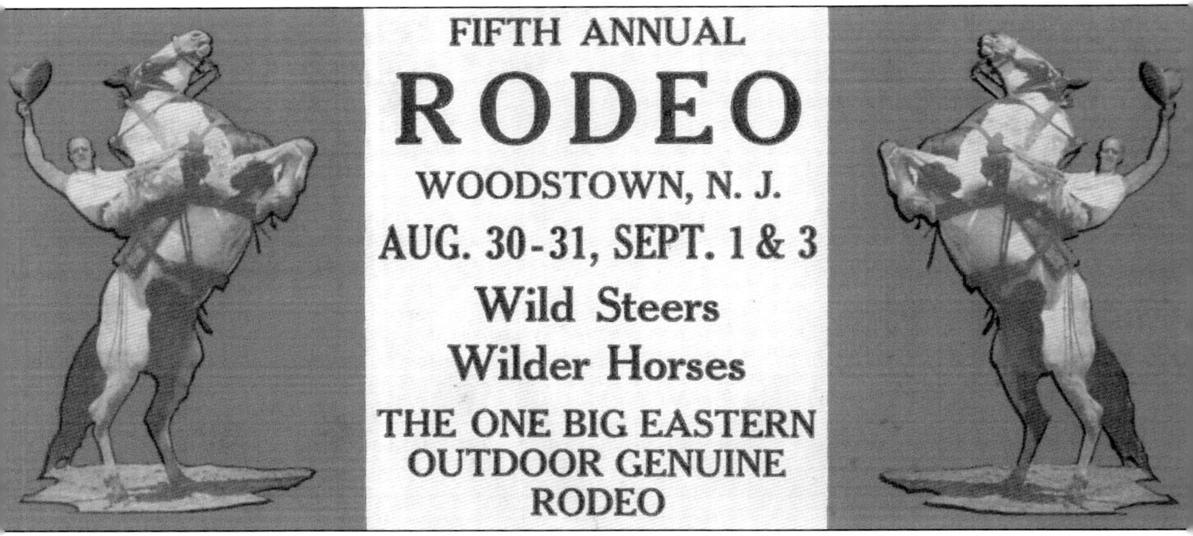

GETTING INTO THE FAIR. This entry ticket for the fifth annual rodeo features Stoney Harris. The annual fair and rodeo was a huge event for Salem County. It was well attended, despite the fact that it was held during the Great Depression.

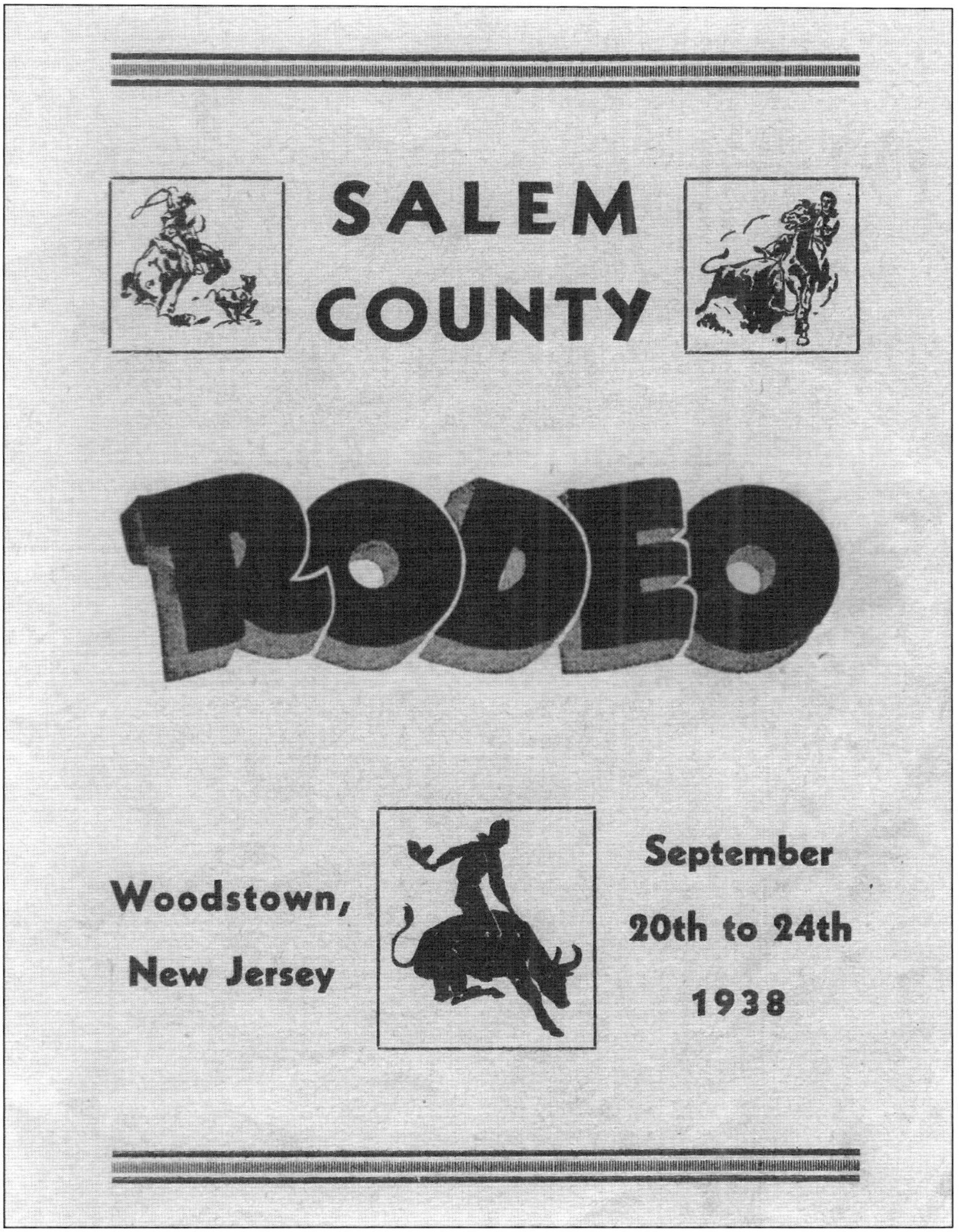

STEER RIDING. The cover of this rodeo program shows a man that was likely riding a steer, not a bull. Inside the program, the event was referred to as steer riding, not bull riding. Steers were used early on in traveling rodeo shows in the West, mostly because they were easier to transport and handle. Even though both steers and bulls are male bovines, they are different. Bulls are capable of reproducing and still have testicles, while steers have been castrated. Because castration is performed at a young age, bull and steer body shapes are different. But body shape is not the only difference. Bulls have more testosterone than steers, which leads to bulls being more aggressive. Bull riding grew in popularity in the 1930s because it was more of a challenge for both bull riders and bullfighters.

'Beleive It Or Not'

YOU can trade in your livestock for

GOODYEAR

Farm Tractor Tires, Farm Implement Tires, Truck Tires or Allis-Chalmers Tractors and Farm Implements here.

(HERE'S ONE FOR WINCHELL)

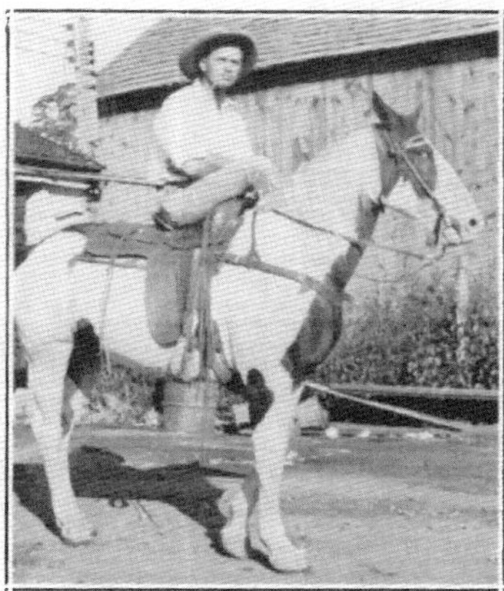

HOWARD "STONEY" HARRIS, JR.

REAL SAFETY PROTECTION

SAFE ON LIFEGUARD!

● It's sweeping the country — this amazing new safety "tire within a tire." You're not really safe unless you have Goodyear Life-Guards.

GOODYEAR LIFEGUARDS

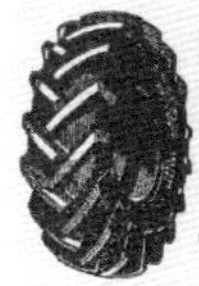

FARMERS! GOODYEAR SURE-GRIP TRACTOR TIRES

● Goodyear Sure-Grip tractor tires dig in, pull right through—even in mud, wet clay and gumbo! The open-center tread is self-cleaning. Let us prove that Sure-Grips will save you money.

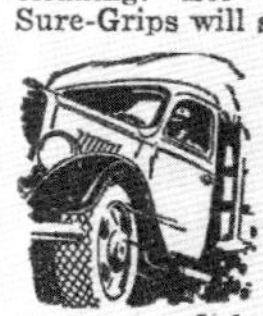

GOODYEAR TRUCK TIRES

● Let us help you select the right Goodyear Truck Tire to fit your hauling need. A slight change of size or type can mean dollars in your pocket! Come in —no obligation.

Complete line of

GOODYEAR

BATTERIES

We Service All Makes of Batteries

HARRIS SERVICE COMPANY

16 WEST AVE. WOODSTOWN, N. J. OPPOSITE THE POST OFFICE

Phone 351

Woodstown's Only 24-hour Service, just Phone 351

HOWARD HARRIS, JR., Prop. HOWARD REID, Mgr.

3

Harris Sales Co. Trading Opportunities. The first advertisement in the 1938 rodeo program was for Harris Service Co. Stoney Harris is featured in the advertisement. Since Harris Sales Co. ran both the livestock auction and the service station, consumers were encouraged to consider trading livestock for tire and vehicle equipment.

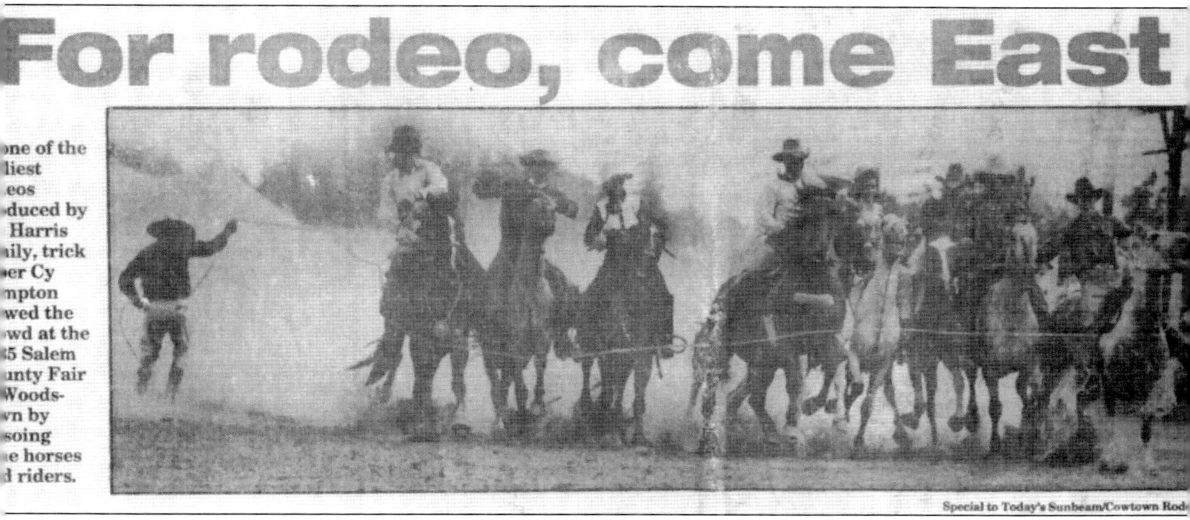

For rodeo, come East

one of the
liest
eos
duced by
Harris
ily, trick
er Cy
npton
wed the
wd at the
5 Salem
nty Fair
Woods-
vn by
soing
e horses
d riders.

Special to Today's Sunbeam/Cowtown Rod

1935 Trick Roping. In an early rodeo organized by Stoney Harris and the Harris Sales Co. staff, Cy Compton performed. Compton, a trick roper, managed to lasso nine horses and nine riders at one time. Trick ropers use lassos or lariats to wow crowds by swinging ropes. Trick roping is often associated with western or rodeo shows.

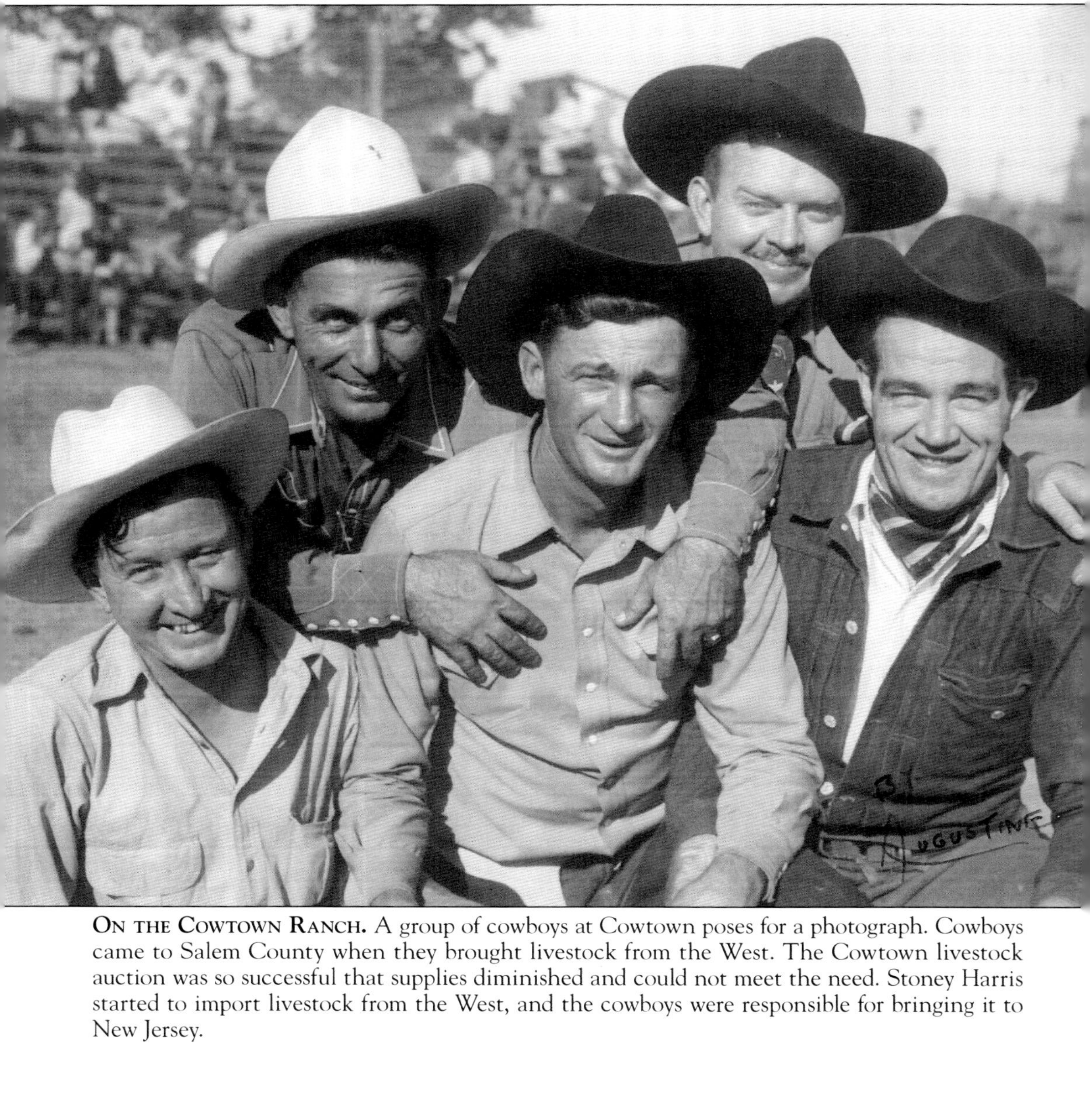

On the Cowtown Ranch. A group of cowboys at Cowtown poses for a photograph. Cowboys came to Salem County when they brought livestock from the West. The Cowtown livestock auction was so successful that supplies diminished and could not meet the need. Stoney Harris started to import livestock from the West, and the cowboys were responsible for bringing it to New Jersey.

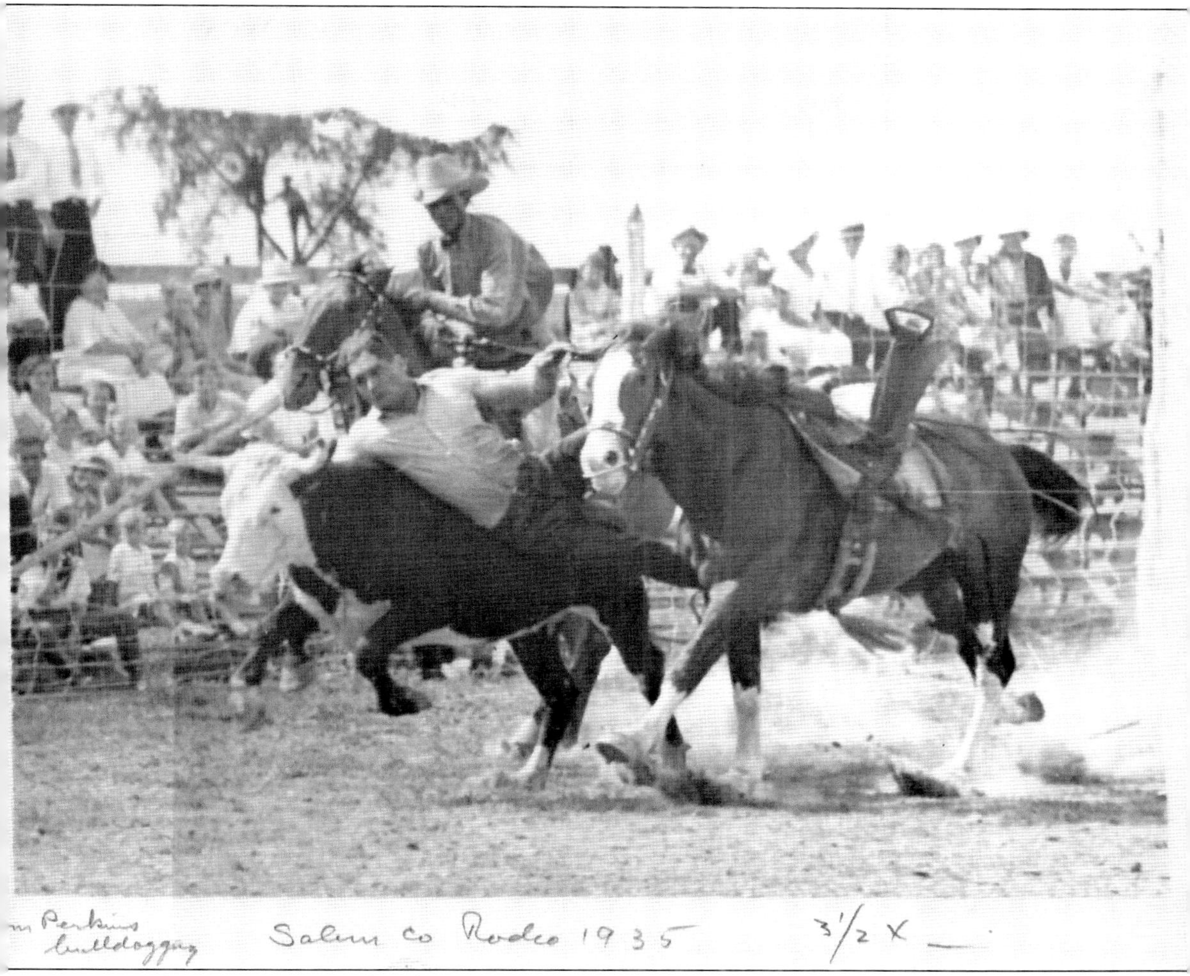

All the Seats Are Full. Rodeos have been a popular form of entertainment for many years. During the Depression, the popularity of rodeos grew across the country. Cowtown was no exception. In the 1930s, the Cowtown Rodeo had been revived in conjunction with the Salem County Fair. When the rodeo was in Woodstown, most of the town attended. Tom Perkins is seen here bulldogging at the 1935 Cowtown Rodeo. Behind him, the stands are packed with spectators.

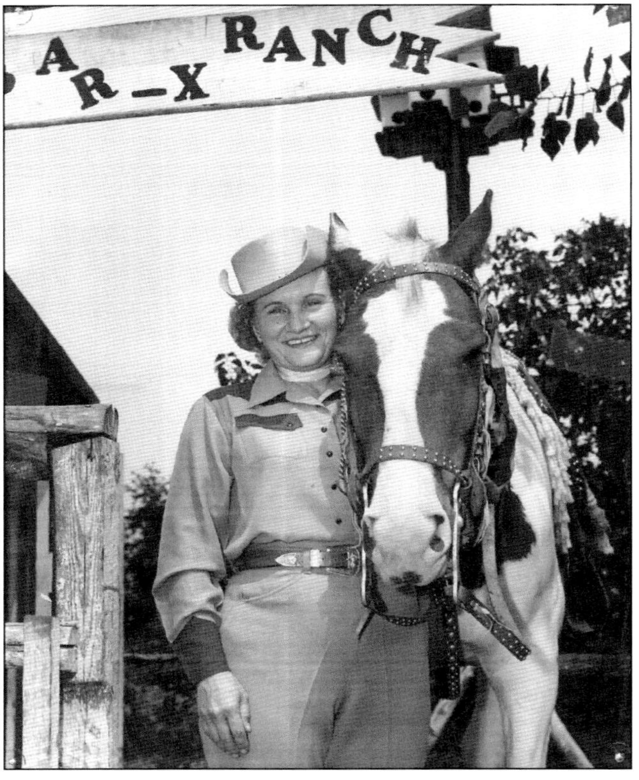

A Love of Horses. Frances Curry of Penns Grove, New Jersey, loved horses and instilled a love of riding in her son Lee. When she took Lee to the annual rodeo in the 1930s, he knew he wanted to ride in the Cowtown Rodeo someday. Eventually, he did. (Photograph by Willard Green; courtesy of Lee and Lorraine Curry.)

Not Just Horses. Bill Gallo Sr. sits on his trained Brahma bull and poses for a picture. Training a bull follows the same steps for training any animal. It is best to start when the animal is young, and it is also best to break the training into increments so the steps can be followed on a regular basis. (Courtesy of Emily Walker.)

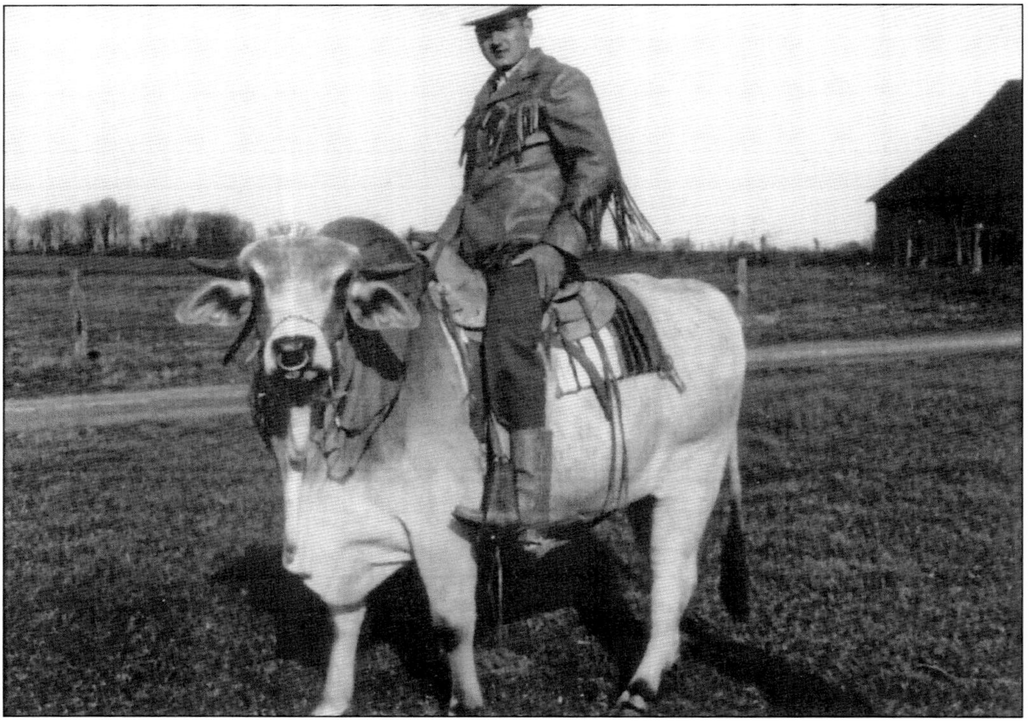

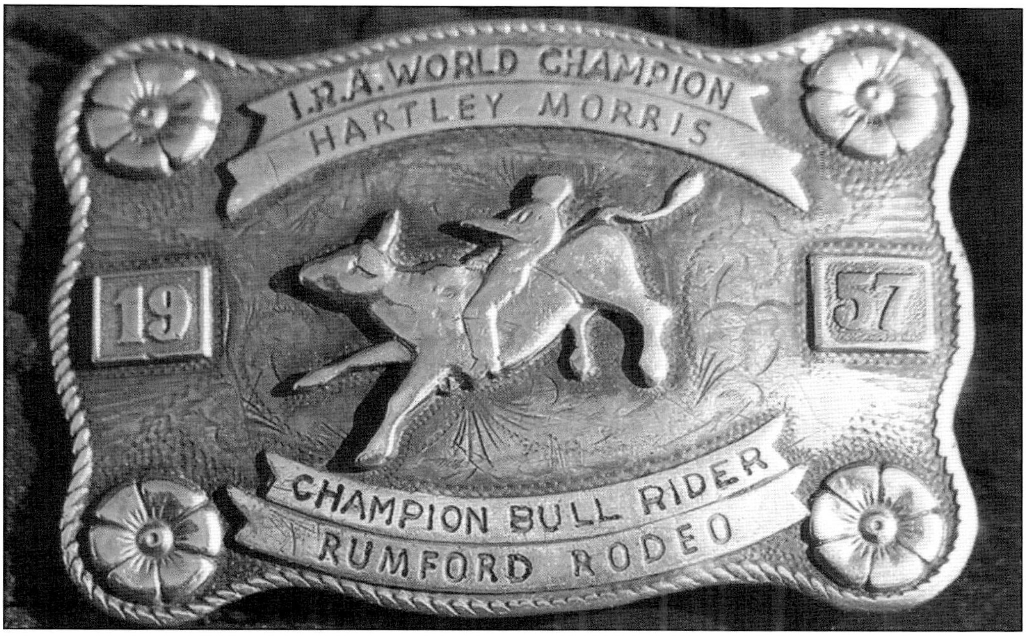

THE INTERSTATE RODEO ASSOCIATION. The Interstate Rodeo Association (IRA) was formed in 1957 to ensure consistency and standards among the quickly expanding venues. The organization began awarding points that year, the same year several Cowtown Rodeo regulars competed. William "Hartley" Morris Sr. won the RCA Championship in 1957, receiving the winning buckle. (Courtesy of Hartley and Denise Morris.)

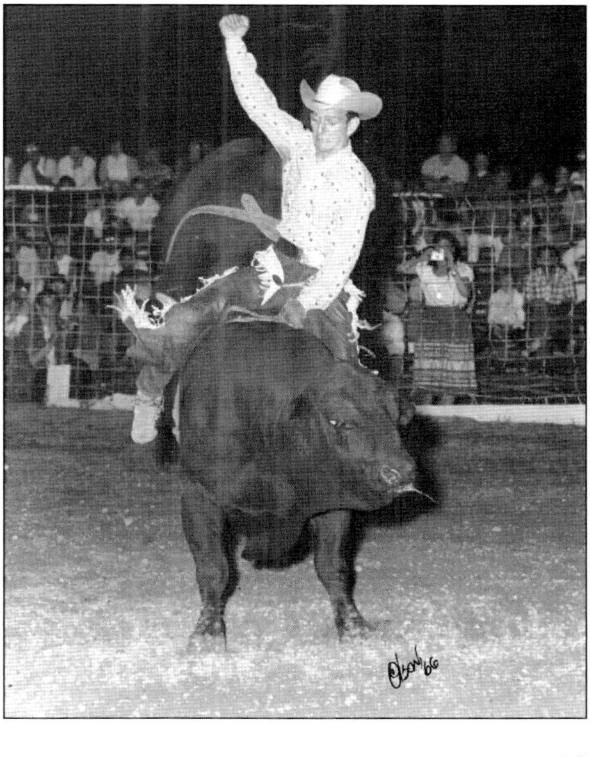

THE COWTOWN RODEO ARENA. Many of the competitors and members of the local community, like Hartley Morris Sr. (pictured), Al Krumm, and Lee Curry, helped build the new arena in 1965. The first year in the new arena, the rodeo hosted a large benefit for the Friends Home, a local assisted living facility. (Photograph by Olson; courtesy of Hartley and Denise Morris.)

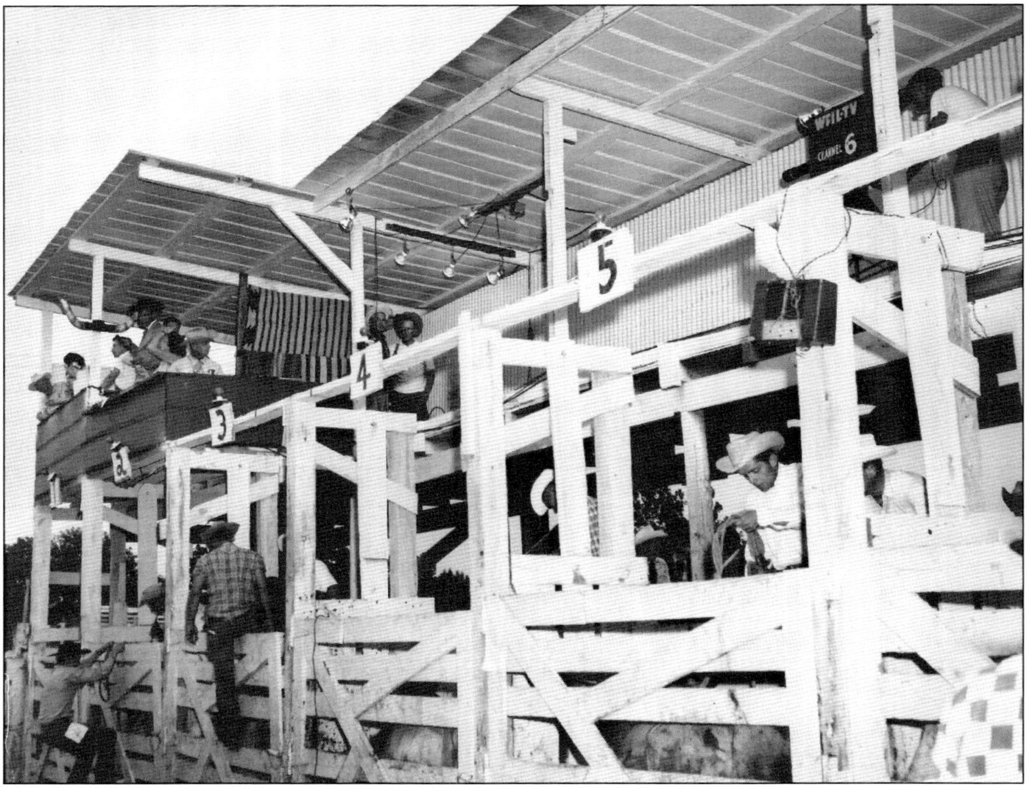

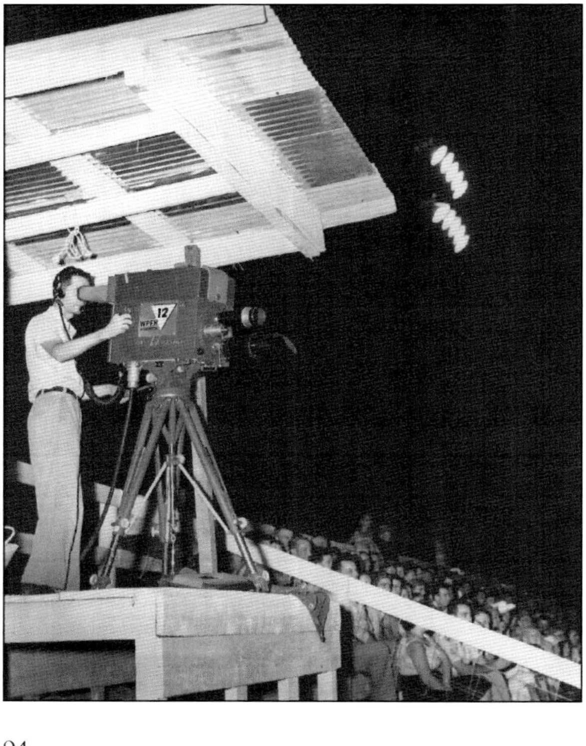

Cowtown on National Television. The Cowtown Rodeo was broadcast on live television nationwide in 1957 and 1958. Live broadcasting was a fairly new endeavor at that time. The Cowtown Rodeo was one of the first sporting events aired on live television. Channel 6 WFIL aired the rodeo. In the late 1960s, Channel 6 aired a taped version of the rodeo.

Local TV. Later, Channel 12 WPFH, a local Wilmington station, aired the rodeo. As more and more people purchased televisions, there were concerns about whether television owners would continue to attend the live shows. Rodeos were no exception; there was hesitancy from some to broadcast the show on television.

Dangerous Profession. Bull riding has been described as one of the most dangerous professional sports out there. Cowboys know just how dangerous it can be. Pictured is Lee Curry, who decided that he was going to ride bulls before his 10th birthday. Curry has ridden bulls all over the country. He frequently rode at Cowtown. (Courtesy of Lee and Lorraine Curry.)

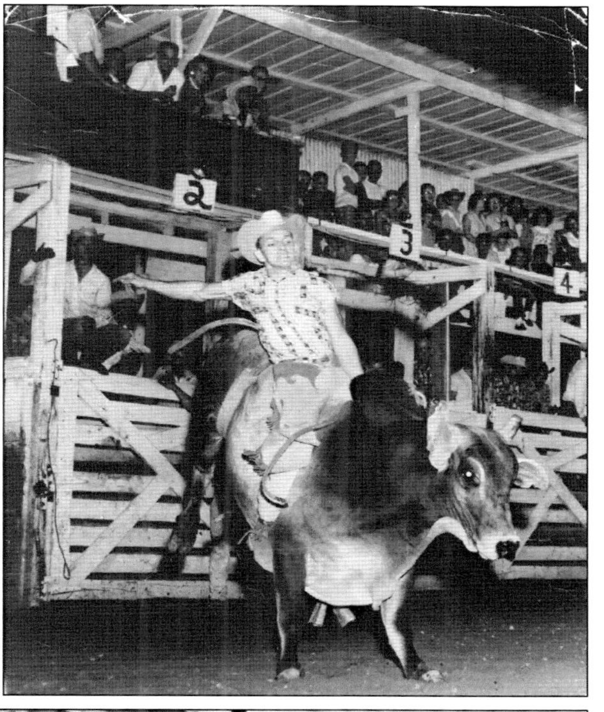

One Hand Only. Curry, who was a rodeo competitor for 15 years, rides a bucking bull. When bull riding, only one hand can hold the bull rope, the primary piece of equipment that a bull rider uses. If the other hand touches any part of the bull or equipment, the rider is disqualified. (Courtesy of Lee and Lorraine Curry.)

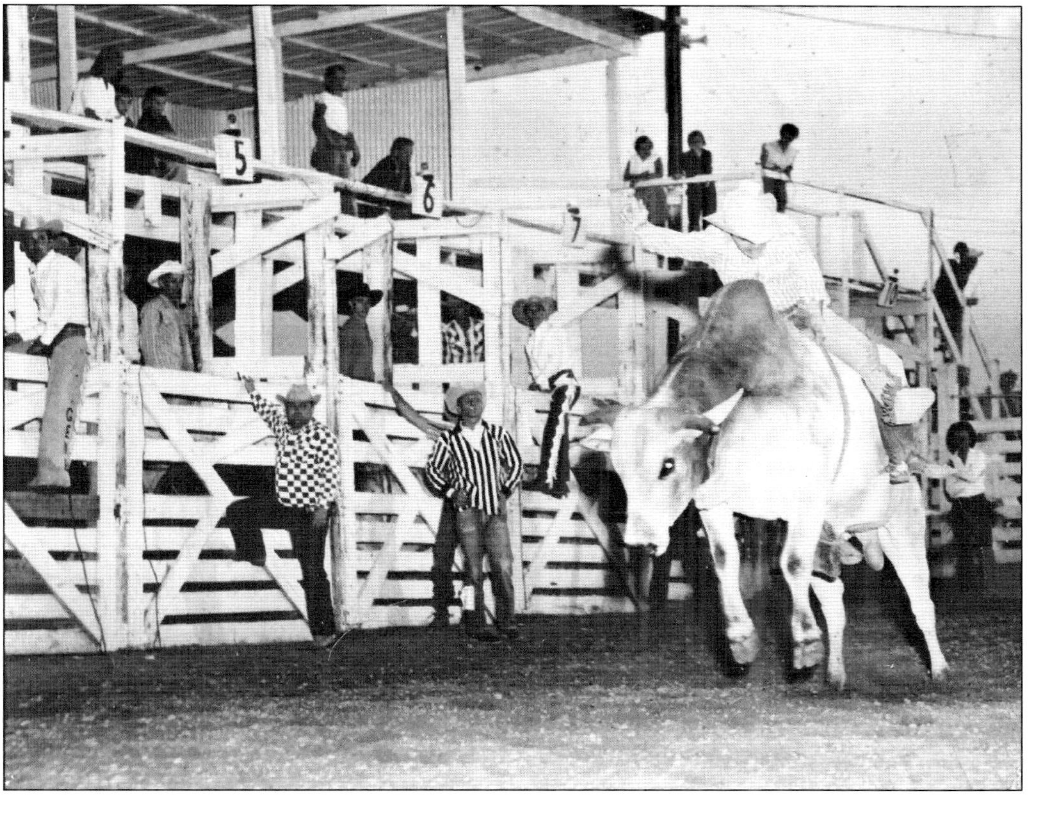

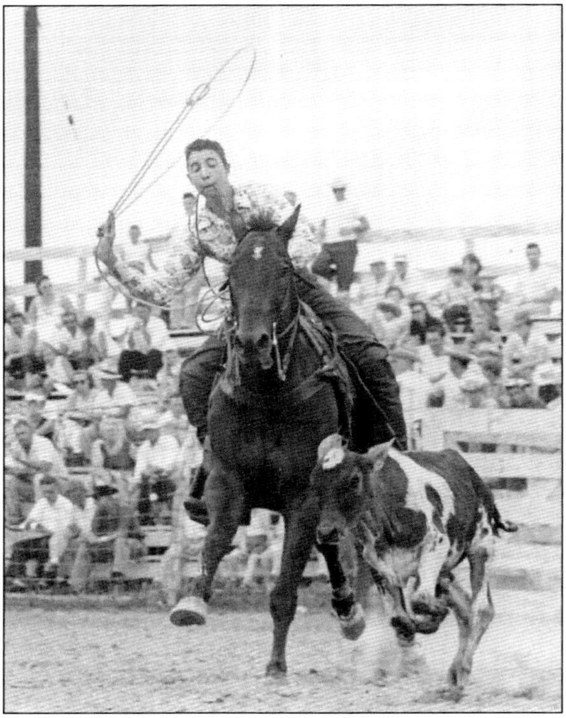

Ranch Work. Calf roper and Salem County native Joe Merola has a "piggin' string" in his teeth, which is a short nylon rope that will be used to tie three of the calf's legs together. Calf roping is sometimes referred to as the most pure event at the rodeo, closest to the original responsibilities of the cowboy. Rodeo events are based on real events that cowboys were responsible for on ranches. (Photograph by Teitsworth; courtesy of the Harris family.)

Short Interview for the Crowd. Jerry Alden was the in-house announcer and was often associated with the Cowtown Rodeo. Alden (right) interviews a cowboy for the WFIL camera and the crowd. Alden and the cowboy stand on the arena floor, which is dirt.

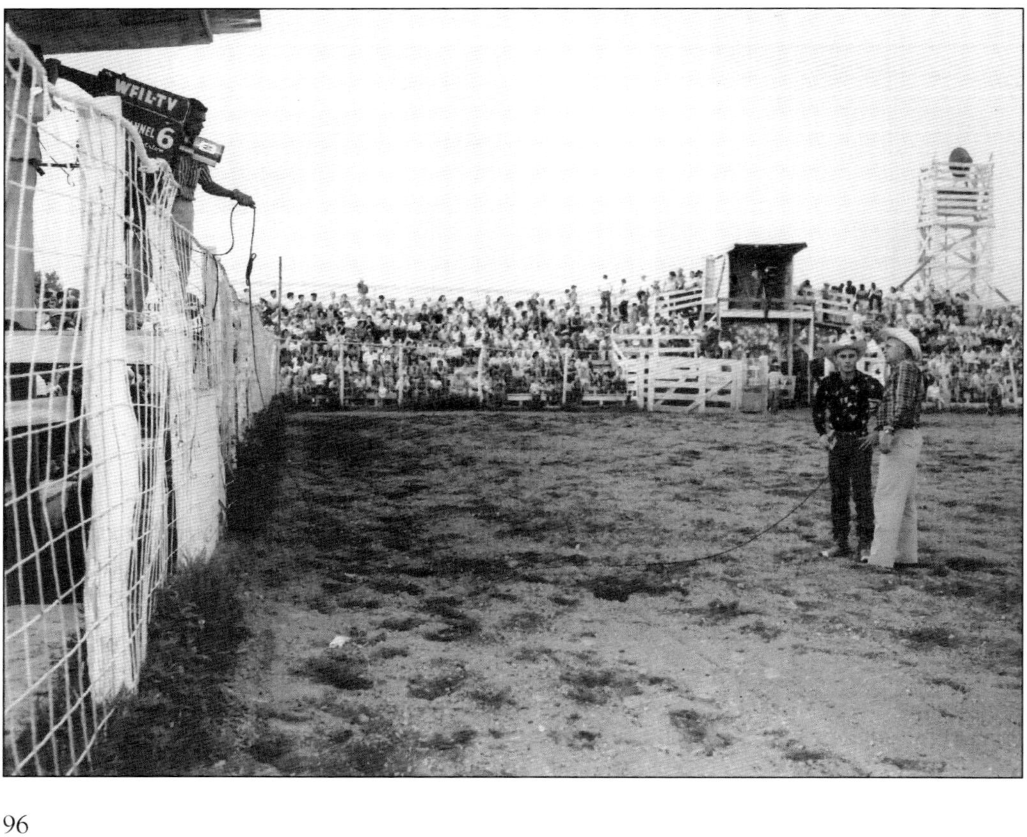

HUB HUBBELL, LONGTIME RODEO ANNOUNCER. Over the years, Hubbell announced at the Cowtown road shows and occasionally at the Cowtown arena. In addition to being a well-known rodeo announcer, he was an exhibition shooter and trick roper. Judith Leipold wrote Hubbell's biography, *Straight from the Horse's Mouth*, in 2013. (Courtesy of Judith Leipold.)

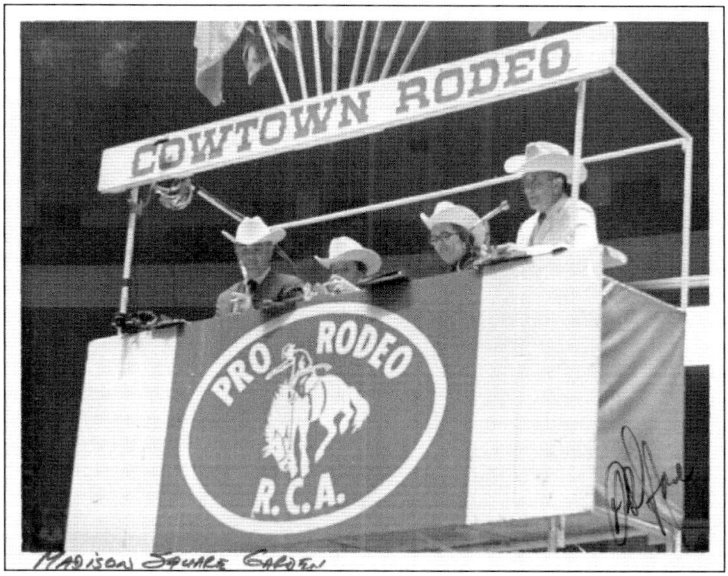

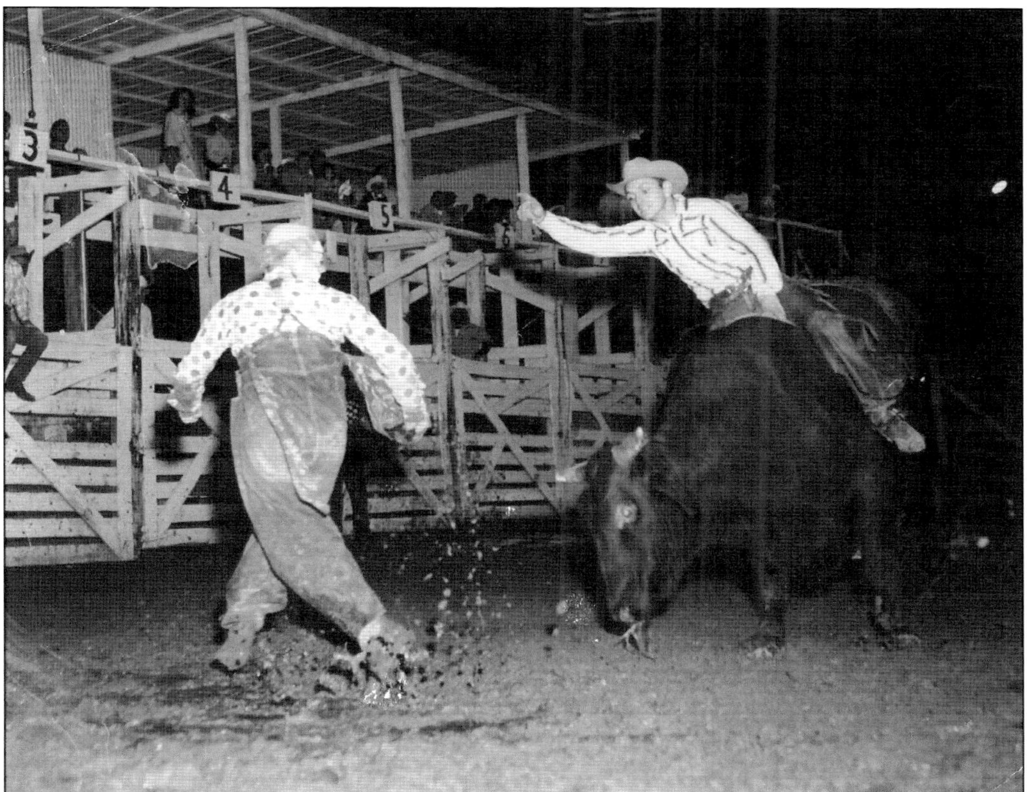

CLOWN STANDING BY. Lee Curry rides while George Doak clowns at Cowtown. Bulls and riders are matched up at random before the rodeo begins. Bulls do not all perform the same. Some are known to be particularly aggressive, and a cowboy is often well aware of the reputations of those bulls before they hop on. (Courtesy of Lee and Lorraine Curry.)

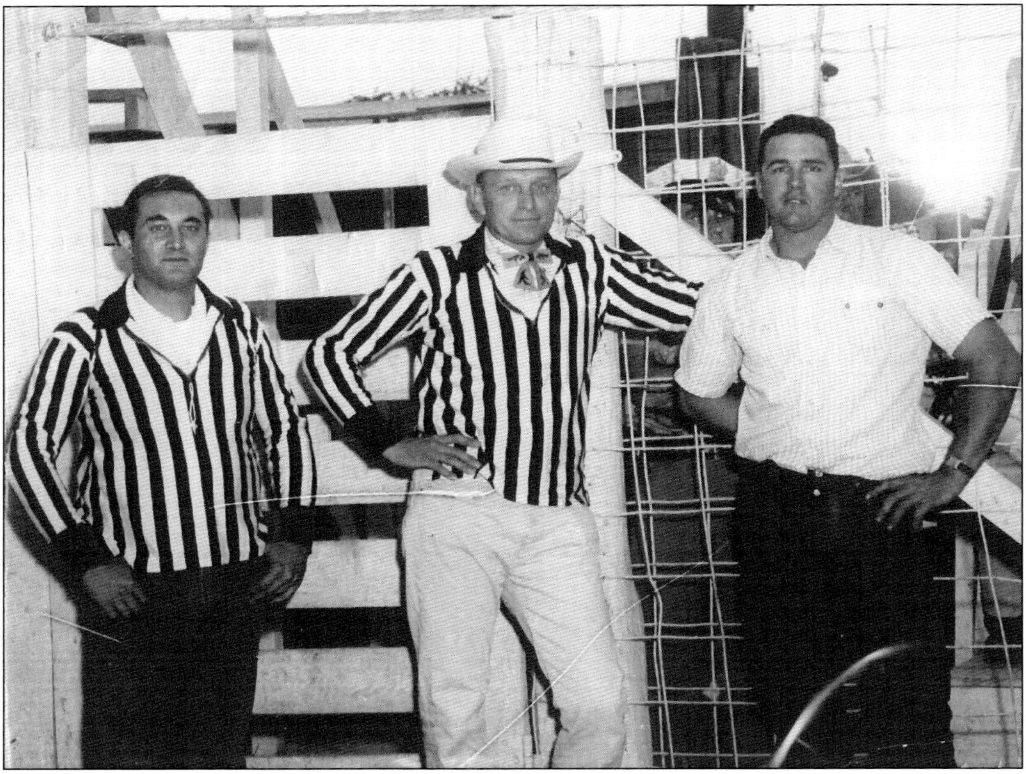

Smart Judges. The intelligence of the rodeo judges was once called into question at a Cowtown rodeo, which offended owner Stoney Harris. He went out and found the two most educated people in town, Dr. Gordon Ostrum (left) and Dr. Art Gemberling (center), to act as rodeo judges. On the right is Eddie Foster. (Courtesy of Dr. Mickey Ostrum.)

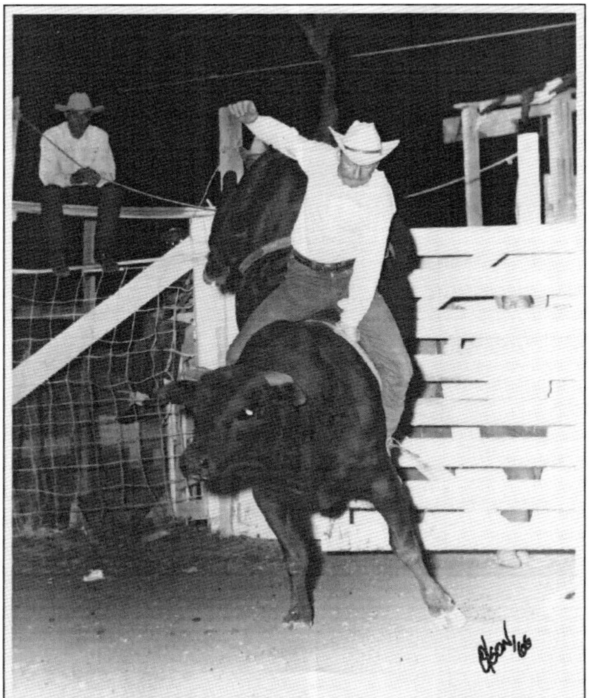

Hanging On. Dave Appleby rides Gil the bull at Cowtown. He wears his cowboy hat, a shirt, and jeans. Today, many competitors wear helmets and protective rodeo vests to increase protection if they are thrown from the bull and stepped on or gored. (Photograph by Olson; courtesy of Dr. Mickey Ostrum.)

Hit the Road. The Cowtown road show brought the spirit of Cowtown to all different parts of the country. Behind the rider, who is likely John Constantinople, the road show crow's nest is occupied by the announcer, the timer, and the secretary. The Cowtown staff and competitors would travel with the show, setting up in new towns for each competition. (Photograph by Olson; courtesy of Dr. Mickey Ostrum.)

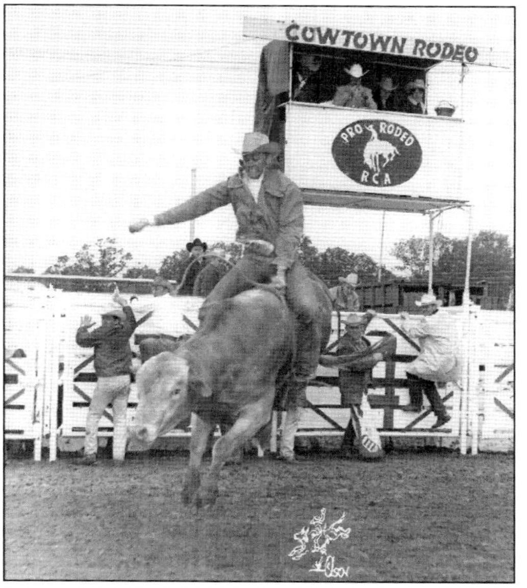

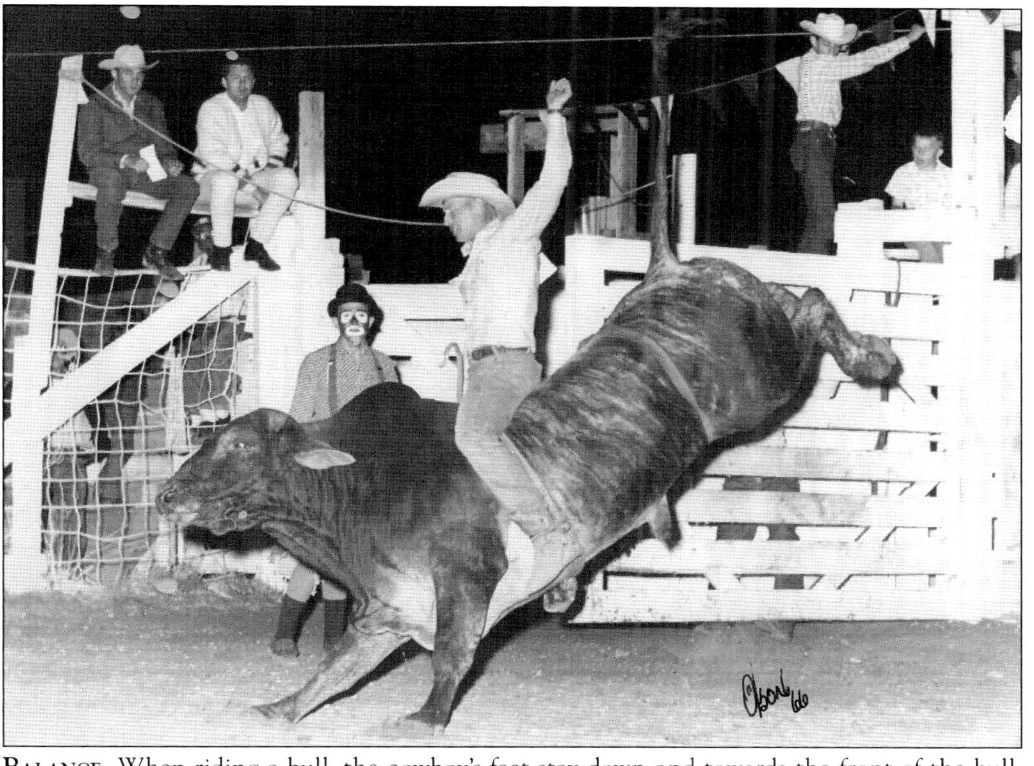

Balance. When riding a bull, the cowboy's feet stay down and towards the front of the bull, and the cowboy's toes may point slightly upward. Some experienced riders use spurs on the back of their boots to get the bull to kick harder, but the spurs are purposefully dull. Bull riders are encouraged to keep their eyes on the back of the bull to help them keep their balance. The bull rider here, likely Marion England, tries to stay balanced. (Photograph by Olson; courtesy of Dr. Mickey Ostrum.)

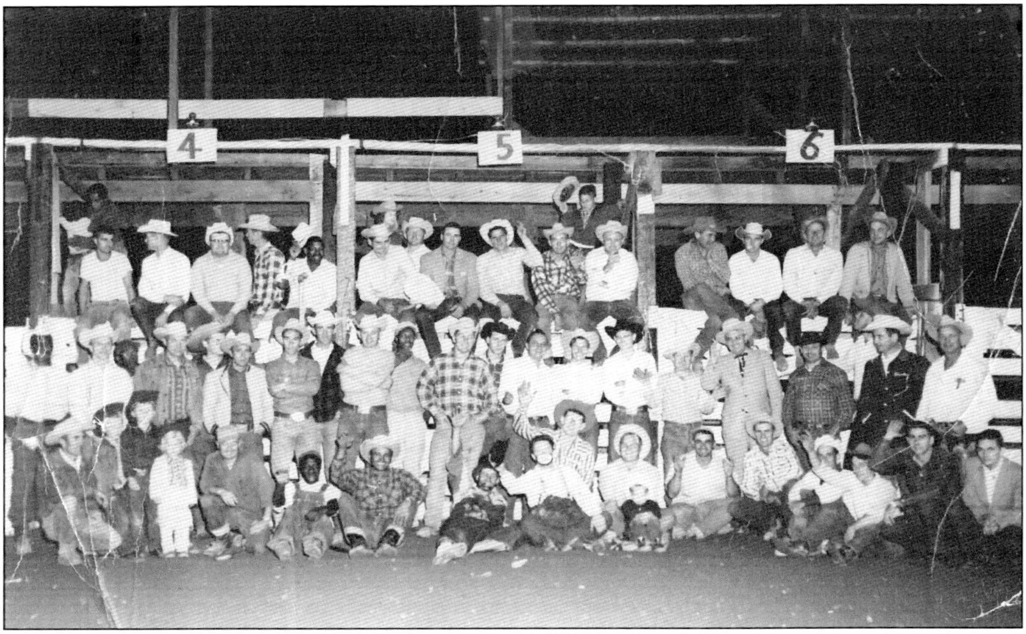

"**Everybody Say Cheese.**" At the end of a long and exciting rodeo night, rodeo contestants and staff would get together and pose for a group shot. The picture above was taken in the original Cowtown arena. The Cowtown team, riders and staff alike, were a big family. Kids would attend with their parents, and friends and family would sit in the stands and cheer on the riders. Like any sporting activity, the athletes and those that are an integral part of the event are aware of the rigors and demands of the rodeo life. Lifelong bonds formed between many of the Cowtown Rodeo team. (Above, courtesy of Lee and Lorraine Curry; below, courtesy of Dr. Mickey Ostrum.)

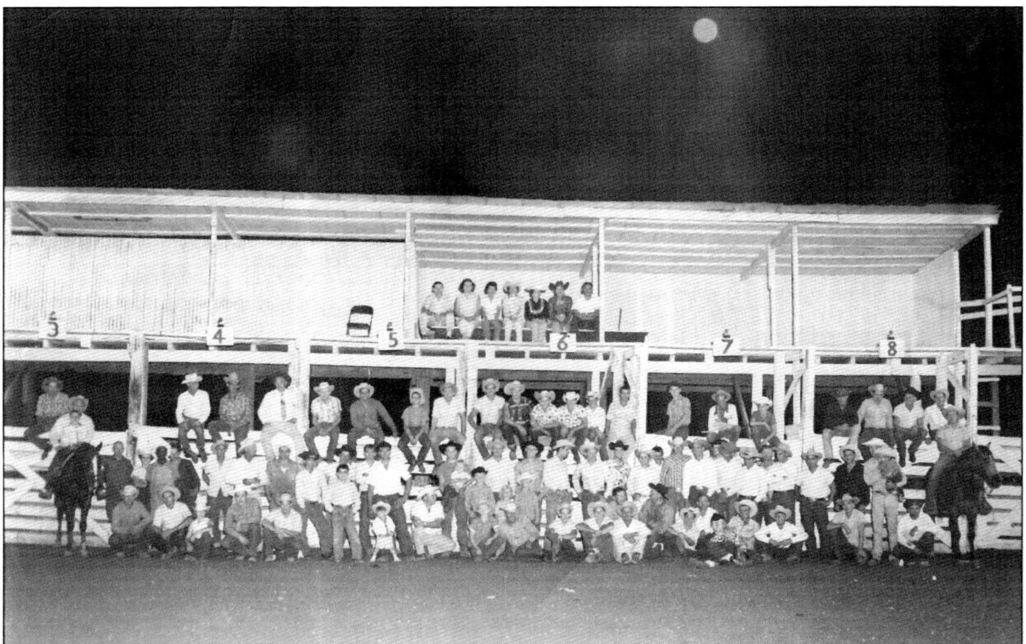

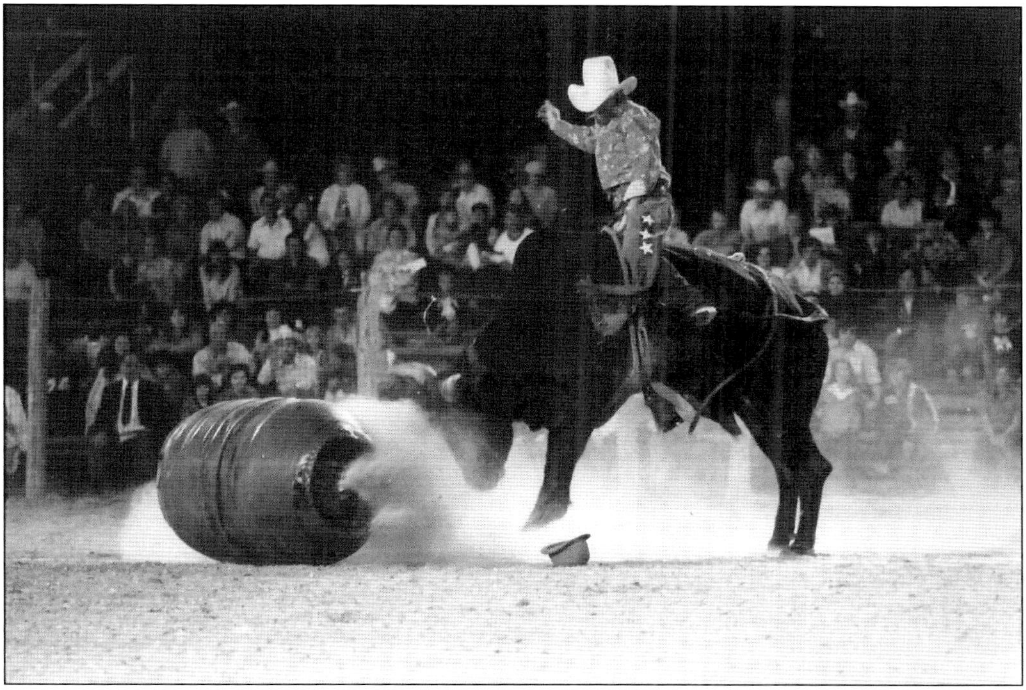

Riding High. George Doak likely clowned prior to his ride on this evening, and he may have stayed on this bull for the full eight seconds. The taming of bulls goes back to the Minoan civilization, but bull riding probably originated in Mexico. Friendly ranching competitions developed into the rodeos of the American Old West, which have since grown in popularity throughout the 1800s and 1900s and into the 2000s. (Courtesy of George Doak.)

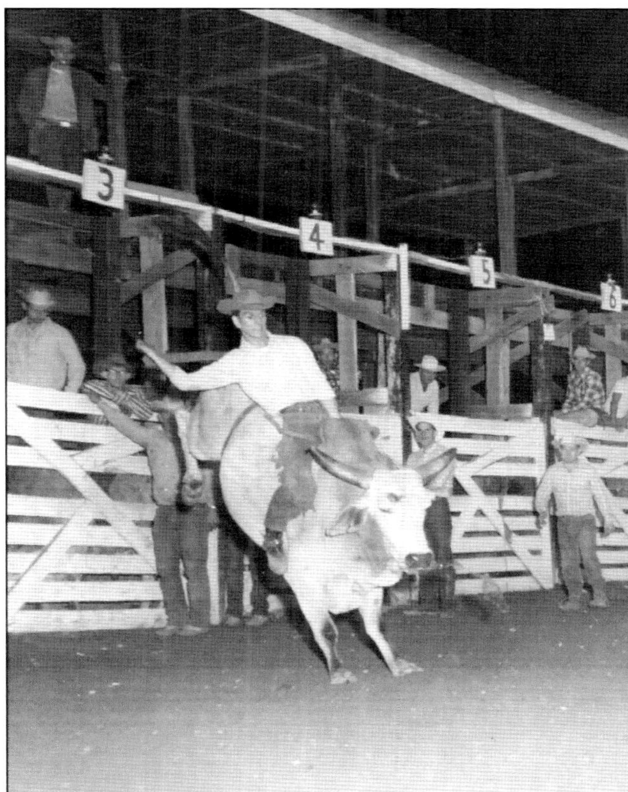

The Team. There are many men in the arena and bucking chutes behind Hartley Morris, who rides the bull. Each person has a different responsibility. Judges stay in the arena, and a flagman drops the flag once the event is over. It is important for rodeo staff to be alert during each competitor's ride, for scoring and safety. (Courtesy of Hartley and Denise Morris.)

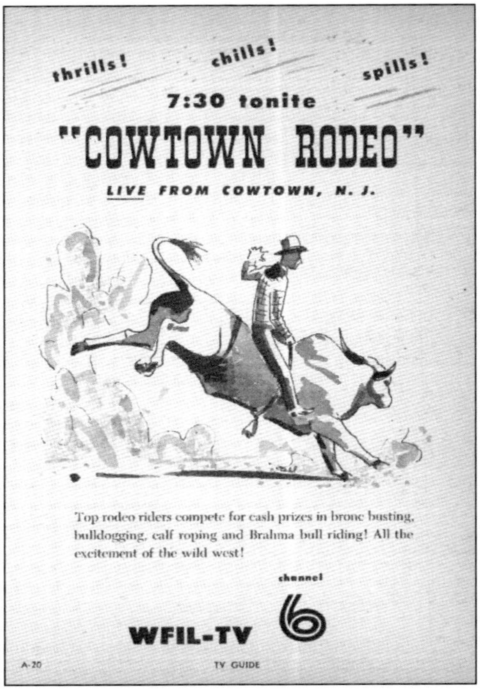

THRILLS, CHILLS, AND SPILLS. *TV Guide* featured the Cowtown Rodeo in 1958. National live television exposure propelled Cowtown from being a regional activity to a destination spot for tourists and travelers. Even today, the rodeo attracts visitors from around the country and the world.

BELT BUCKLES. Barney Faircloth, a well-known cowboy at Cowtown, poses with Cowtown owner Irene Harris (right) and Mary Ann Ostrum, the wife of Dr. Gordon Ostrum, a Cowtown Rodeo judge, at a rodeo in Harrisburg, Pennsylvania. Belt buckles are often associated with rodeos and western wear. (Photograph by Bryant Foster; courtesy of Dr. Mickey Ostrum.)

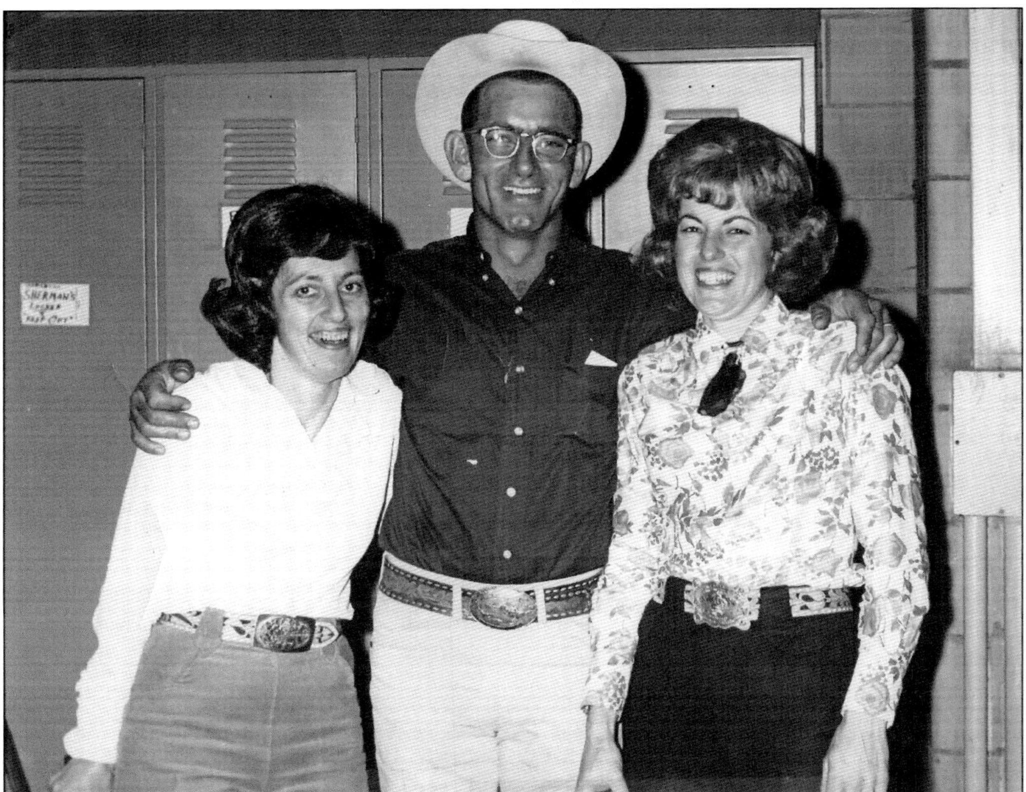

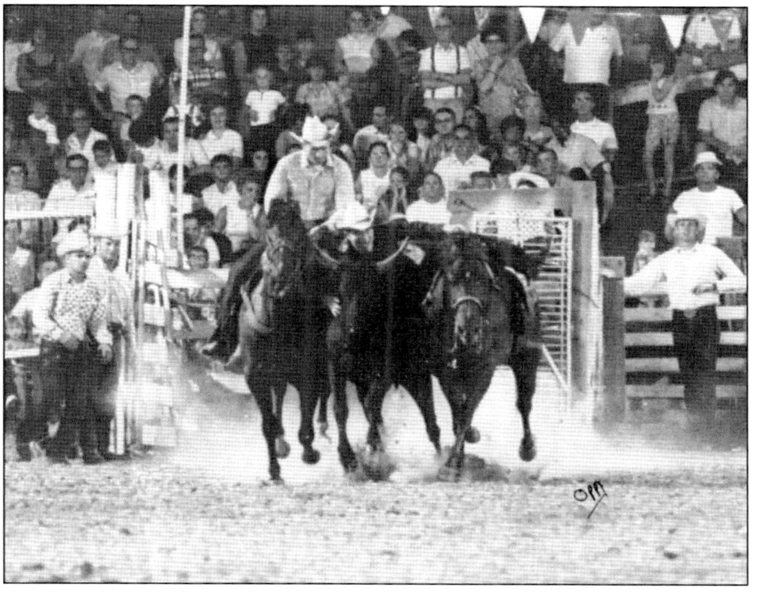

Steer Wrestling. Sometimes called bulldogging, steer wrestling developed from when cowboys in the West would have to catch large steer. Once the steer runs out of the chute, the bulldogger then starts the chase with support from the hazer, a rider on another horse that is on the other side of the steer. Bill Hamer Sr. is seen here bulldogging while another cowboy hazes. (Courtesy of Bill Hamer Sr.)

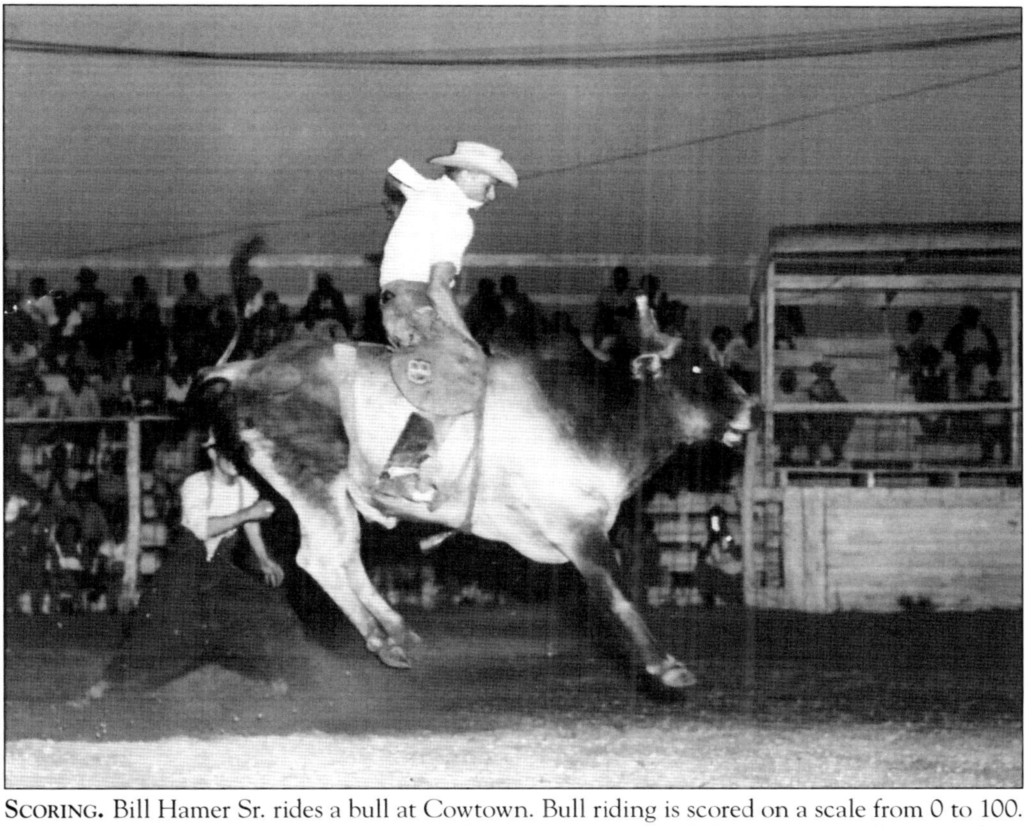

Scoring. Bill Hamer Sr. rides a bull at Cowtown. Bull riding is scored on a scale from 0 to 100. The bull and the rider can each be awarded up to 50 points, and there are typically two judges. Generally, a good bull ride achieves points in the 70s, a great bull ride achieves points in the 80s, and an amazing bull ride achieves points in the 90s. (Courtesy of Bill Hamer Sr.)

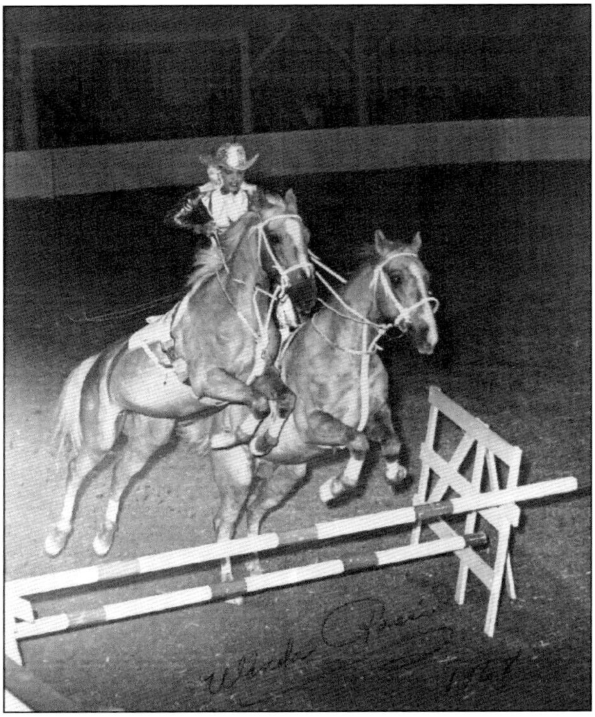

Riding Two Horses at Once. Wanda Rossi, a regular at the Cowtown Rodeo, is pictured Roman riding. Rossi and her husband, Rex, often performed together, moving from rodeo to rodeo. Many performers would stay at one rodeo for a week or two and then move on to the next one. Rodeo managers wanted to give the crowd something new and exciting each week throughout the season.

Amazing Stunts. Rex Rossi was a world champion trick rider and a Stuntmen's Hall of Fame inductee that performed in rodeos all over the country, including at Cowtown and Madison Square Garden. The Rossi family was made up of trick riders. Trick riding, the act of performing stunts while riding, originated in Russia.

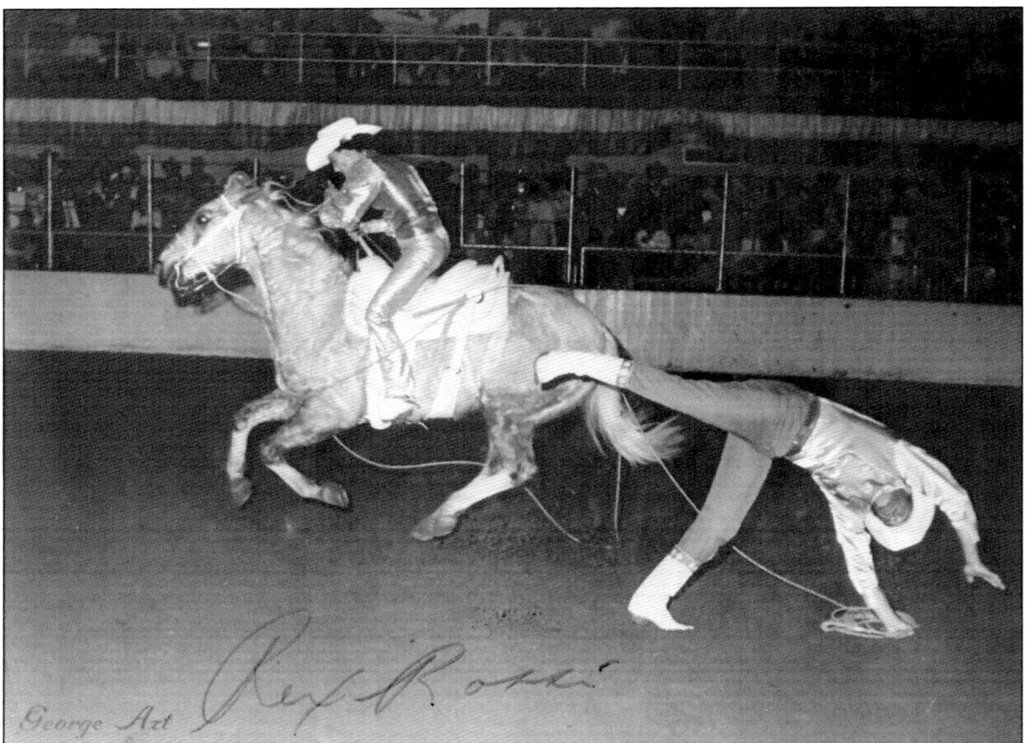

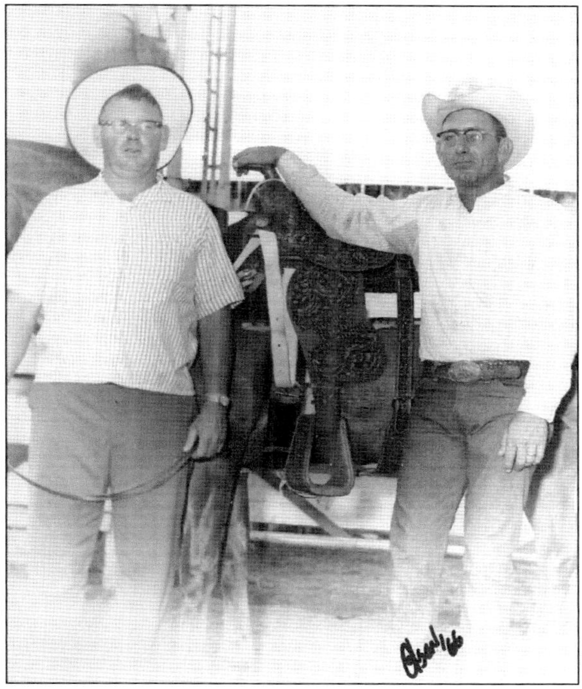

COMPETITION. Barney Faircloth (right) and another cowboy stand in front of a saddle as they prepare for a rodeo. Today, it is uncommon for rodeo competitors to compete in more than one event, but they used to. Faircloth was a calf roper as well as a steer wrestler.

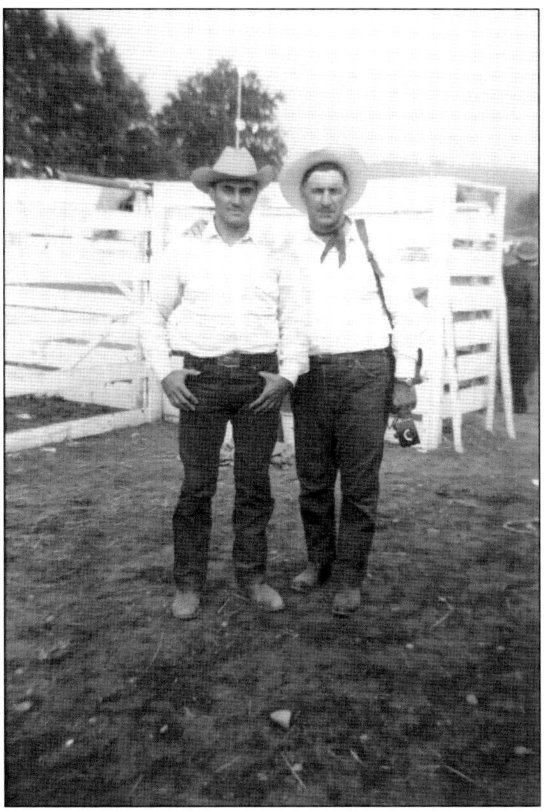

SCHEDULE. Dr. Gordon Ostrum (left), a rodeo event judge at Cowtown, stands next to Joseph Muscarello Jr. behind the chutes. In the original arena, the rodeo season started in May and went to the end of August. Once the new arena was built, the season extended to September. PRCA finals were held at Cowtown until the 2000s. Today, the rodeo finals are held in Harrisburg, Pennsylvania. (Courtesy of Dr. Mickey Ostrum and Joseph Muscarello Jr.)

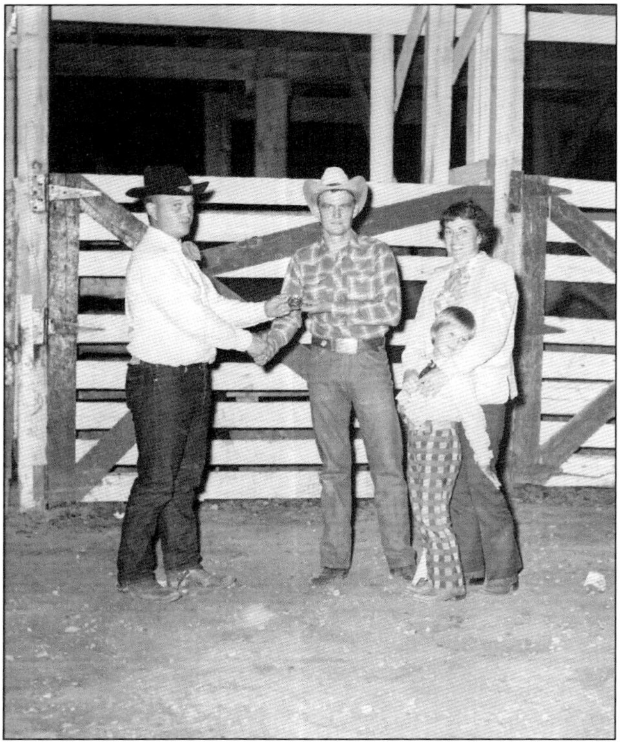

Presenting a Winning Buckle. Jimmy Rogers (center) was an all-star champion in the 1960s. Because of his athletic abilities, he performed well in all five of the events he entered. Howard Harris III (left) shakes Rogers's hand and awards him with a buckle. Irene Harris and daughter Kathy stand next to Jimmy. (Photograph by Bryant Foster; courtesy of the Harris family.)

Rough Stock and Timed. Cowtown rodeo contestants, like the ones seen here posing for a picture with some Cowtown staff, would compete in either rough stock events, timed events, or both. Bull and bronc riding (saddle and bareback) were rough stock events, while barrel racing, calf roping, steer wrestling, and team roping are timed events.

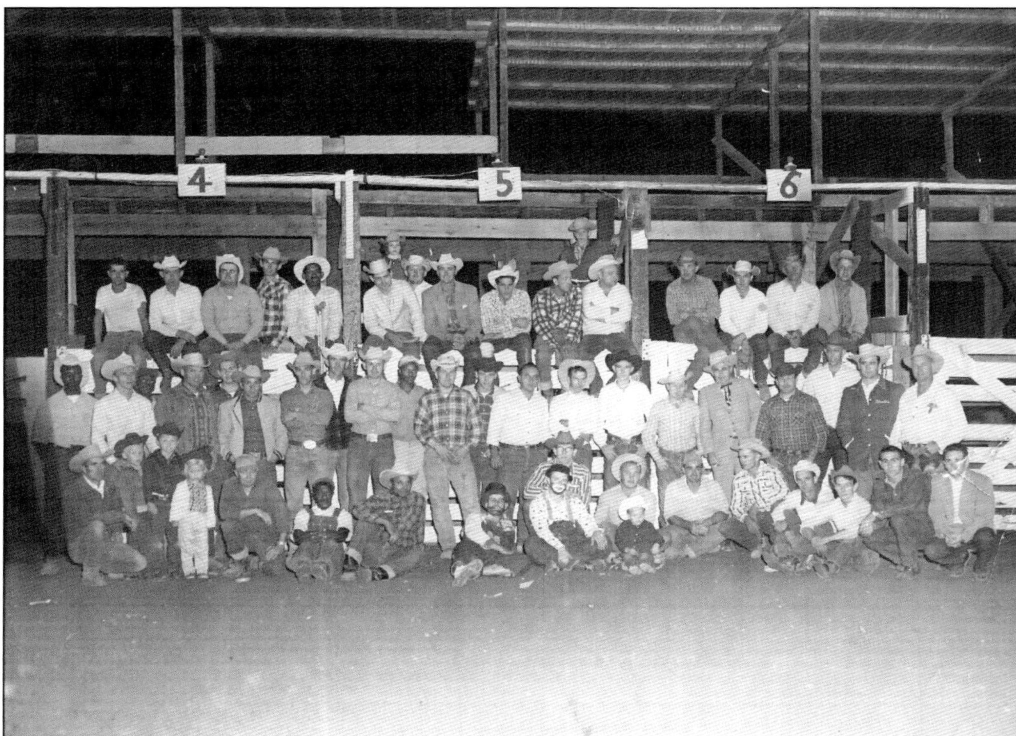

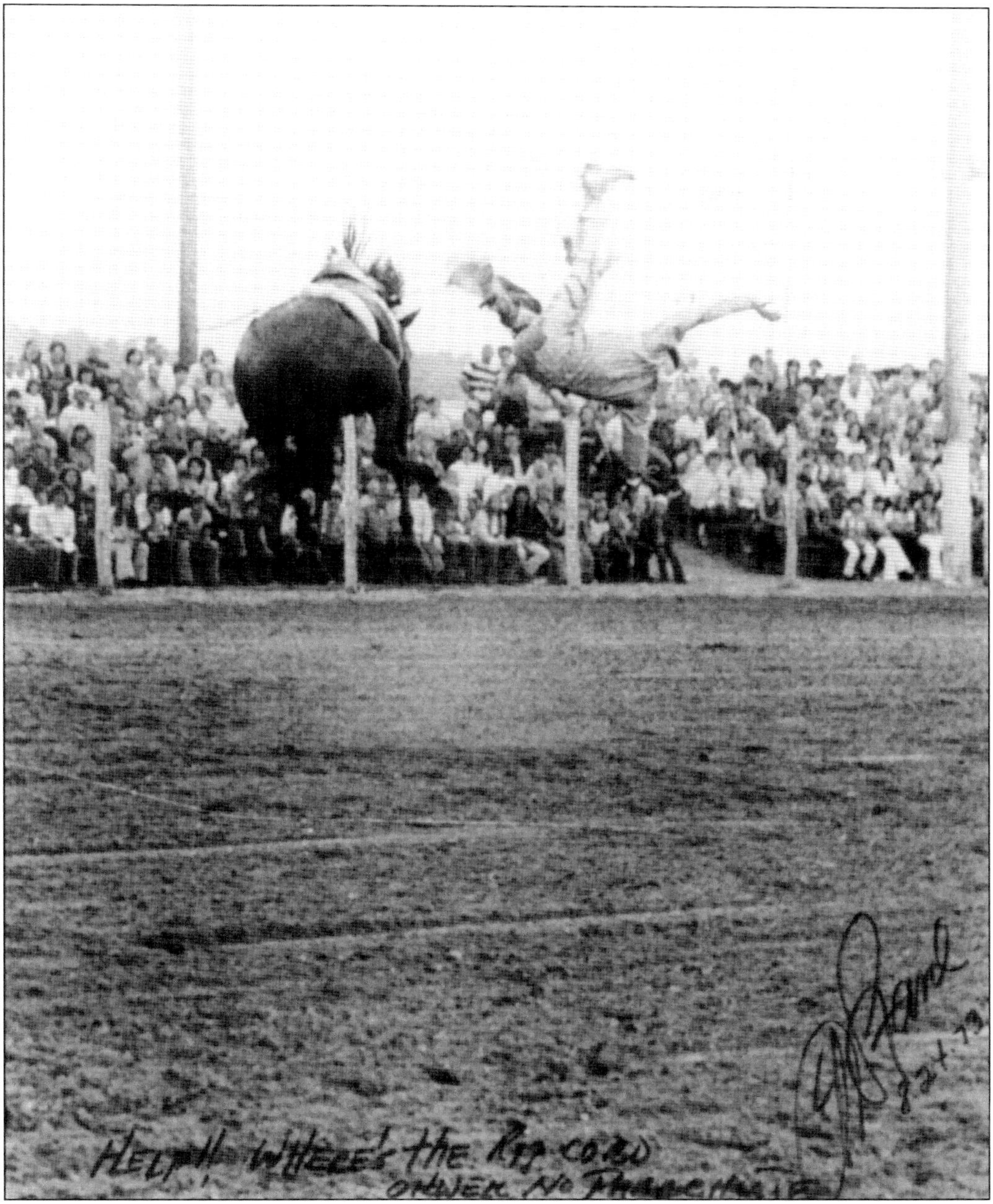

Up in the Air. Hank Molfetto is airborne after a not-so-successful saddle bronc ride. It was not Molfetto's first competitive ride, but it was the horse's first. Saddle bronc riding and bareback riding both involve bucking horses. Both are rough stock events that are based on the Old West ranch duties of breaking wild horses so they become suitable to ride. The big difference between saddle bronc and bareback is that there is no saddle during bareback and there is during saddle bronc. During bareback, a suitcase-style handle is provided to the rider to hold on to during the ride. That handle is located behind the horse's withers (the ridge behind the shoulder blades). During saddle bronc, the rider grips a rein with one hand while remaining seated in a specialized saddle. Different riding techniques are associated with each. (Courtesy of Henry Molfetto.)

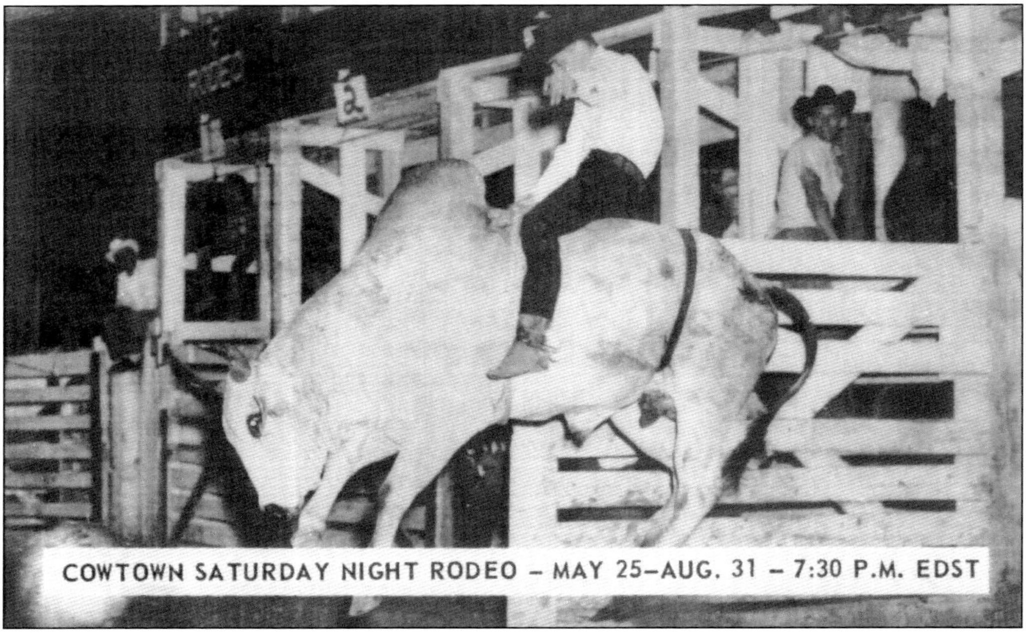

Personal Invitation. Postcards were sent out in the early years of the rodeo to invite people to visit Cowtown. Cowtown owner Howard Harris III handwrote each postcard. A picture of a bull rider with the event information was provided on the front of the card, as well as a description of the rodeo experience. Over the years, Cowtown has advertised the rodeo and market in a variety of ways. Newspaper advertisements, distributing promotional material, and contributing to local events are all ways Cowtown has gotten the word out to its fans. Today, Cowtown has a website, www.cowtownrodeo.com, where folks from all over the world can learn more about Cowtown.

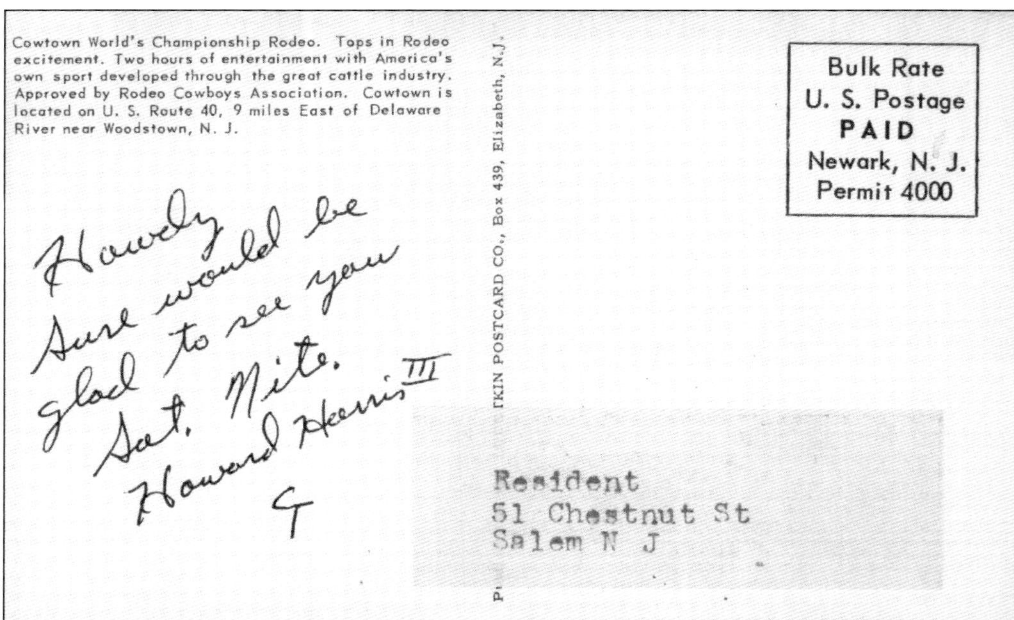

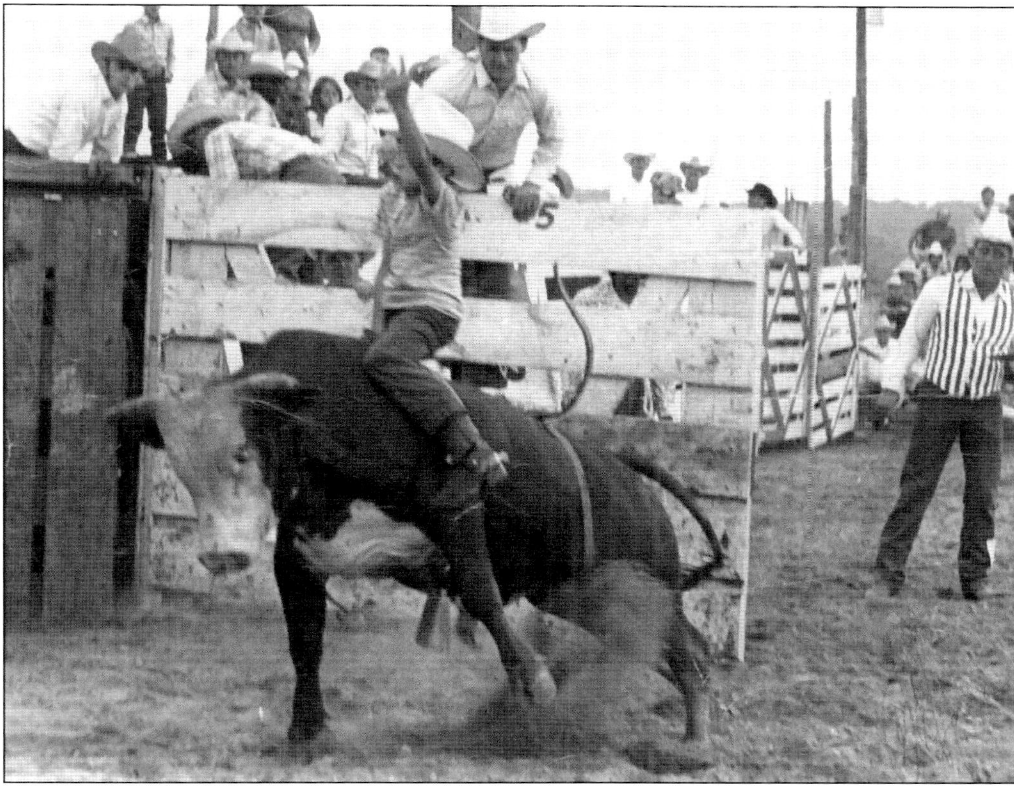

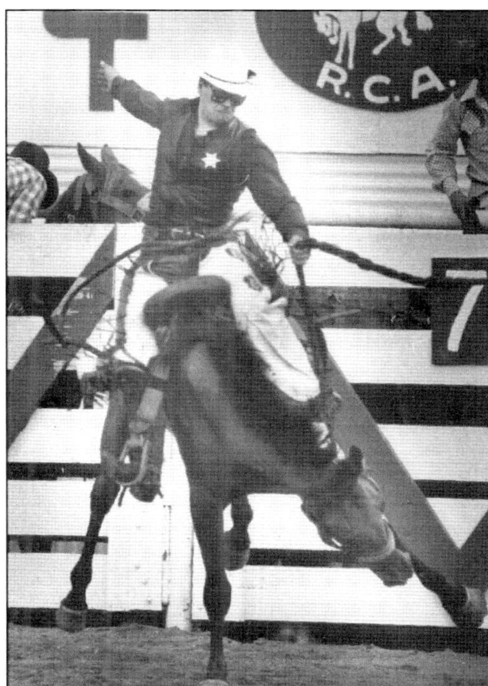

Generations of Riders. Many mothers and fathers pass their love of the rodeo on to sons and daughters. Bill Hamer Jr., seen in both these pictures, rides a bull as a youngster and a bronc as an adult. His father, Bill Hamer Sr., rode in the rodeo as well. Some children who grow up around the excitement of the rodeo eventually want to try it out for themselves. (Above photograph by Bob Hill; both courtesy of Bill Hamer Sr.)

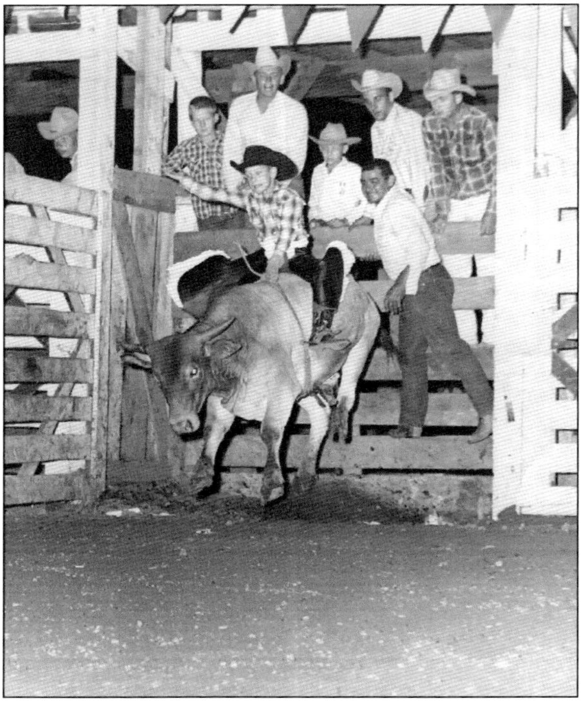

Young Rider. Hartley Morris Jr. wanted to ride, just like his father, Hartley Morris Sr. Behind Morris Jr. and the bull, Jack Bitter stands on the fence to the right. Young Morris appears fearful, but he must have enjoyed it since he went on to ride again at Cowtown. (Courtesy of Hartley and Denise Morris.)

Family of Riders. Jeffery Wayne Morris Sr. rides in a juvenile bull-riding event while Hartley Morris Jr. and Hartley Morris Sr. (both to the right of the bull) watch. It is common in the sport of rodeo to see members of the same family, and even multiple generations of families, compete. For many who participate, rodeo is not just a profession, but also a lifestyle. (Photograph by Olson; courtesy of Hartley and Denise Morris.)

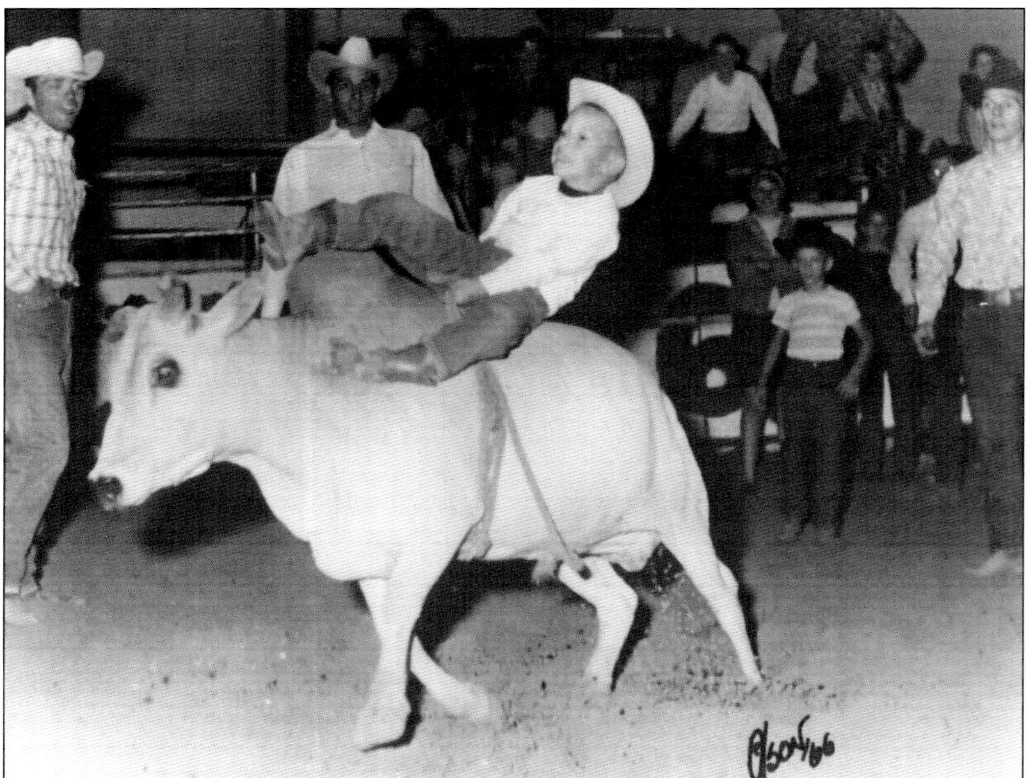

Cowtown in New York City. The Cowtown Rodeo crew made the yearly trip to the Cowtown-produced championship rodeo, held at New York City's Madison Square Garden in the late 1960s and 1970s. In the 1975 official souvenir program, pictured here, an interview with Cowtown owners Howard and Irene Harris is the first featured article. Interviewer Bob Goldwater asked them about trends in rodeo and about the events. At the Madison Square Garden rodeo, Howard was the sole stock contractor, and Irene was the official rodeo secretary. The group picture below was likely taken at the Madison Square Garden event. Howard is lying on the ground in the front center, and Irene (left of Howard) wears a patterned shirt.

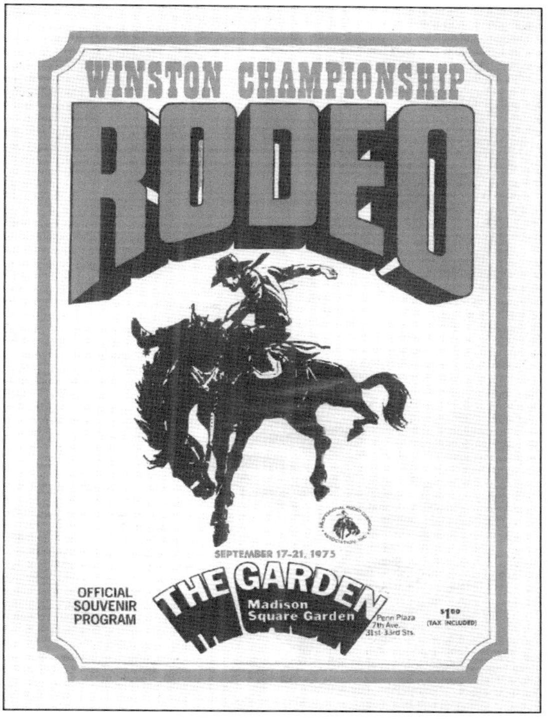

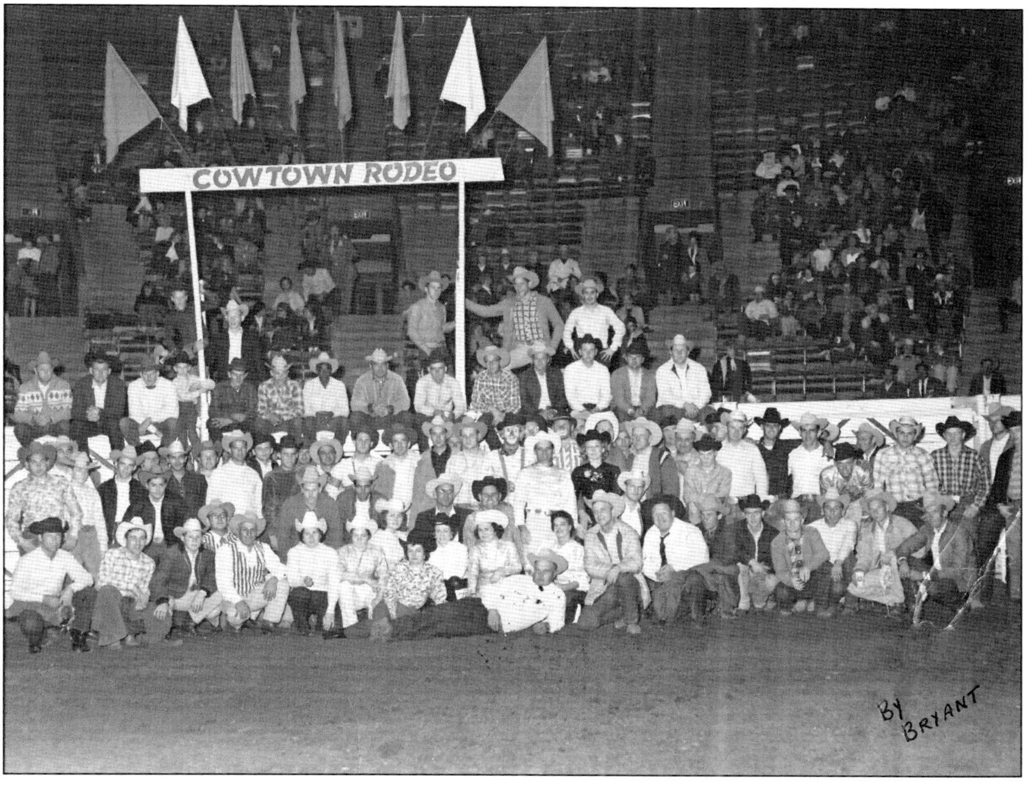

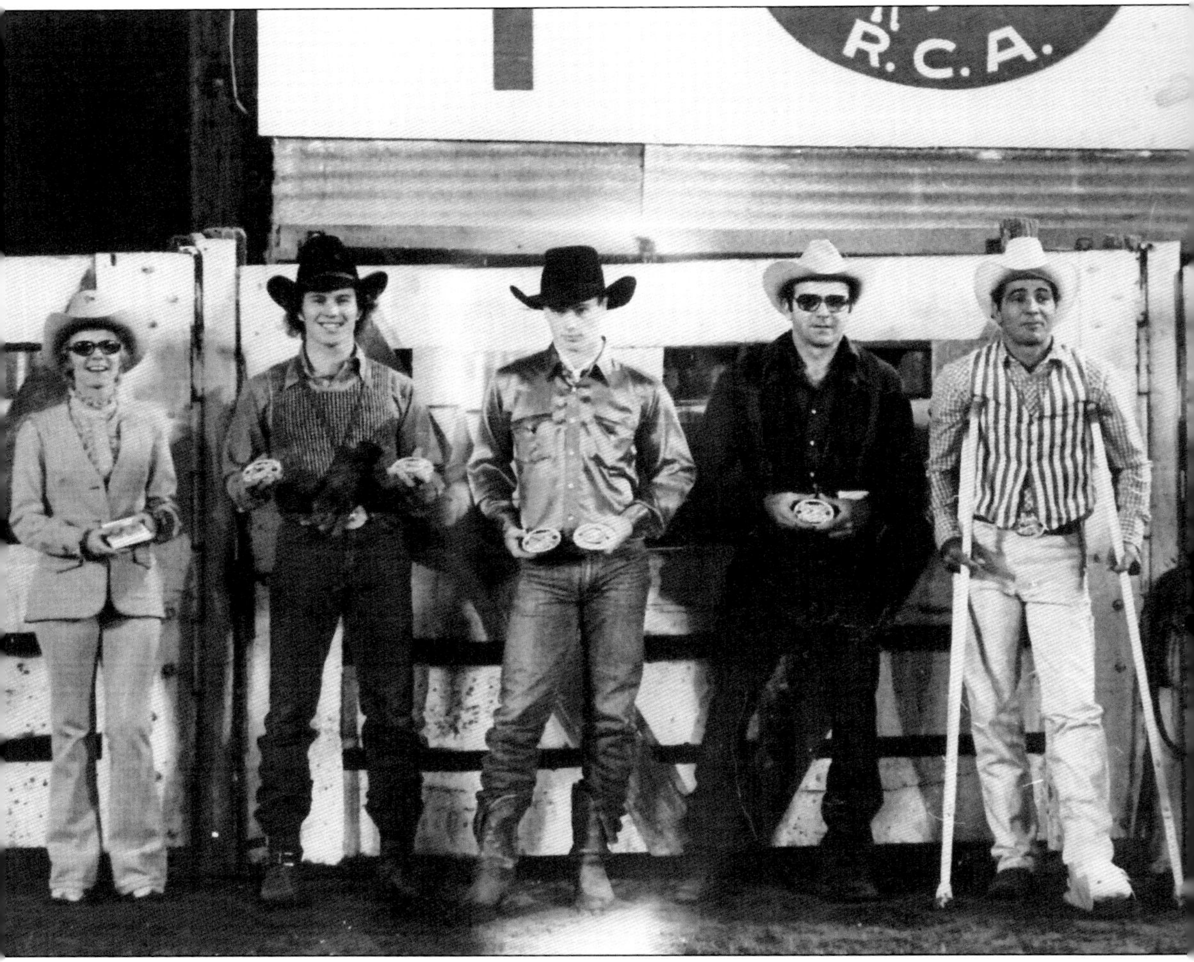

Championships. Buckles are traditionally awarded to event winners on the championship level. Winning buckles were given out to, from left to right, Diane Sleeter, Andy Harris, Grant Harris, Quinn D'Imperio, and Jack Meli. The PRCA sign appears above them at Cowtown.

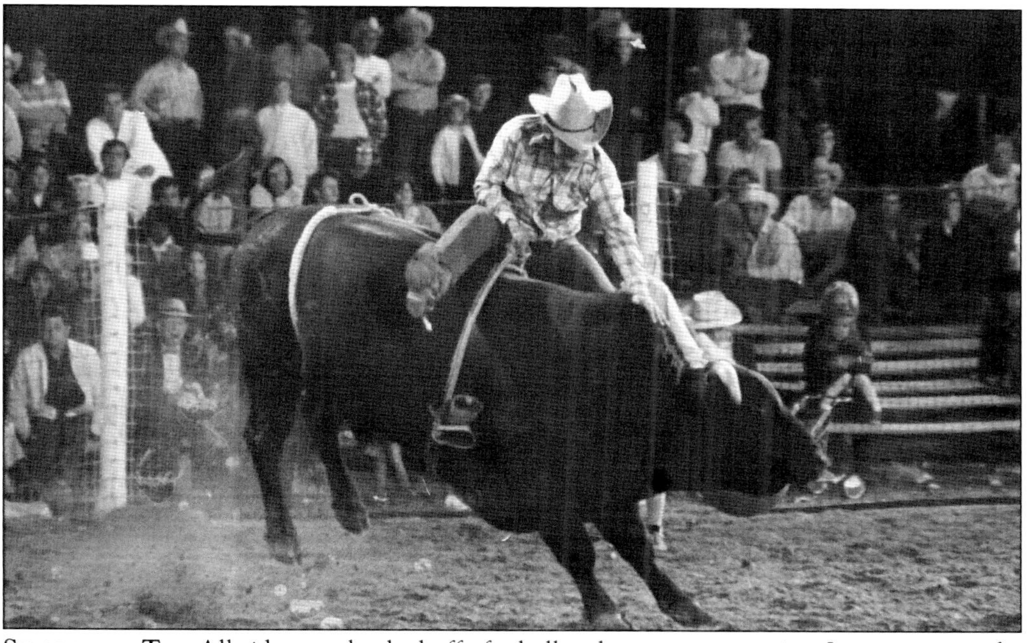

Staying on Top. All riders get bucked off of a bull or horse at some point. It is important for riders to train to gain the experience necessary to be able to continue to ride and eventually stay on the animal for eight seconds, which is a complete ride. In this photograph, Dave Cawman is trying to stay on the bull. (Photograph by Ken Carver; courtesy of Jimmy Lee Walker.)

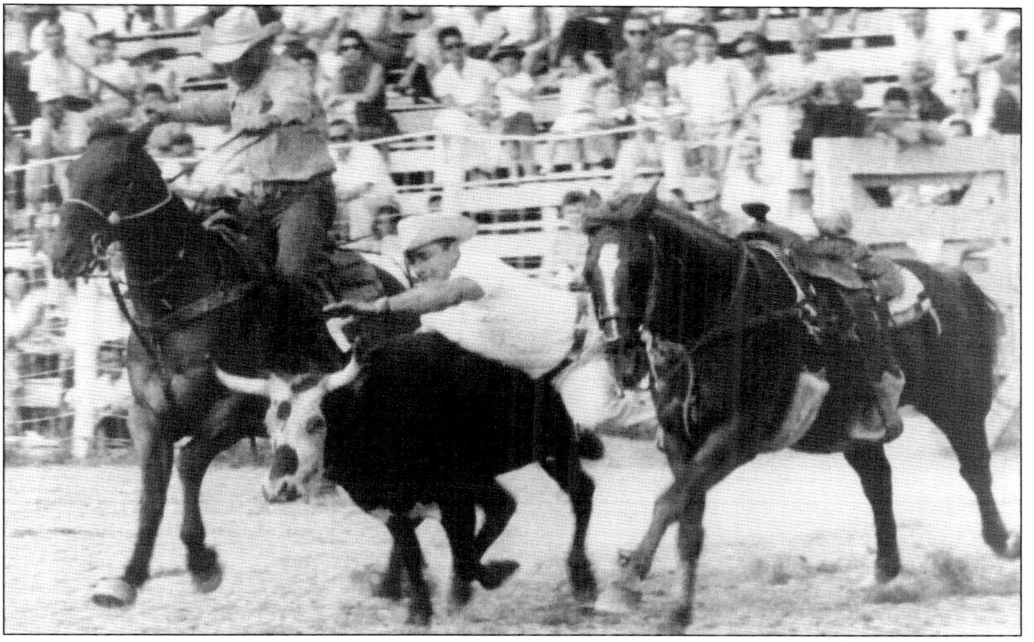

Getting the Steer Down. Eddie Foster Sr. tries to get the steer to the ground in the steer wrestling event. All four of the steer's legs must be facing the same direction to stop the clock. The hazer, who helps keep the steer from running away by staying on the other side of it, is Henry Kroll. (Courtesy of Jimmy Lee Walker.)

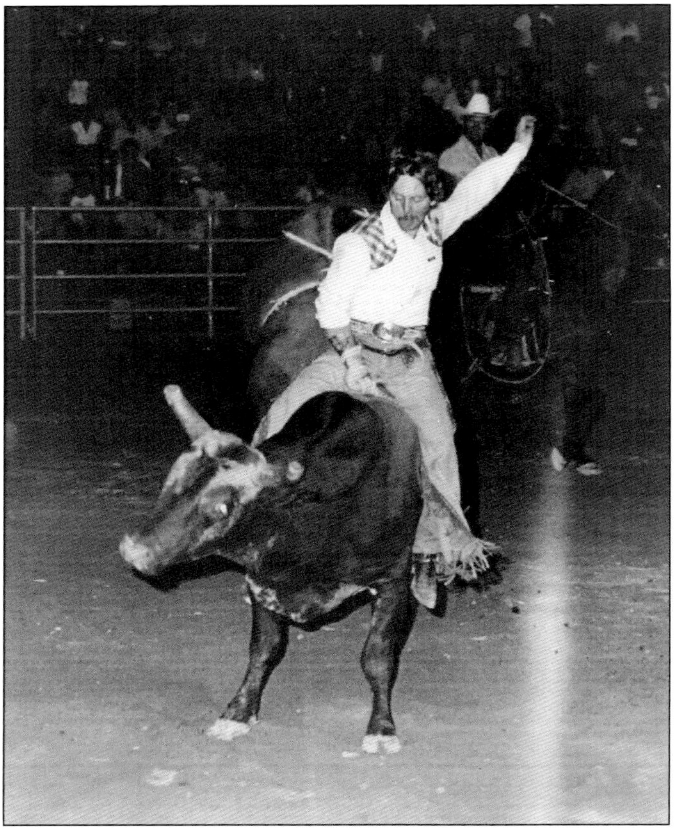

Rodeo Season. Barry Tharp rides a bull at Cowtown. The Cowtown Rodeo season runs from Memorial Day weekend to the last weekend in September. In 1957 and 1958, since the season was televised, qualifying rodeo events were held on Tuesday and Thursday nights to determine who was riding on Saturday nights. (Courtesy of the Cokenakes family and Palace Restaurant & Outfitters.)

Next Rider, Please. Jimmy Lee Walker stands closest to the bull in the arena. The ride was over, and it was time for the bull to be corralled to the open gate leading out of the arena so the next competitor could ride. Bulls, once their riders are on the ground, tend to calm down and stop bucking. (Courtesy of Jimmy Lee Walker.)

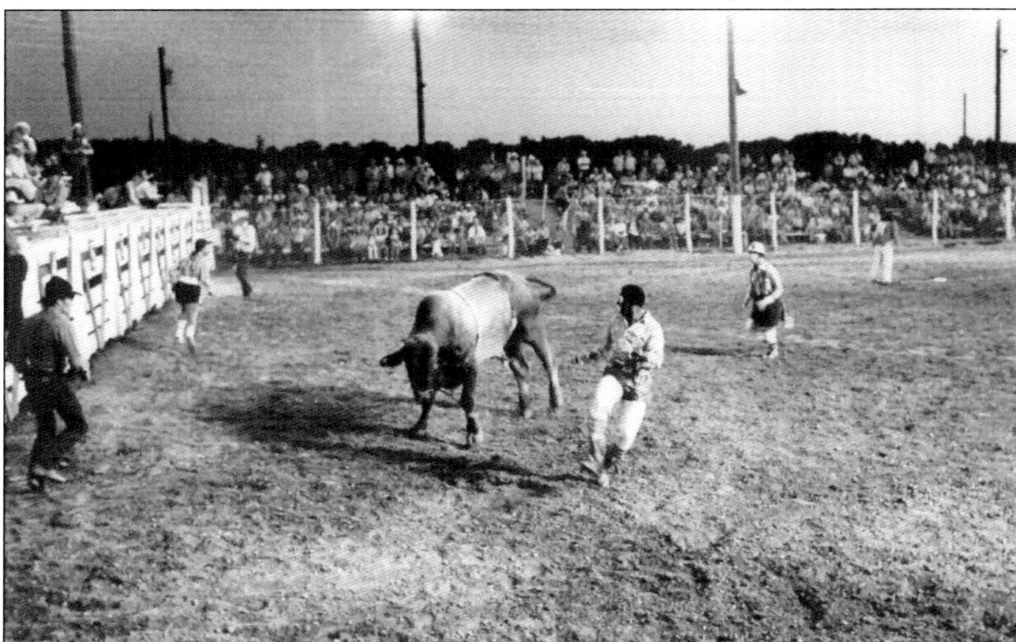

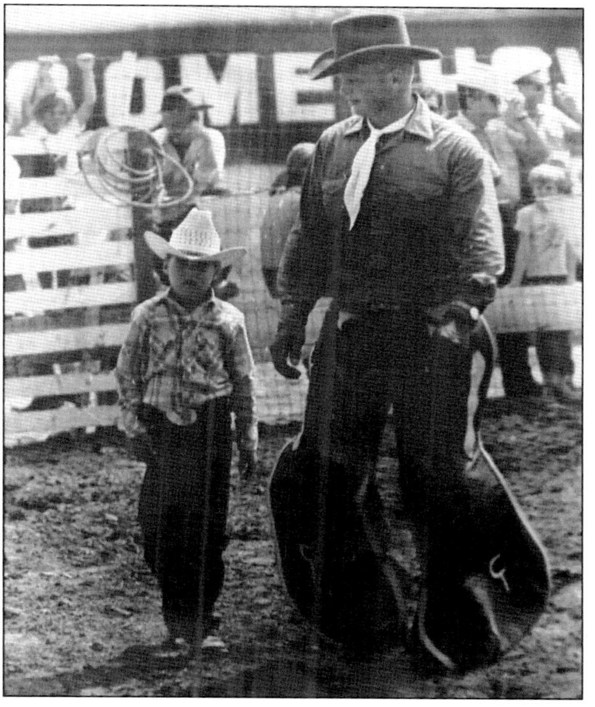

Mentoring Session. Howard Harris III walks alongside Vincent Dolbow in a rodeo arena, likely during a traveling show. Many children love cowboys and rodeos, but not every child that enjoys watching becomes a competitor. Usually, competitors start at a young age, practicing riding and learning technique. There are skills involved with the rodeo that need to be practiced and refined over time to make one a successful competitor. (Courtesy of Richard Dolbow.)

Marking Out. Gene Walker rides bareback at the Cowtown Rodeo. Bareback riders and saddle bronc riders must "mark out," which means they must have both spurs above the horse's shoulders until the horse's feet hit the ground after the initial jump. (Photograph by Frank Dougherty; courtesy of Jimmy Lee Walker.)

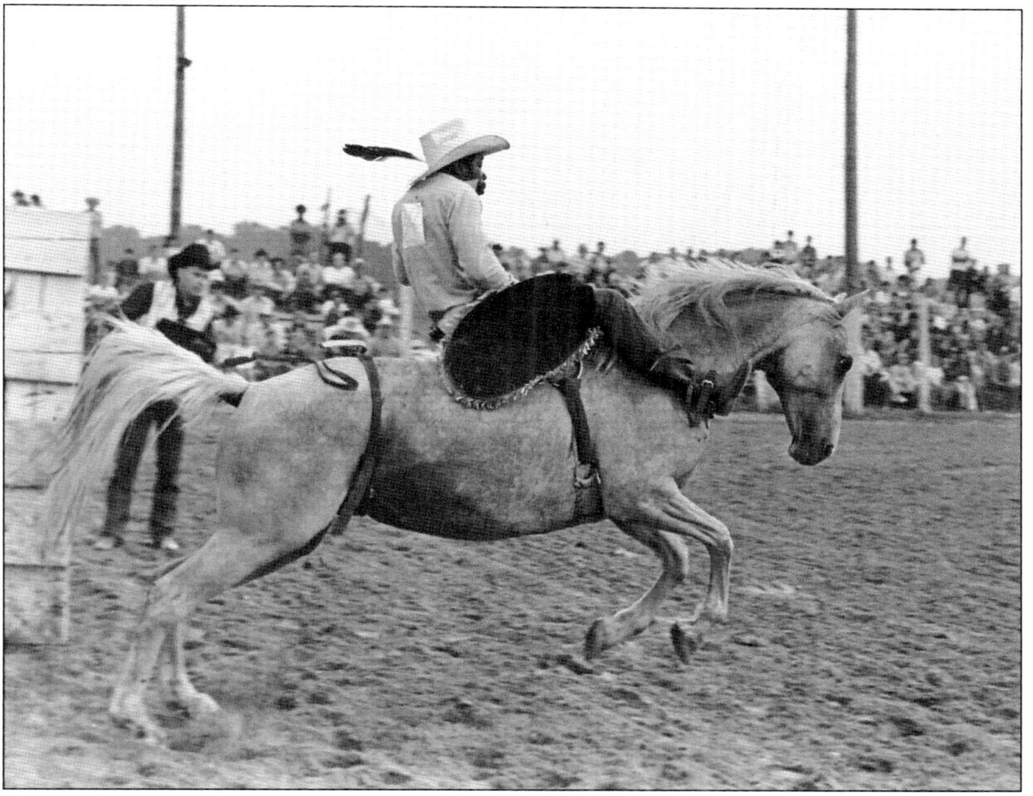

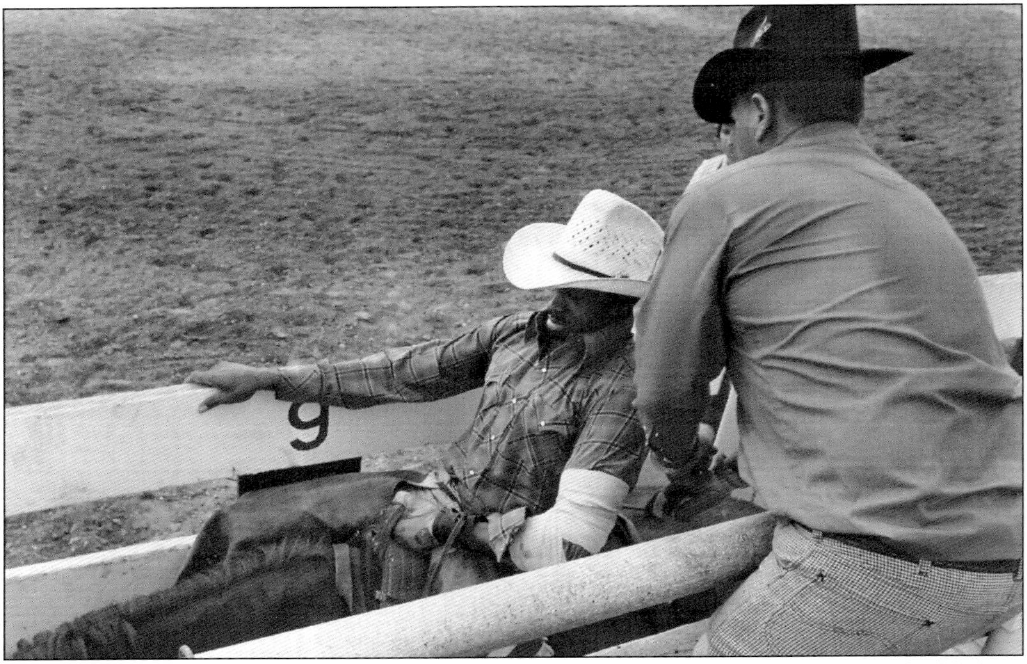

Man of Many Events. Jimmy Lee Walker competed in the Cowtown Rodeo as a bullfighter, bull rider, and saddle bronc rider. His versatility helped him gain experience in multiple events. The Cowtown Rodeo was a family affair for the Walkers, as two of his brothers and cousins also competed. (Courtesy of Jimmy Lee Walker.)

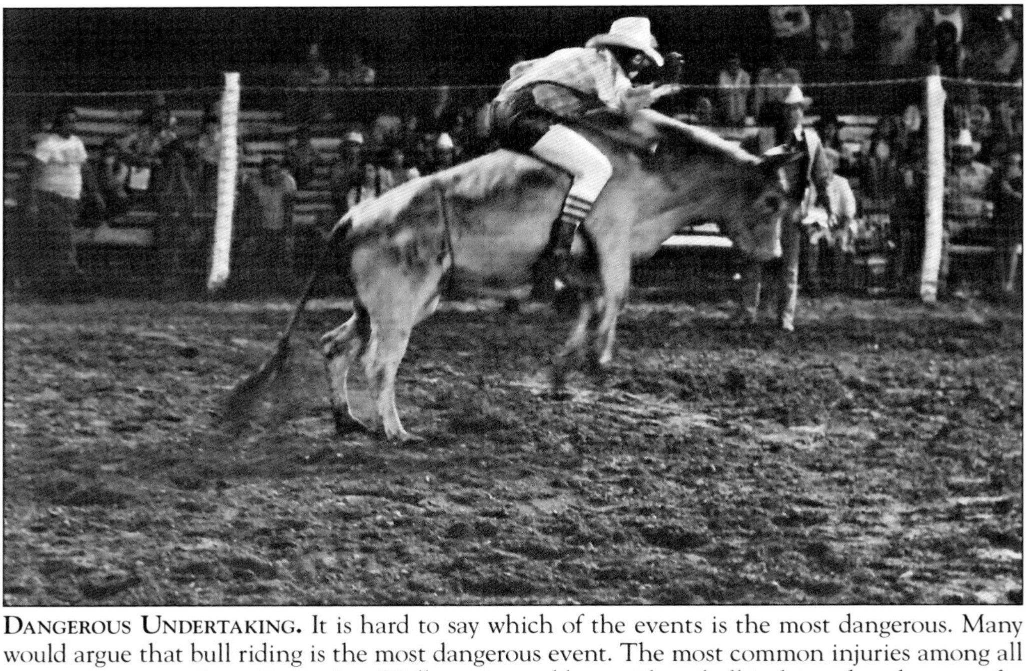

Dangerous Undertaking. It is hard to say which of the events is the most dangerous. Many would argue that bull riding is the most dangerous event. The most common injuries among all events are concussions. Jimmy Lee Walker, pictured here, rides a bull in his rodeo clown outfit, leaning forward as the bull bucks. (Courtesy of Jimmy Lee Walker.)

Bull Horns. This bull, ridden by Rich Keen, was not dehorned. Dehorning bulls is the process of removing or stopping the growth of the horns of livestock. Most rodeo bulls are not dehorned; however, tipping—the process of removing sharp tips that have no nerve endings in them—is sometimes done. (Photograph by Bob Hill; courtesy of Jimmy Lee Walker.)

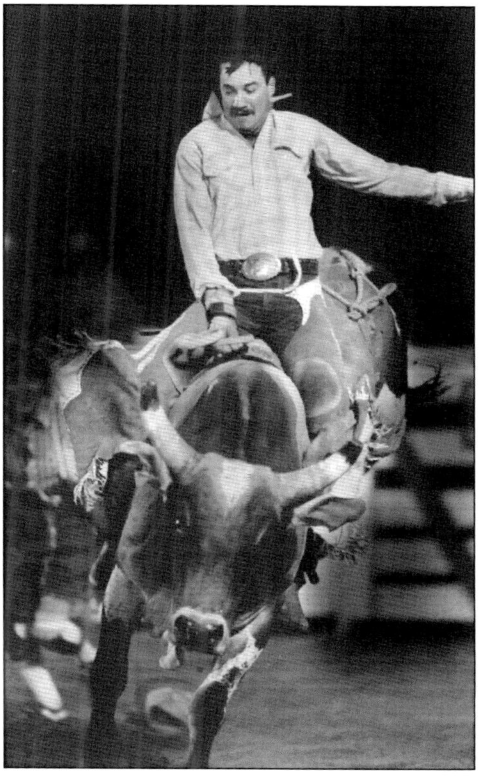

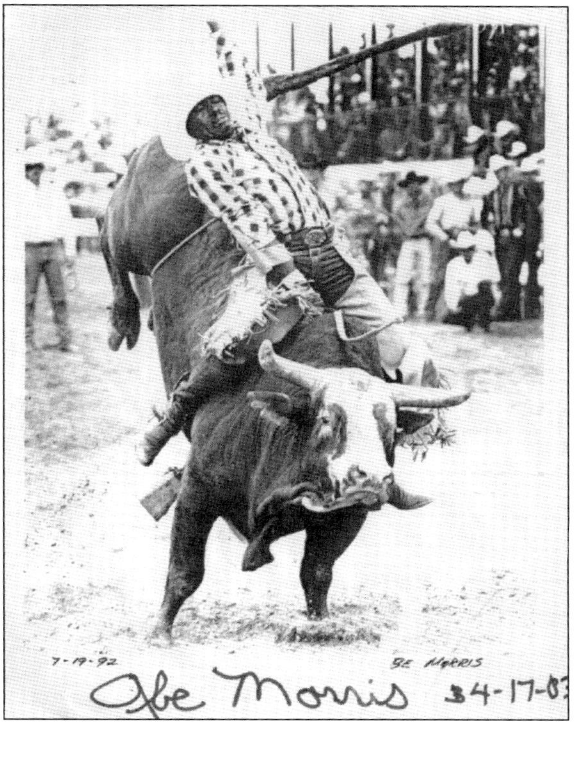

Chaps for Protection. Abe Morris is seen here in the middle of a bull ride. Morris captured his rodeo experiences in his book *My Cowboy Hat Still Fits*. Morris wore chaps during this ride, which are traditional apparel for rough stock events. Sometimes brightly colored and patterned, they are often made of leather and are designed to protect the rider's legs and thighs. (Courtesy of Jimmy Lee Walker.)

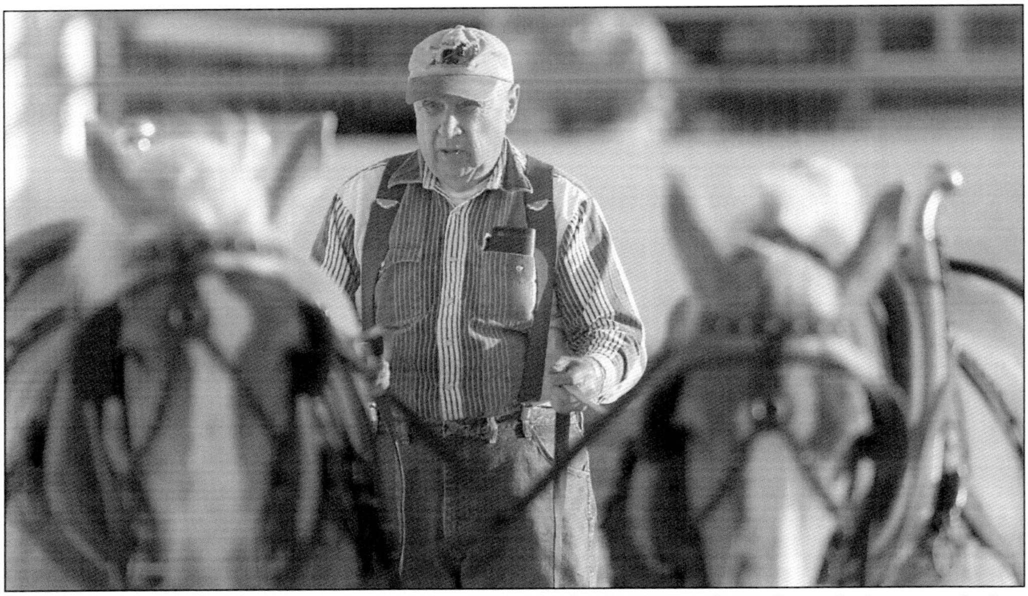

Smoothing the Surface. Bob "Brownie" Brown runs his horse Zamboni through the arena before the start of an event. Since the arena floor is dirt, few cowboys and cowgirls leave the arena as clean as they were when they entered. Dirt, as opposed to other harder surfaces like concrete or asphalt, is ideal for rodeo events, since cowboys are thrown from bulls and horses or have to jump off so frequently. (Photograph by Lisa Soltner.)

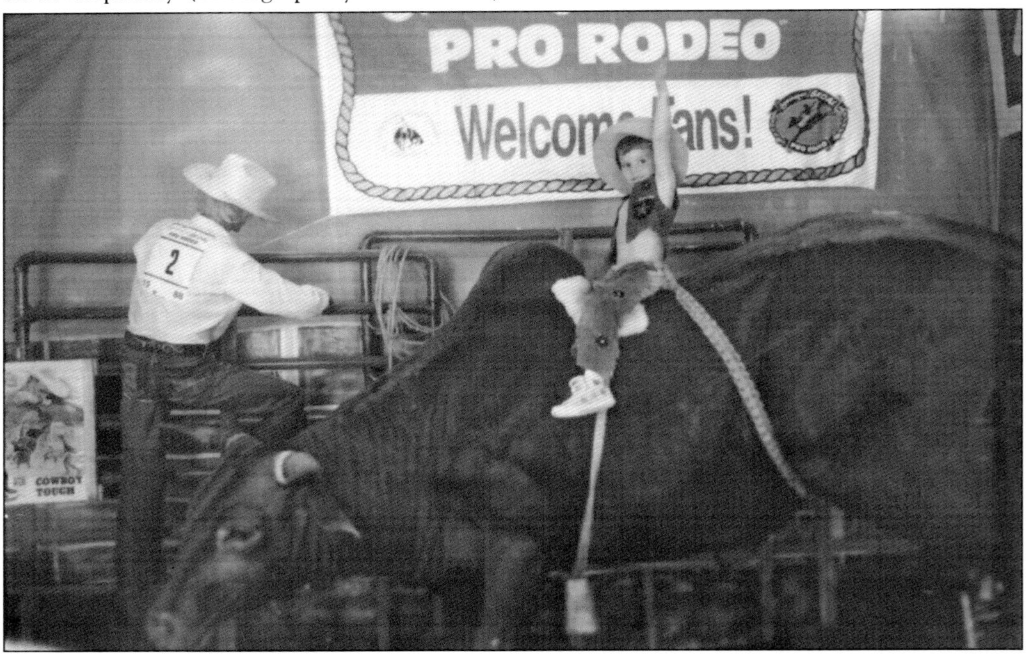

Bull Rider Photo Op. Andrew Burgmuller poses for the camera at the Cowtown Rodeo. Burgmuller attended the rodeo dressed as a cowboy; he even had a sheriff's badge on his vest. A fake cowboy was set up next to the bull and was posed to look like he was climbing up the fence, just like the cowboys in the arena. (Courtesy of Gary and Kim Burgmuller.)

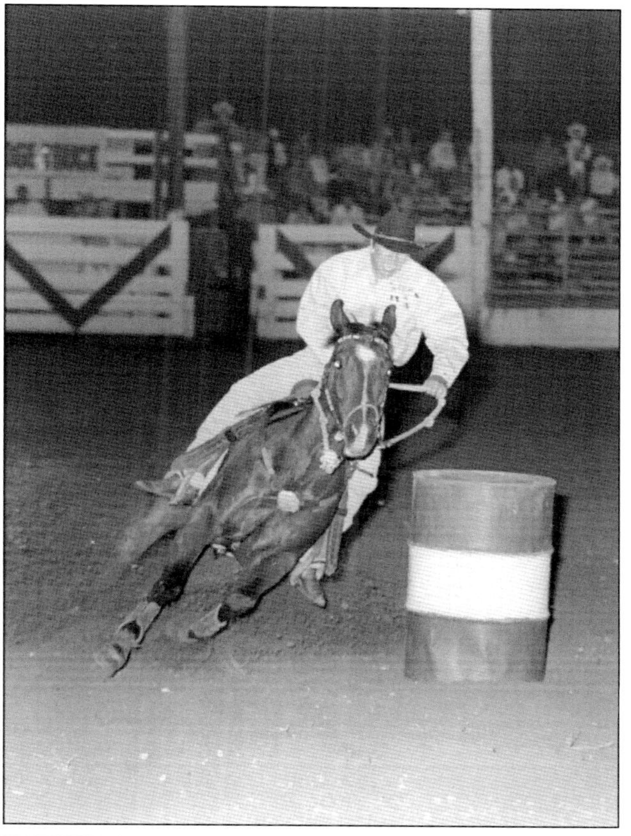

Women in Rodeo. Most participants in the rodeo events are men. There are a few exceptions, as some women have competed in bull and bronc events in recent years. However, rodeoing is a male-dominated sport. The exception to this is barrel racing. Judy Merola is seen here barrel racing at Cowtown. Judy and her husband, Joe, also have both children and grandchildren that compete in various rodeo events. (Courtesy of Joe and Judy Merola.)

Roundup. Before the start of the event, livestock have to be rounded up. The Harris family owns pastures throughout Salem County, where the livestock have plenty of room to graze and roam. Cowtown is a stock contractor, so the organization has its own animals for competition. It has also recently partnered with the Three Hills Rodeo Company in Iowa. (Photograph by Lisa Soltner.)

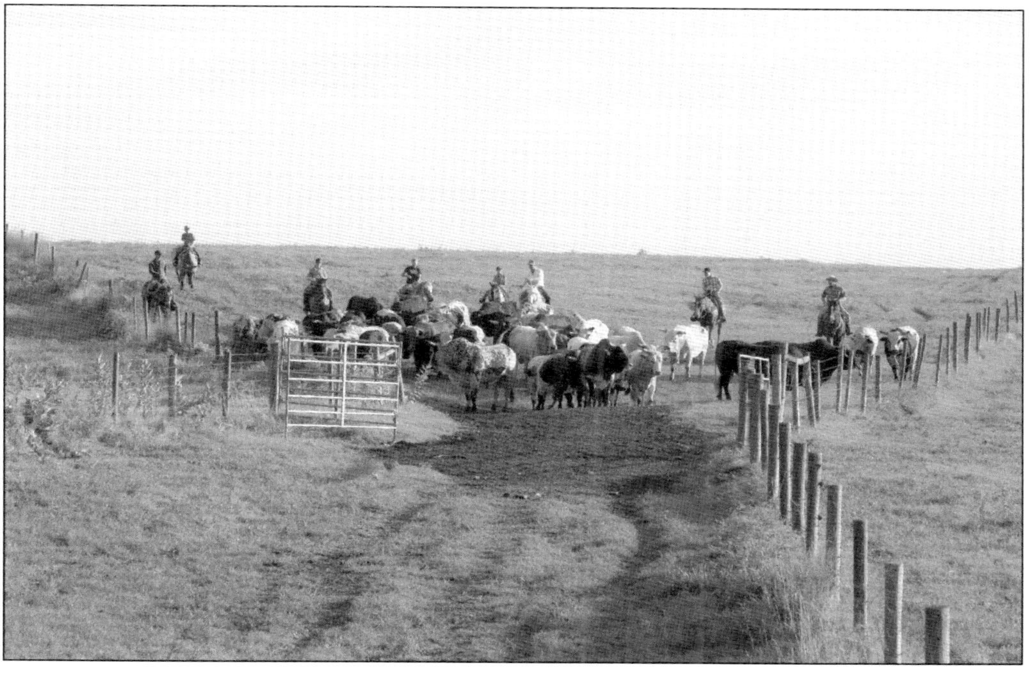

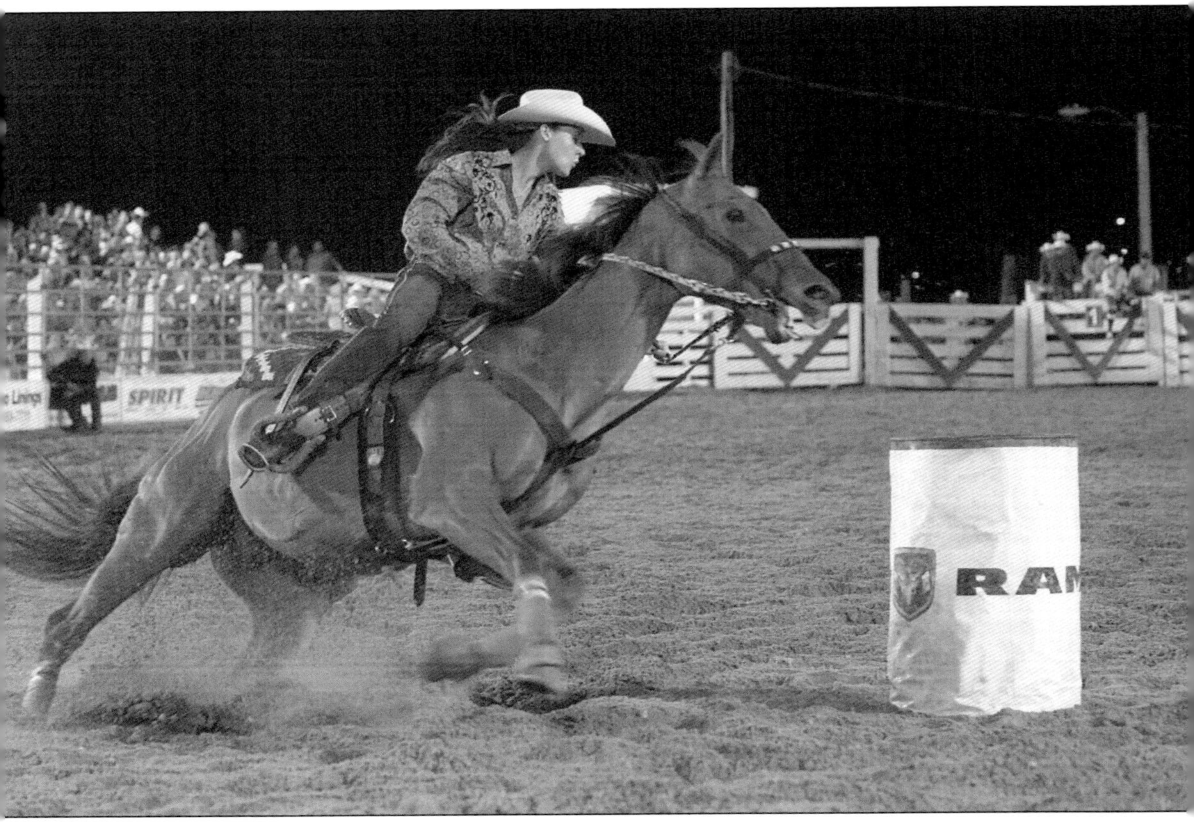

Moving Fast. Barrel racing became a standard event sometime after the new arena at Cowtown was built. Before that, the barrel racing events were only held two or three times each summer. In barrel racing, a horse and rider maneuver around barrels in set locations around the arena. In this photograph, a barrel racer attempts to complete the course in the shortest amount of time. (Photograph by Taylor Ejdys.)

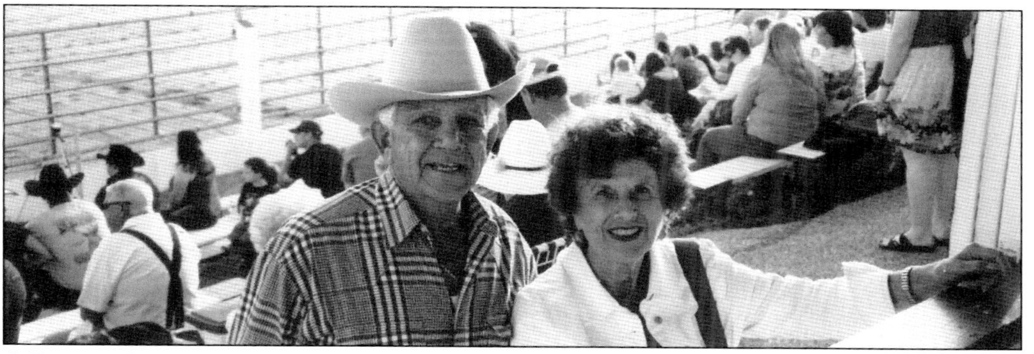

A Former Competitor Visits. Gene Lorenzo, a retired Cowtown cowboy, visits Cowtown with his wife, Janet. Behind the Lorenzos are the bleachers where spectators watch the rodeo. Regular attendees have favorite seats in specific areas of the stadium. The rodeo starts at 7:30 p.m., but spectators try to get good seats as early as 6:00 p.m. (Courtesy of Emily Walker.)

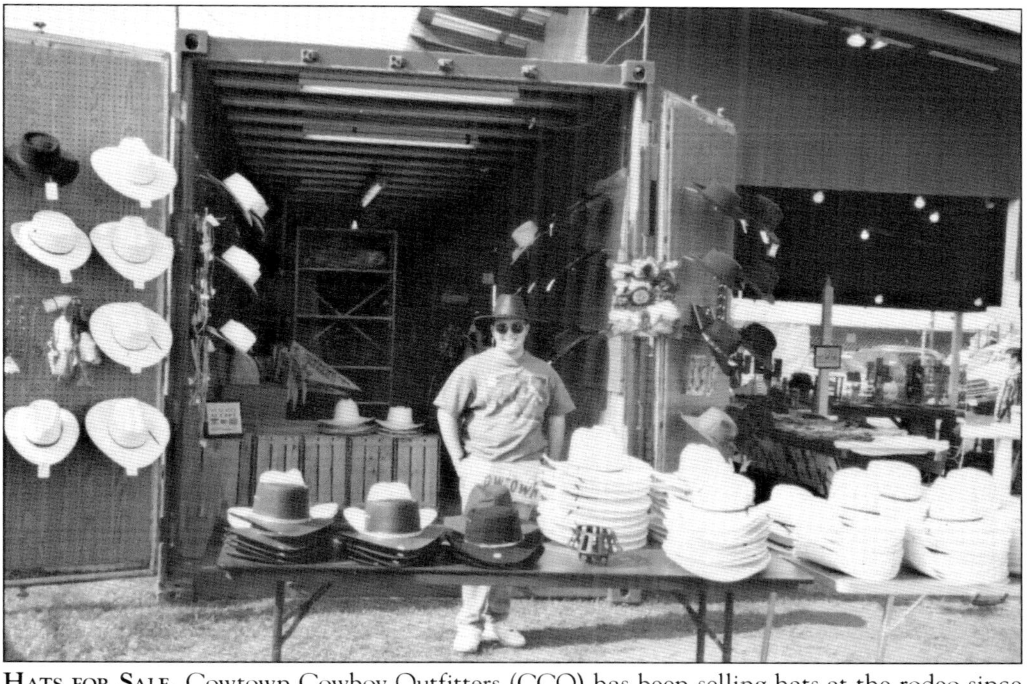

Hats for Sale. Cowtown Cowboy Outfitters (CCO) has been selling hats at the rodeo since 1974. The CCO staff sells cowboy hats before the rodeo begins. Many rodeo attendees, especially the first-timers, see the cowboy hats of the riders and the Cowtown staff and end up buying a hat before they leave. (Courtesy Travis and Suzie Zigo.)

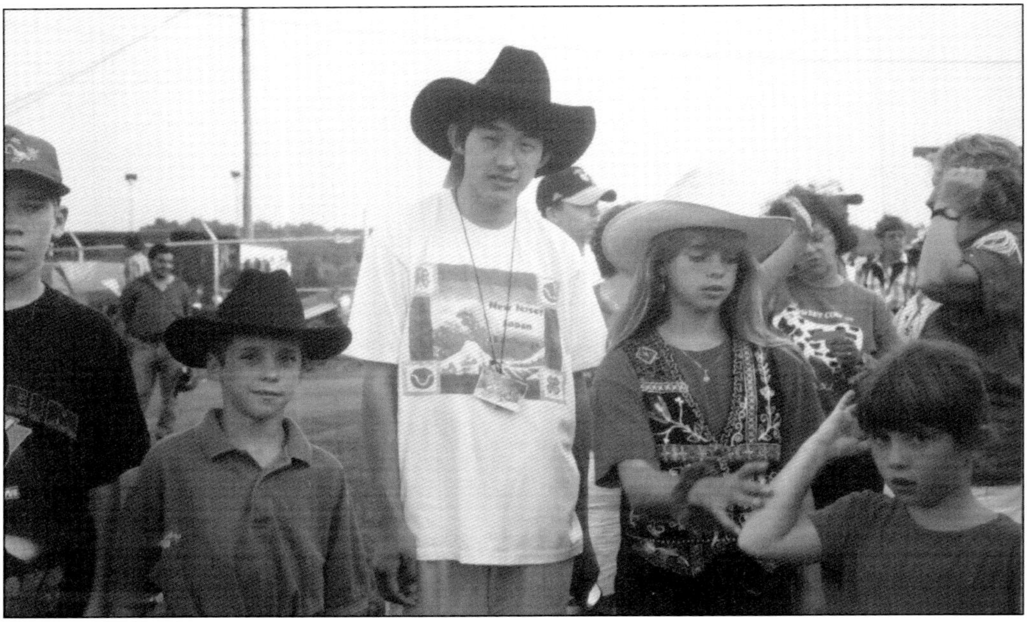

From Japan to Cowtown. Cowtown is a travel destination for many that visit the United States. Minoru Onuki was involved with a foreign exchange program in South Jersey. Onuki (center) and his host family visited the Cowtown Rodeo. Visitors from around the world come to Cowtown each year. (Courtesy of Minoru Onuki.)

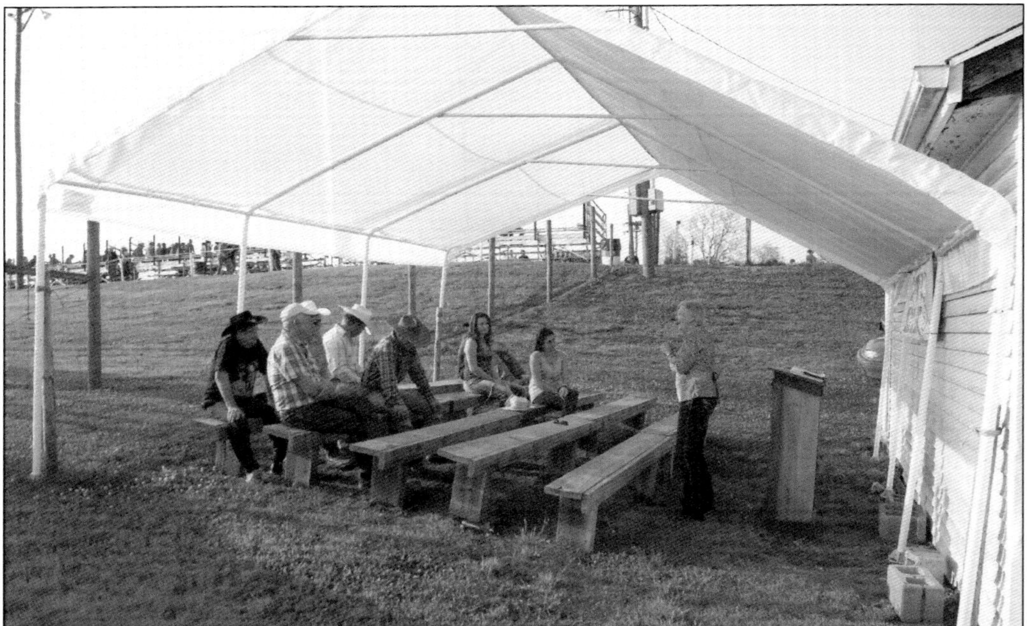

The Cowboy Chapel. The Cowboy Chapel, located on the Cowtown grounds, is open for prayer each week before the start of the rodeo. Rodeo photographer Susie Graham heads up the nondenominational Christian outreach program at Cowtown. Many cowboys and cowgirls stop at the chapel before their event starts. (Photograph by Eva Scofield.)

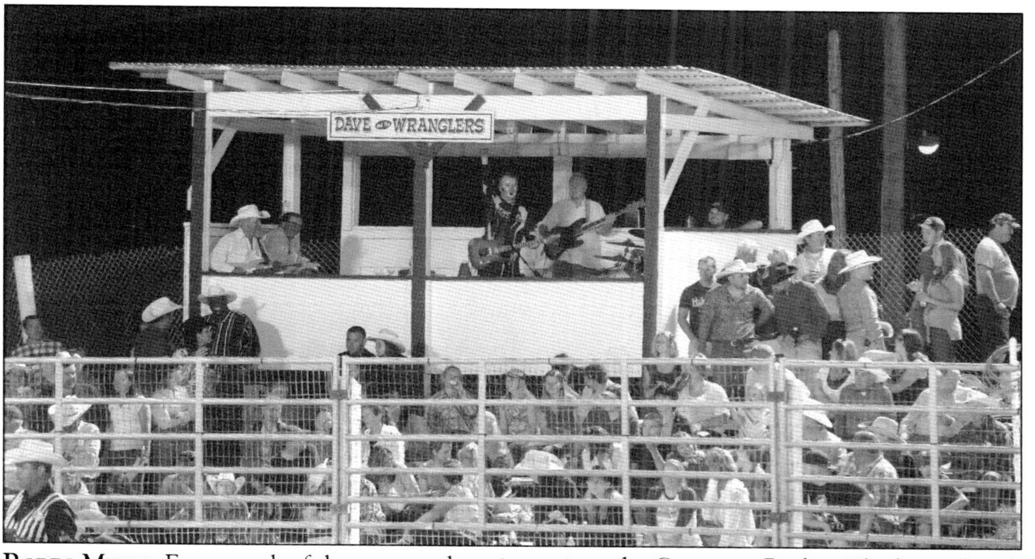

RODEO MUSIC. Every week of the season, there is music at the Cowtown Rodeo. The house band, Dave and the Wranglers, plays covers songs and adds musical riffs during and between events to keep the crowd entertained. Two songs are also traditions at the rodeo: "The Star-Spangled Banner" kicks off the event after Grand Entry, and "Happy Trails" is played each week to indicate the end of the rodeo. (Photograph by Eva Scofield.)

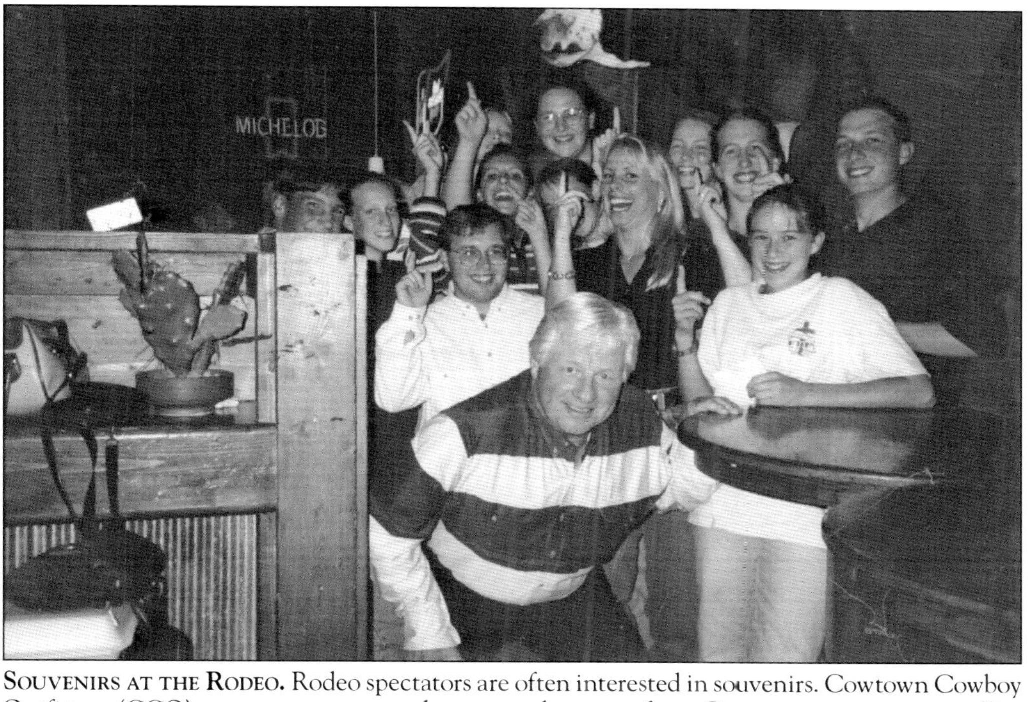

SOUVENIRS AT THE RODEO. Rodeo spectators are often interested in souvenirs. Cowtown Cowboy Outfitters (CCO), a western wear vendor across the street from Cowtown, operates a satellite store at the rodeo each week. In this picture, the rodeo division enjoys an end-of-the-season party. Former Pilesgrove mayor and CCO owner Ernie Bickford (wearing a striped shirt) is in the center of the group. (Courtesy of Travis and Suzanne Zigo.)

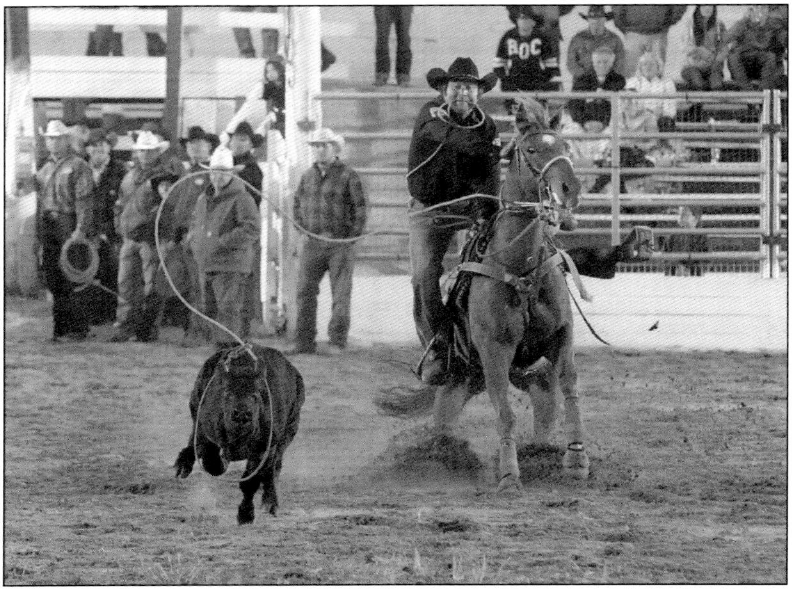

Calf Roping. Calf roping is a timed event that requires a strong cowboy and a well-trained horse. The goal is to throw a looped rope around the calf's neck, dismount from the horse, run to the calf, and then restrain the calf by tying three of its legs together. The calf roper seen here is moving fast. (Photograph by Eva Scofield.)

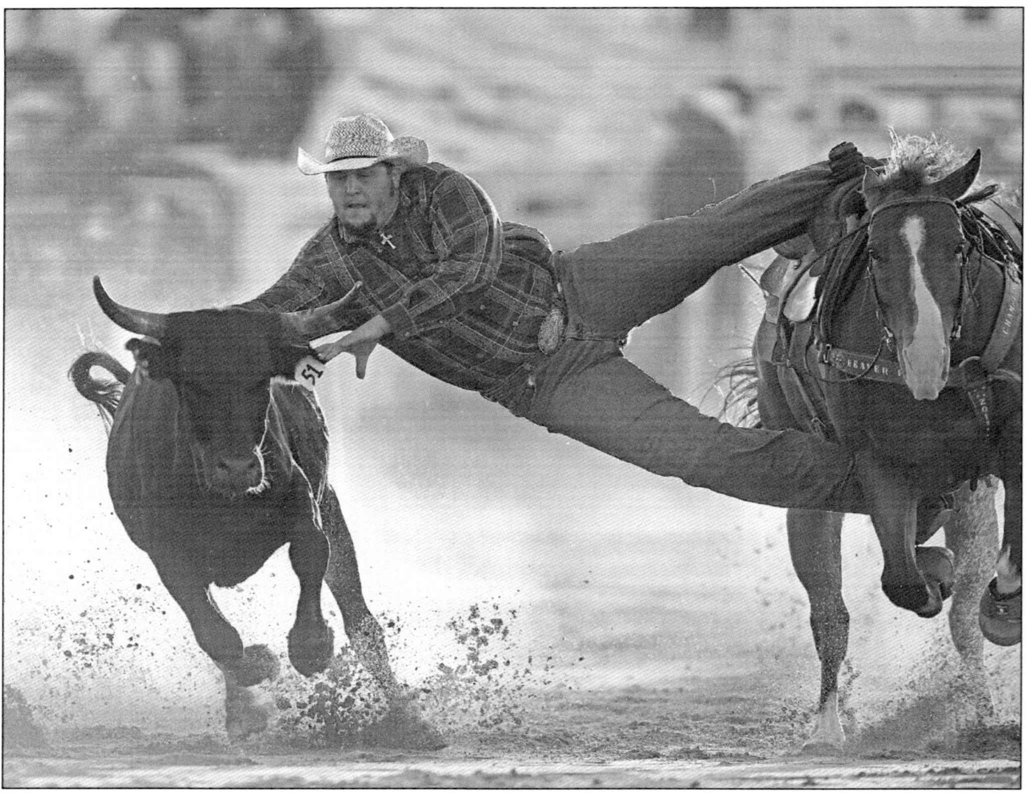

Bulldogging. One of the most important things in the steer wrestling event is the jump. The bulldogger seen here is in mid-jump and has made contact with the steer. Once a rider is off the horse and on the ground, he hooks his arm around the steer's horn and digs his heels into the dirt while pulling the steer to the ground. (Photograph by Don Pivonka.)

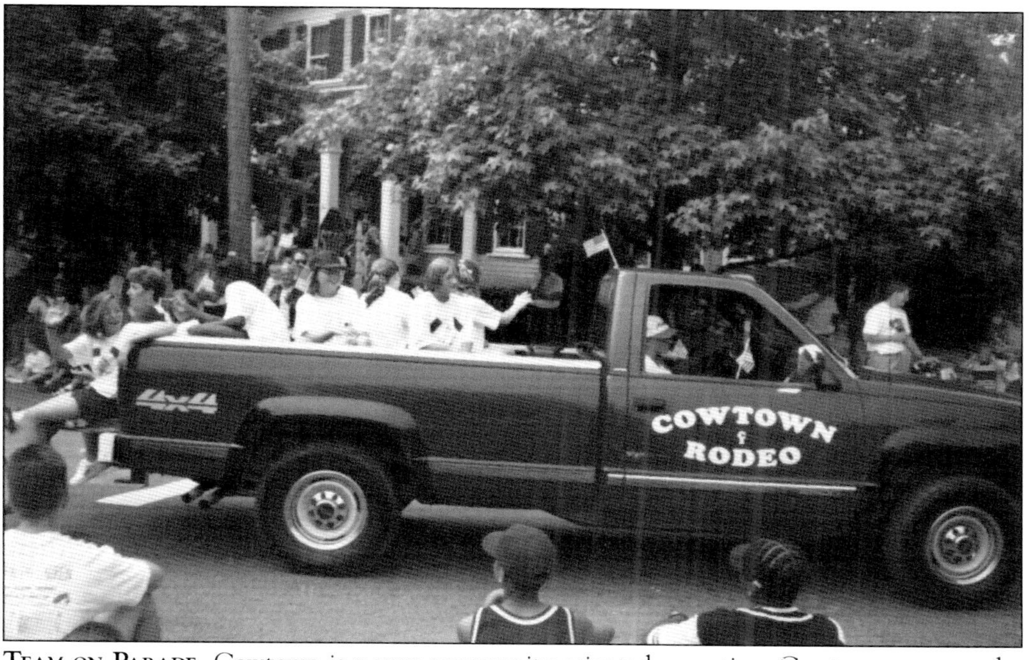

TEAM ON PARADE. Cowtown is a very community-oriented operation. Cowtown sponsored a little league softball team, which entered this local parade. Team members are seen here being driven around in the Cowtown truck during the event. The market and rodeo are visited by just as many locals as out-of-towners. (Courtesy of Lisa Mutter.)

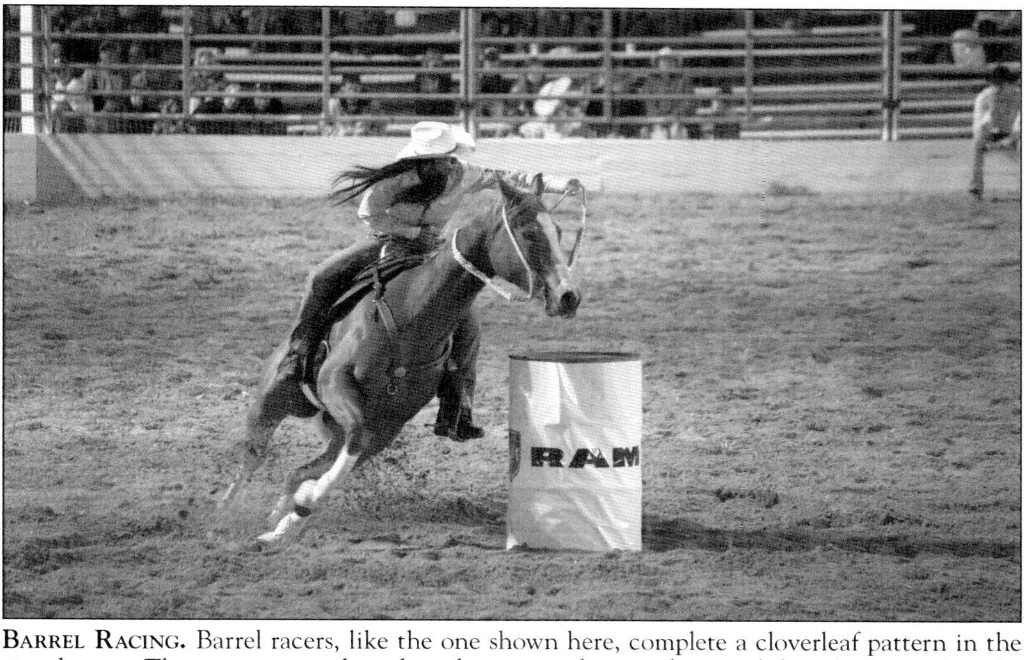

BARREL RACING. Barrel racers, like the one shown here, complete a cloverleaf pattern in the timed event. The timer starts when the rider crosses the start line, and they then complete the pattern and cross over the finish line. This women's event takes practice and skill. Riders attempt to finish as quickly as possible.

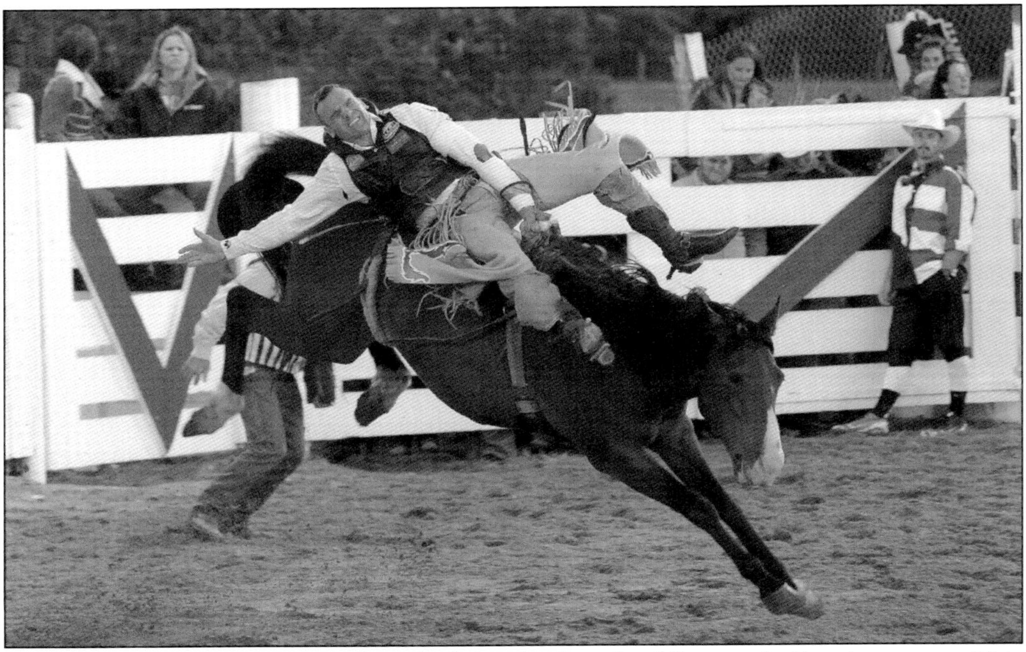

Bucking Excitement. Bronc riding, both bareback and saddle, are challenging events. This bronc rider tries to hold on while the horse bucks hard and fast. Once the bucking chute opens, the horse exits, and the rider tries to hold on for eight seconds. This event, just like all rodeo events, is very exciting to watch. (Photograph by Eva Scofield.)

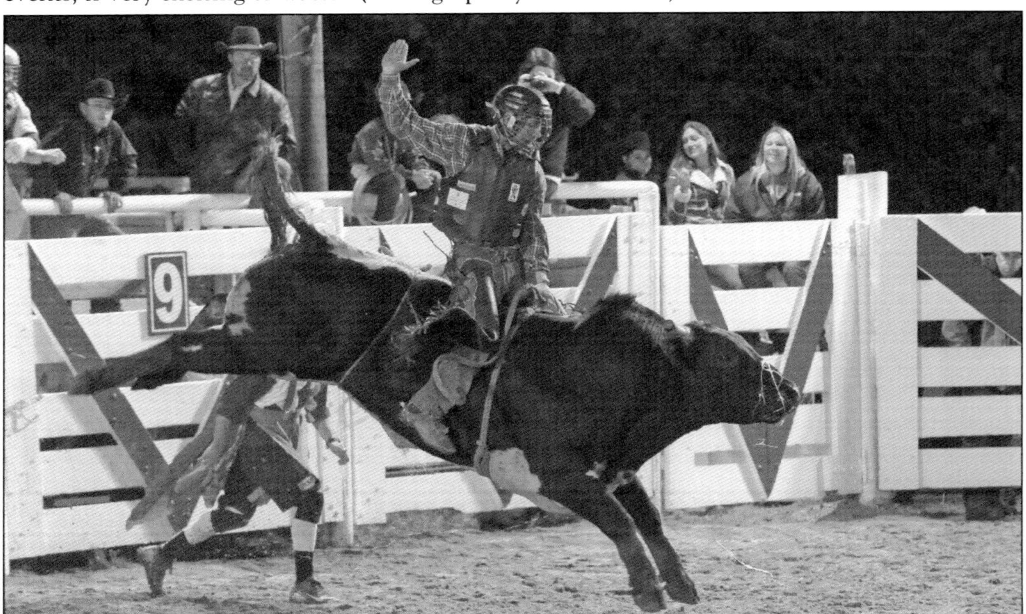

A Bull Rider at Cowtown. Cowtown is well known for its bucking bulls and horses. In 1984 and 1985, one of Cowtown's bulls, appropriately named Cowtown, won the PRCA's Bucking Bull of the Year. The livestock at Cowtown are descendants of the bucking animals that were at the Cowtown ranch 80 years ago. (Photograph by Eva Scofield.)

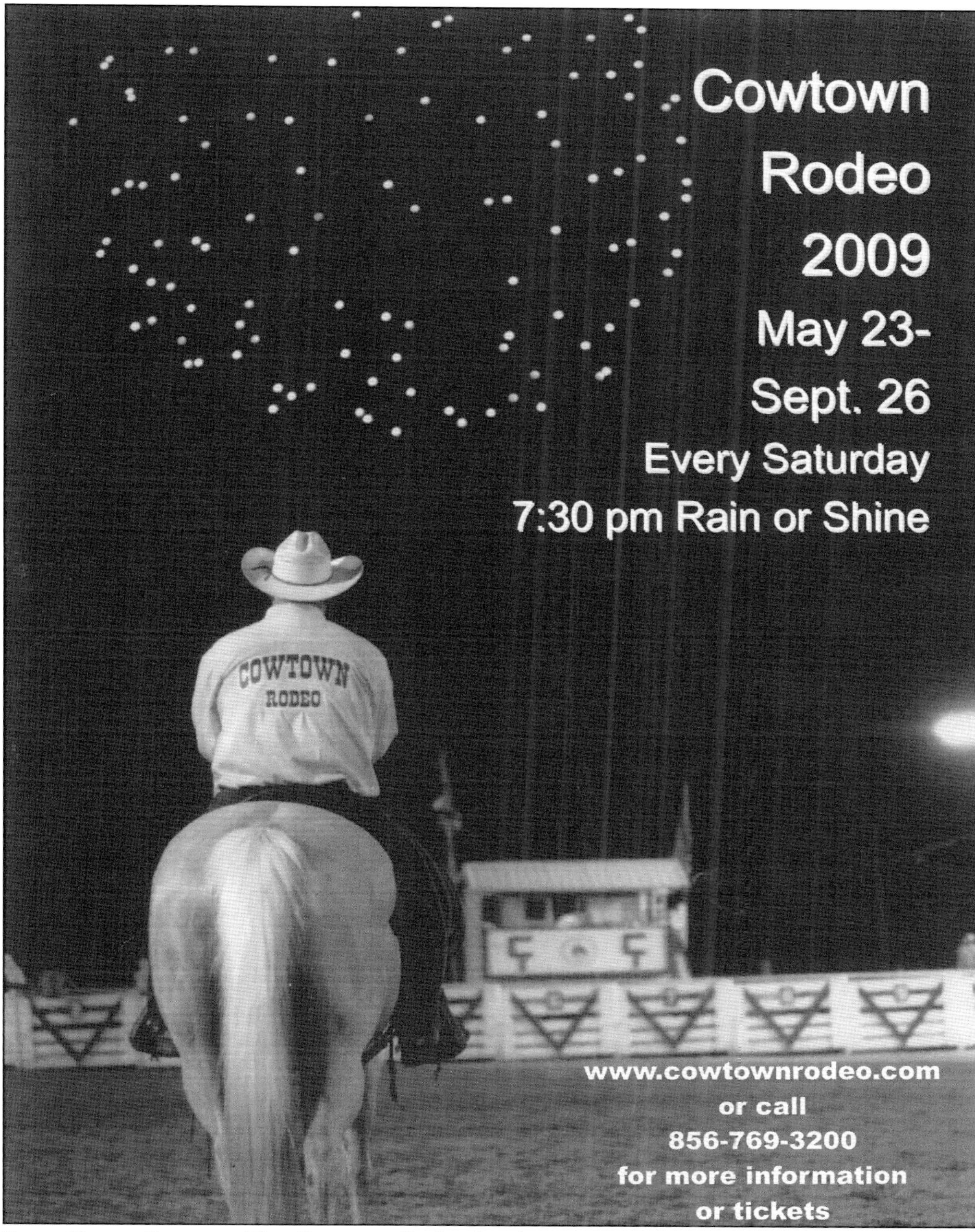

STILL GOING STRONG. The Cowtown Rodeo has been going strong since the late 1920s. Each year brings a new and exciting group of competitors to a sporting event with a rich history. Many would not associate New Jersey with rodeo; however, the Cowtown Rodeo is the longest-running weekly rodeo in the country, and it shows no sign of slowing.